THE WORLDE
WORKSHOP

THE WORLDBUILDING WORKSHOP

Teaching Critical Thinking and Empathy Through World Modeling, Simulation, and Play

Trent Hergenrader and Stephen Slota
foreword by Bryan Alexander

The MIT Press
Cambridge, Massachusetts
London, England

The MIT Press
Massachusetts Institute of Technology
77 Massachusetts Avenue, Cambridge, MA 02139
mitpress.mit.edu

© 2025 Massachusetts Institute of Technology

All rights reserved. No part of this book may be used to train artificial intelligence systems or reproduced in any form by any electronic or mechanical means (including photocopying, recording, or information storage and retrieval) without permission in writing from the publisher.

The MIT Press would like to thank the anonymous peer reviewers who provided comments on drafts of this book. The generous work of academic experts is essential for establishing the authority and quality of our publications. We acknowledge with gratitude the contributions of these otherwise uncredited readers.

This book was set in Stone Serif by Westchester Publishing Services. Printed and bound in the United States of America.

Library of Congress Cataloging-in-Publication Data

Names: Hergenrader, Trent author | Slota, Stephen T. author
Title: The worldbuilding workshop : teaching critical thinking and empathy through world modeling, simulation, and play / Trent Hergenrader and Stephen Slota; foreword by Bryan Alexander.
Description: Cambridge, Massachusetts : The MIT Press, [2025] | Includes bibliographical references and index.
Identifiers: LCCN 2025004427 (print) | LCCN 2025004428 (ebook) | ISBN 9780262553339 paperback | ISBN 9780262384681 pdf | ISBN 9780262384698 epub
Subjects: LCSH: Simulation games in education | Imaginary societies | Critical thinking | Empathy
Classification: LCC LB1029.S53 H47 2025 (print) | LCC LB1029.S53 (ebook)
LC record available at https://lccn.loc.gov/2025004427 LC ebook record available at https://lccn.loc.gov/2025004428

10 9 8 7 6 5 4 3 2 1

EU Authorised Representative: Easy Access System Europe, Mustamäe tee 50, 10621 Tallinn, Estonia | Email: gpsr.requests@easproject.com

For Greyson and Anders, who have their whole lives ahead of them to help build a more just and equal world for us all. It's an impossible job, of course, but the only one worth doing.

For Audrey, whose wonder is equal parts adorable and inspiring to your (cynical but aspiringly hopeful) uncle. May your curiosity and joy persist for decades to come.

Reality is a fallacy
An agreed-upon construction
Fear and greed's a melody
Worthy of destruction
We've been raised to behave in ways
To keep the system going
Pray to the Gods of power
To keep the money flowing

—Langhorne Slim, "For the Children"

CONTENTS

FOREWORD xiii
ACKNOWLEDGMENTS xix
PROLOGUE xxi

I FOUNDATION

1. AROUND THE WORLD IN 300 PAGES 3
A Simple Cup of Coffee 8
Complexity, Generalizations, and Stereotypes 12
Critical Thinking and Empathy 15
What Is Worldbuilding (and What Can We Do with It)? 17

2. ROAD TO CONTEMPORARY LEARNING THEORY 23
Where Did You Come From, Where Did You Go? 23
One Fateful Day 25
Roots of Educational Psychology 26
The Learning Theorists 28
To The Information Age and Beyond 31
Situating Cognition 33
What About Worldbuilding? 38
Onward and Upward 40

3. THEORY TO PRACTICE 43
Targeting Transfer 44
Welcome to Pripyat 47
Philosophy and Psychology 48
Introducing ADDIE 55
Designing Instruction 57
A Theory of Worldbuilding 59
Pulling It All Together 65
What's Next? 67

4. COLLABORATION AND COMMUNITY   69
　　Identity, Positioning, and Social Constructivism   70
　　Of Termites and Men   71
　　Communities of Practice   73
　　CoPs for the Classroom   76
　　From Here to There   78

5. ASSESSMENT   79
　　Alphanumeric Grading   79
　　Standards-Based Assessment   80
　　Ungrading   86
　　Feedback   92
　　Scaling Assessment   94
　　On the Horizon   95

II CONCEPTS

6. WORLDS IN SPACE AND TIME   99
　　Scope: Worlds in Space   101
　　Sequence: Worlds in Time   105
　　Macro and Micro   106

7. STRUCTURES AND SUBSTRUCTURES   109
　　Governance   109
　　Economics   111
　　Social Relations   111
　　Cultural Influences   113
　　Synthesis   113
　　Social Forces   117
　　In Closing   119

8. EXAMINING LIFE-WORLDS THROUGH DEMOGRAPHICS   121
　　Nominal and Quantitative Descriptions   122
　　Narrative and Qualitative Descriptions   124
　　Essentialisms, Stereotypes, and Drawing Wrong Conclusions   124
　　Using Demographics to Explore Lived Experiences   128
　　Someone Else's Shoes   133

9. CLASS PREPARATIONS   137
　　Developing Your Project Overview   138
　　Stage One: Project Purpose and Length   138
　　Stage Two: Scheduling   139

contents   xi

      Primary and Secondary Sources   140
      Unlearn What You Have Learned   143
      Wikipedia as a Source of Information   144
      Stage Three: Introducing the Project   145
      Preparations Complete   146

10. WIKIPEDIA AS A MODEL FOR WORLDBUILDING   149
      Getting Started   149
      Organizing Entries   152
      Wiki Management   154

 III   WORLD MODELING

11. CONSTRUCTING THE WORLD NARRATIVE   161
      Charting Complexity   161
      Quantitative Approaches to Modeling Worlds   163
      Qualitative Approaches to Modeling Worlds   164
      Drafting the World Metanarrative   166

12. CATALOGING PEOPLE, PLACES, AND THINGS   173
      How Many Entries?   174
      Entries for People   175
      Entries for Places   179
      Entries for Things   181
      Groups, Events, and Other Types of Entries   183
      You've Got a World…Now What?   184

13. SIMULATIONS   187
      The Sims   188
      Simulations for Worldbuilding   189
      Social and Environmental Changes on a Timeline   189
      Black Swan Events   193
      Wicked Problems   194
      Simulations in the Classroom   197

14. ROLE-PLAY   199
      A Cautionary Tale   201
      Role-Playing Perspectives   204
      The Worlds of *El Cid*   206
      Consequences for Actions   214
      Successes and Failures   215
      Using Role-Play to Virtually Experience Worlds   217

15. WRAP-UP AND CRITICAL REFLECTION   219
    Large-Group Debriefing   220
    Self-Accounting   220
    Peer Evaluation   221
    Big, Messy Affairs   222

EPILOGUE: NOTES FROM THE END OF THE WORLD   225

IV   CASE STUDIES

CASE STUDY I: HISTORY   233
Eric J. Morgan

CASE STUDY II: BRITISH LITERATURE   239
Luke Strohm

CASE STUDY III: PHILOSOPHY   245
Rebecca Scott

CASE STUDY IV: PHYSICS   251
Tori Wagner

CASE STUDY V: HONORS   257
Wendi Sierra

CASE STUDY VI: LABOR STORIES   261
Ching-In Chen

NOTES   265
INDEX   275

FOREWORD

Bryan Alexander

Can we teach worldbuilding?

It's a challenging question for anyone interested in education. The notion might sound strange—a kind of category error, like adding phenomenology to a car. But it has the potential to make us rethink how and why learning happens.

Education already involves worldbuilding, especially from the student's perspective. Like a reader, viewer, or player immersing themselves in a deeply constructed fantasy, historical, or science fiction world, students have to make sense of a large array of new or reimagined objects and places, characters and controversies, references and languages. They need to parse maps, sometimes conceptually and sometimes literally. Studying anatomy or a new language is very much about learning a vast, complex world. And faculty do some of the same worldbuilding via their research (adding details to the world's map) and class designs (walking students through the cartography).

This process evokes a reader's or learner's agency. We often explore new worlds by actively poking into them, organizing and reorganizing our experiences, and making "stuff" in response. Computer game players have for decades created their own maps and guides for games that unfold in complicated worlds. Fantasy novels are so frequently accompanied by an introductory map that it's become something of a cliché. Especially enthusiastic readers (watchers, players, listeners) create their own derivative works, from stories and visual art to fan pages and costumes. Travelers who physically visit faraway lands famously document the experience through photographs, journals, souvenirs, and stories. Apprehending a new world can be exciting, inspiring, and creative.

It's in such a spirit that the following book greets you.

Trent Hergenrader and Stephen Slota introduce not just a new world but a *pedagogical metaworld* wherein instructors teach students how to inhabit and cocreate understanding. This is based on the authors' years of joint research, refinement, passion, and experimentation. Their framework is replete with reimagined practices and objects for us to navigate, including new conceptual (and occasionally visual) maps to survey. They are able guides on an exciting road ahead.

"Hang on," you might say. "Why should educators, students, and support staff spend time on . . . worldbuilding? We're already at full capacity with our curricula, emerging technologies, and an expectation to provide escalating services—not to mention all the financial, cultural, and political issues in education. Why should we add another item to our overfull, tottering plates?"

Because teaching with worldbuilding *works*. And it works well.

Hergenrader and Slota clearly identify a stream of benefits for learners grown out of contemporary pedagogical theory and practice. The act of navigating and learning a world is one that responds well to inquiry. Modeling a world allows for the interrogation of complex systems, and such interrogation develops our cognitive muscles. This is where we get meaningful stories, both contained in a particular world and developed during a world's cocreation. Students learn how to learn while crafting personalized narratives.

In my own work on digital storytelling, I've found many student gains on this particular score. Learners who create digital stories benefit from rethinking class materials, practicing media literacy, working on storytelling technologies and techniques, and developing voice and self. That last piece is incredibly important to Hergenrader and Slota. In their view, identity is a key component of worldbuilding (cf. chapter 4, "Collaboration and Community" and elsewhere), and they describe the necessity of developing a world's characters using qualitative and quantitative evaluation of demographic, cultural, and political data. They connect student identities to cocreation in sensitive, careful ways.

There are multiple advantages to this approach, as detailed through case studies and examples drawn from both fiction and nonfiction. Recall that fiction itself is borne of reality—even the most fantastical worlds are grounded in lived experience, situating the strange and unreal with the familiar and real, as J. R. R. Tolkien taught us.[1] And that is why Hergenrader and Slota focus on a combination of forms and subjects, including and especially history. Studying a world in class sheds insights into the world(s) we inhabit elsewhere. Indeed, the richer the world(s) we study, the more educational and broadly applicable they become.

Worldbuilding is also a fine example of interdisciplinary work. No single discipline owns all worlds or all of one world, and the act of building demands expertise from multiple fields. If I were to teach a course centered on a future version of Earth wracked by climate change, I would need to draw upon Earth science, meteorology, oceanography, and cryosphere studies just as a foundation. Then, I'd need to apply political science to model changed governments, sociology and psychology to anticipate human responses to the crisis, economics to describe changes to business and finance, and religion to examine how faith might be transformed. My students would have to make similar interdisciplinary moves to cocreate, learn about, and build upon that world.

All of this enables learners to grow their personal capacities. Cocreating a world in good faith requires some degree of empathy for us to imagine how humans can and will act or react. As I write these words, our inhabited reality is undergoing an acute empathy shortage and could well use some more of it. Although we tend to think of empathy on a micro, personal level, it likewise connects with a macro, sociopolitical level. That is, a student who develops a sense of what it means to be, say, a shipbreaker in my climate crisis class will be primed to link their experiences to the political and natural structures in which their life is actually embedded. Echoing that micro-macro dual movement, students shift between personal and group learning (per Hergenrader and Slota's guidance). This is key to modeling and exploring interconnected systems—as students engage in such activities, they develop vital problem-solving skills while being roused to become the best version of themselves.

I've written first about worldbuilding's benefits for students because students are my focus as an instructor, but this book is particularly well prepared for teacher use. Hergenrader and Slota walk through an excellent summary of pedagogical theories (which should be of great utility to early career instructors) while setting up a range of ways to interact with worldbuilding (constructivism looming largest). These pages are rich with practical advice derived from years of trialing assessment measures, scheduling worldbuilding tasks in undergraduate and graduate classes, and describing these ideas to other academics. The authors also recommend complementary digital tools like wikis and cowriting software (viz. Google Docs), which are time-tested educational technologies with their own benefits (e.g., teaching coauthorship, annotation, and cooperation).

I've repeatedly used words like "cocreation" and "cooperation" throughout this introduction, and I want to dwell briefly on their implications for pedagogical worldbuilding. It is vital for the reader to understand that this book is not about a faculty member obtaining a fully realized world and delivering it unto a class. Rather, Hergenrader and Slota envision a practice of **shared creation and development**. To oversimplify, the instructor sets up one world idea (or several from which students choose), provides a basic framework (drawing to some extent from preceding topics and lessons), and encourages the students to build it out by developing characters, key objects, locations, and more—always as a team. Throughout creation, the instructor guides from the side, giving feedback and pointers, connecting students with each other, conducting some assessment, and facilitating rather than pontificating. They ask students to answer questions about assumptions and gaps in their presentation of the world, which is, incidentally, excellent critical thinking practice. The class engages in *active learning*. The teacher is decentered as font of all wisdom, and students are recognized as makers. Creators. Not just receptacles for curricular content.

As you might expect, the authors link this type of democratic pedagogy to a keen sense of social justice. They take care to establish that worlds are often unequal and the characters inhabiting them appear in various forms of advantage and oppression. At one point, Hergenrader and Slota recommend that while using demographic information to create characters, students should focus more on minorities than majorities so they will remain mindful of the marginalized and minoritized. This helps establish the direct connection between fictional(ized) worlds and our lived reality, which is a highlight of the authors' words of wisdom for educators whose own students are privileged or marginalized by all-too-familiar structural dynamics.

I've mentioned the pedagogies of storytelling and collaborative writing but feel I must add another for worldbuilding: educational gaming. Game worlds are learned through play, such as those conjured in tabletop role-playing games (*Dungeons & Dragons*, the most famous) and computer role-playing games (the authors are rightly fond of the *Fallout* series). There is a substantial and still-growing body of scholarly literature and practice about teaching with games, which Hergenrader and Slota knowledgeably refer to, before focusing on two such modes: "the best games for learning were simulations and role-plays, flexible experiences that provided space for students to reflect on their learning." Simulations and role-play emerge in the following pages as lively and synthetic mechanisms of learning—interdisciplinary engines for creative study. They allow students to internalize a world and then voyage through it in a productive and inquiring manner. They summon a spirit of friendly competition that the instructor may referee, and they bring a joyful, liberated feeling to learning.

Let me close by returning to a broad idea. Yes, this book offers theoretical and practical details for teaching worldbuilding, from assessment design to syllabus reconfiguration. But it also aims high, linking pedagogy to our times. In chapter 1, "Around the World in 300 Pages," the authors pause to pose an ambitious question: "What can be done to reconfigure education for the challenges of modernity?" You may anticipate their answer to be "teach worldbuilding," but read how Hergenrader and Slota actually respond: "We believe it vital to help educators at every level and in every discipline revise their instruction for critical thinking and its less-talked-about sibling, empathy. As you will see, our strategy is built on deconstructing and analyzing the planet's most mind-bogglingly complex, urgent questions through a combination of collaboration, inquiry, and reflection—a process we call worldbuilding."

Note the soaring ambition. They seek to grapple with this era's deepest dilemmas (recall my example of a climate change class), not by simplification but by expanding the educational space. They want to rethink how we teach that most cherished, argued about, and often difficult topic of critical thinking. And they hope to achieve all this while focused on better understanding and connecting to fellow humans through empathy. I know of few other educators who so successfully bridge their classrooms with the world, with such ethical soundness, and with such a commitment to their students' thoughtful, playful flourishing.

In other words, the world needs more worldbuilding. Read on to see what you can cocreate.

Bryan Alexander, PhD
Senior Scholar, Georgetown University
Futurist, author, and creator of the Future
of Higher Education Observatory

ACKNOWLEDGMENTS

Writing this book in the wake of COVID-19 turned out to be a more formidable task than either of us expected.

Consider that an academic's labor is typically divided between teaching, research, and service at a 40-40-20 ratio. That figure has changed dramatically since the spring of 2020. Teaching obligations have ballooned beyond comprehension, time and funding for research have become increasingly scarce, and service obligations have skyrocketed (due in no small part to perpetual hiring freezes—faculty who quit or retired were not, and in many cases still have not been, replaced). If the adage says many hands make light work, it is equally true that fewer hands make work heavier, and we are still coming to grips with the shock and trauma of this (hopefully once-in-a-lifetime) event. We have limped back to something vaguely resembling our pre-2020 routines, but we have not returned to anything resembling "normal" (leaving aside the argument that pre-2020 "normal" might not be something we should yearn for anyway).

Both of us—Trent and Stephen—owe immense gratitude to the many people in our professional and personal networks who helped us overcome the aforementioned challenges to get this book across the finish line.

First and foremost, we thank Susan Buckley and the MIT Press for choosing to publish our work, facilitating peer review, and making our wacky ideas available to the broader field of education. We thank our families and friends for exercising incredible patience in listening to our rambling, reading our drafts, and providing feedback throughout the years-long stop-start process. We thank our students, who joined us in putting our worldbuilding, simulation, and role-play machinations into motion. We thank our closest colleagues (and Slack confidants) Kevin Ballestrini, Mark Pearsall, Lindsay Sears, and Roger Travis, who have tolerated our nonstop banter, faux bickering, and curmudgeonly grousing for more than a decade, all without releasing the mountain of blackmail material they have undoubtedly accumulated in that time.

We also want to thank the network of scholars, instructors, and enthusiasts who volunteered to write case studies for this project. Although space prevents us from publishing all of them in the appendix (and the pandemic prevented some from being completed), each of you was instrumental to our thinking and writing. This includes Brent Ryan Bellamy, Ross H. Brubaker, Julialicia Case, Ching-In Chen, Katrin Geneuss, Shelly Jones, Noelle Kaiami, Andrea Kelley, Adam Liszkiewicz, Beatrix Livesey-Stephens, Siobhan Lyons, Brian McKenzie, Kevin Moberly, Eric Morgan, David Ng, Roberto Lint Sagrena, Tammie Schraeder, Rebecca Scott, Wendi Sierra, Luke Strohm, Mira Sucharov, Tori Wagner, and Bob Weiman.

Additionally, Trent would like to thank his students, friends, and colleagues in the University of Wisconsin–Milwaukee Department of English and Creative Writing Program where he began his work on worldbuilding; the Department of English, Creative Writing Program, and the College of Liberal Arts at the Rochester Institute of Technology, whose support has allowed him to continue to develop this line of research; his partner, Amy Mueller, and his sons, Greyson and Anders, for abiding his general absent-mindedness, grumpy mood swings, and corny dad jokes. Finally, he would like to thank the Adirondack Mountains, tabletop role-playing games by Free League Publishing, and the video games *Valheim* and *Minecraft* for keeping him somewhat sane during months of mandatory lockdown.

Stephen would like to thank their parents, Michael and JoAnn, as well as their sister, Shannon, for shaping them into the person they are today; Amy Freeman for being a loving and caring partner in crime; Michael F. Young for his long-time mentorship and friendship; and the many game design, educational technology, and learning science undergraduate and graduate students who have believed in the project and what it stands for. Last but not least, they would like to thank caffeine, duloxetine, and the various animators, authors, filmmakers, game developers, and other artists who make life worth living.

PROLOGUE

If you want to make an experienced games and education researcher groan, utter the phrase "chocolate-covered broccoli."

The descriptor was coined during Amy Bruckman's (1999) Game Developers Conference presentation entitled "Can Educational Be Fun?" In her remarks, Bruckman bemoaned the state of "edutainment" and the community's increasing supersaturation with subpar educational games. She described these media as a kind of chocolate-covered broccoli—the masking of something undesirable-but-good-for-us (i.e., broccoli, school) with something desirable-but-not-as-good-for-us (i.e., chocolate, gaming).[1]

To paraphrase the ever-sardonic chaotician Ian Malcolm from Steven Spielberg's (1993) *Jurassic Park*, edutainment developers had become so preoccupied with whether or not they could that they didn't stop to think if they should.[2] Their products, which purportedly made learning "fun," were seldom fun or educative, and they were rapidly piling onto an already overflowing stack of chocolatey florets in the vegetable crisper of K–12 education.

By 2012, those of us attracted to the promise of game-based learning grew weary of responding to suspicious (or downright hostile) colleagues who routinely invoked the concept of chocolate-covered broccoli to ask why educators should be responsible for making learning fun when what students *really* needed was less coddling, fewer distractions, and more rigor. These were often the same colleagues who defended one-to-many lectures, multiple-choice exams, and five-paragraph essays as the "correct" route to a "good education."

What such conversations revealed was not a fatal flaw in games and/or education but rather a fundamental lack of understanding about how human beings learn. Humans find joy in discovery. We develop knowledge through trial and error, and we derive pleasure from building competence (if not mastery) across domains. Understanding how and why learning happens allows us to design instructional methods that successfully motivate people to pursue new skills and subjects. As highlighted in James Paul Gee's (2003) landmark *What Video Games Have to Teach Us About Learning and Literacy*, the book that launched a thousand researchers, games create satisfying reinforcement loops capable of tuning perception and testing our abilities.[3] His (commonly misrepresented) point was not that games can brute force learning into being "fun" but that educators can borrow particular game mechanics and design strategies to make learning more fulfilling and transferable.

The following prologue introduces the authors of this book and our positioning vis-à-vis the world of game-based learning. Neither of us self-identify as fad enthusiasts, so we did not jump on the games and education bandwagon because chocolate-covered broccoli struck us as an easy way to achieve riches and fame (we both find profit motives in education to be equal parts foreign and nauseating). Instead, we stumbled into playful learning through a blend of personal interest and classroom experimentation, shifting away from the dissatisfactory elements of our own K–12 experiences and toward more stimulating (and, to our minds, intellectually rich) ways of thinking about "school." Like many of our colleagues, we became invested in the idea that well-crafted game narratives and rulesets could help learners take ownership of their learning, and we sought partners to strategically develop game-based tools for our own classrooms. Extending from Gee's thesis, we initiated a collaborative effort to make good educational games from good learning theory.

These are our stories.

STEPHEN'S ORIGIN

"SKUNKED!"

My aunts and uncles crack up as my father collects the cards. He stacks them, does a few quick riffle shuffles, and ends with an overhand shuffle.

". . . Again?"

He deals the cards around the table, circling from person to person. There are six players in two teams of three. My aunt resets the "29"-shaped wooden pegboard while everyone else examines the hand they have been dealt—a bit of mental math to decide what to keep or toss.

"Four."

". . . Nine."

"Fifteen for two!"

"Already? Come on . . ."

An eyeroll followed by more laughter.

Gaming has been a constant in my life as far back as I can remember. My father was an avid soccer player and semi-professional referee, and my mother was a former cheerleader raised in a game-friendly environment (her uncle was a celebrated baseballer turned bowling alley owner, and her father was a champion candlepin bowler). Together, my parents, sister, and I would regularly play *Trouble*, *Candy Land*, and *Chutes & Ladders*, and as we all changed with age, so too did our preferences (*Pictionary*, *Scattergories*, *Rummikub*, and *Farkle* remain popular among the four of us). Both sides of my extended family have always enjoyed *Cribbage*, and my maternal relations continue passing down the playful sixteenth-century Welsh tradition of *snapdragon* (i.e., pouring raisins onto a baking sheet, covering them in brandy, lighting them on fire, and reaching in to grab and eat the flaming fruits).

It should be no wonder that child me went on to develop a fondness for games—not just tabletop games but *digital* ones whose pixels presented one puzzle-solving opportunity after another to satiate my (then-undiagnosed) neurodivergence. Of course, my parents never loved that I was burning so much of my youth with eyes glued to a screen, but the joke's on them: It turned out to be a more viable career path than any of us could have imagined. And to give credit where due, they did a pretty great job supporting my interest (read: hyperfixation) despite any misgivings.

I vividly remember my dad bringing six-year-old me on a "mystery ride" to the 1990 Nintendo World Championships in Worcester, Massachusetts. A 20-foot tall inflatable Mario stood sentinel at the Worcester Centrum gate, and as we passed onto the concrete concourse, we were wowed by the beeps and boops of hundreds of consoles and CRT TV booths. *Castlevania III*, *Super Mario Bros. 3*, and countless other games that had gripped me through the pages of *Nintendo Power Magazine* were available for playtesting, and the event's sheer scale—you mean to tell me that this many other people love games TOO?—imprinted upon me a deep fascination with the development process.

The subsequent year, I was gifted a Super Nintendo Entertainment System for Christmas, and it was not long before we were *Mario Kart*-ing it up on a regular basis. More than once, I gave my sister an unplugged controller so she could pretend she was at the wheel while I did the actual driving, and I may or may not have tricked her into sitting on a bunch of rocks I painted to resemble Yoshi eggs (I convinced her that they would hatch if she just kept them warm). As we completed a few more revolutions around the sun, we picked up a used Nintendo Entertainment System from a nearby video rental store (I loved *Mega Man*), Santa landed another slam dunk with the delivery of a *Nintendo 64*, and my mother surprised my friend and me with a trip to Northampton, Massachusetts, where we got to meet the design team at Cyberlore Studios (makers of [2000] *Majesty: The Fantasy Kingdom Sim*).[4]

At the same time, I was leaning into my other obsessions—illustration, animation, and puppetry—to design games of my own. William Sleater's (1984) *Interstellar Pig* inspired me to create a real-life version complete with plasticine figurines,[5] and I became the first team member at our middle school newspaper to run a regular fun-and-play page. Eventually, I worked up the courage to send Nintendo of America a letter begging them to make a paleontology-based game that taught players how to dig up dinosaur bones and organize them as complete skeletons.

However much I loved and wanted to make a career out of interactive media, gaming and storytelling remained fanciful hobbies rather than anything resembling a profession. Not only was I in a small, rural part of Connecticut with limited access to relevant mentors, but it just never seemed like something I could do—the studios were few, they mostly operated on the opposite coastline, and it was difficult to learn anything about them when the internet mostly consisted of anonymous message boards, chat rooms, and user-made GeoCities websites. "Instead," I told myself, "I'll be a cartoonist. Or a music teacher. Or a scientist. Or, or, or . . ."

It was college that changed my mind. There, I found a community that would transform my Mario-provoked pipedreams about game design into something more.

The first of many *Dungeons & Dragons* adventures unfolded with friends I met through the University of Connecticut Marching Band, and we frequently hosted LAN parties to test our mettle via *Starcraft*. By 2005, a half-dozen of us were actively subscribed to Blizzard Entertainment's (2004) *World of Warcraft* (*WoW*),[6] which had introduced us to an extremely diverse global community (initially a small-ish guild called Inspire, then a larger guild called the Church, and finally our own guild, Death Star Orphans). Although it would be a while before I made the connection to K–12 and higher education, *WoW* was providing us with innumerable opportunities to socialize and build community as well as refine our leadership abilities and engage in collaborative problem-solving. The game was not just fun—it was instructional.

By the time I was set to graduate with my bachelor of science in molecular and cell biology, I realized that I was much less invested in the incremental, lonely work of growing mouse cells under a fume hood than in shaping other people's lives through education. I reoriented my honors thesis from laboratory research to an evaluation of in-service educators' attitudes toward internet and multimedia use, and I enrolled in a one-year master of arts program that could propel me into teaching high school life science. What distinguished my instructional approach from that of my peers was an eagerness to interconnect popular culture—including graphic novels, films, and video games—with concepts drawn from the standard life science curriculum. Rather than simply describing the scientific method, we watched portions of the (1993) stop-motion animated musical *The Nightmare Before Christmas*;[7] to structure a hypothesis, we brainstormed strategies for fighting big, bad *WoW* bosses before putting those ideas into action and evaluating the outcomes; to grapple with distinctions between Darwinian evolution by natural selection and so-called intelligent design, we played Maxis's (2008) life simulation game *Spore* and debated how, in the real world, limiting environmental factors would affect the long-term viability of our various Frankenstein-ian creations.[8]

For the two years I remained in that job, very few constraints were imposed on my pedagogical designs, and my supervising vice principal was so pleased with their effectiveness that he invited me to run district-wide professional development workshops about my methods. It was not long before colleagues began requesting that I punch up their syllabi and classroom activities, which piqued my interest in larger-scale instructional design and the possibility of sharing my strategy with a broader audience.

One chilly afternoon in November 2008, my then-roommate entered our apartment and tossed a copy of the *UConn Advance* into my lap. He pointed me to an article featuring two of my former professors, Roger Travis and Michael F. Young, who were spearheading something called the Video Games and Human Values Initiative—an endeavor to spur interdisciplinary discussion about games and play for higher-quality, more engaging instruction. He urged me to reach out to the duo given the obvious overlap in our goals.

I knew both men reasonably well: Roger led my ancient Greek civilization and mythology courses during undergrad, and Mike taught educational technology during my master's program. Although he did not know it at the time, the former had been the greatest influence on my own approach to teaching—he often used movies and games as exemplars during discussions about historical, sociocultural, and theological themes—and the latter had dramatically reframed my conception of what "educational technology" actually means; our conversations about *WoW* led me to better understand the connection between in-game learning and out-of-game action. This new Video Games and Human Values Initiative synthesized several ideas I was independently exploring with my high school students, and it made me optimistic there was a path into game development that I had not previously anticipated.

My 2009–2010 school year rapidly transformed into a testing ground for home-brewed tabletop role-playing and alternate reality experiences. In addition to teaching topics like human health and sexually transmitted diseases via a *Dungeons & Dragons* adventure (e.g., investigating and quashing a pandemic outbreak), I poured hours into crafting an overarching narrative for all of our lectures, lab experiments, and assessments. During the first week of class, students were invited to follow up on their work, complete journal entries, and discuss findings through a text-based forum, and a plucky scientist narrator named Dr. Cornelius Beakerstink (played by me) could respond with tips, feedback, and resources. Beakerstink's insights emphasized the connections between content units, gradually constructing a long-form story in partnership with the learners themselves (a form of colearning).

Emboldened by my students' success, I spoke with Roger and Mike about enrolling in UConn's Educational Psychology doctoral program to further explore the affordances of games, stories, and play in instructional contexts. Not only did they welcome me with open arms, but by June 2010, I had cofounded an educational design company—The Pericles Group, LLC—along with Roger and several other classicists; was preparing to leave K–12 education for the foreseeable future; and was learning the ropes as a new member of UConn's educational technology team. My first academic presentation took place that July when Roger and I expounded on the potential utility of (the now-defunct) Google Wave collaborative writing platform to a room of blue-haired retirees at a local conference about gifted and talented education.

The following four years formed a crucible for my study of theory, pedagogy, evaluation techniques, and technology integration, and I maintained hope that an improved holistic understanding of instructional design would allow me to break through the Borg-like conformity and resistance to innovation that defined education's century-old structure and function. Games and storytelling, I believed, were going to change "school" forever. My colleagues and I just needed allies who could assist in drafting and enacting a plan.

FIGURE 0.1
A (1995) photo of eleven-year-old Stephen playing chess with their father, Michael (left); a (1981) photo of seven-year-old Trent posing atop a soccer ball (right).

TRENT'S ORIGIN

Since childhood, I have been enthralled by both storytelling and games. I was a voracious reader of books and comics and a huge fan of science fiction and fantasy movies and TV shows. As a child of the 1980s, I grew up with a steady diet of Atari, Coleco, and eventually Nintendo video gaming consoles, and I played a ton of tabletop role-playing games—not just *Dungeons & Dragons* but many games published by TSR Hobbies in many different genres: the Western-themed *Boot Hill*, the postapocalyptic mutant-filled *Gamma World*, the spy and espionage *Top Secret*, the deep space sci-fi *Star Frontiers*, and my personal favorite, *Marvel Super Heroes*. I was also a rabid soccer fan, an eccentricity in my football-mad hometown of Green Bay, Wisconsin.

Despite having a good group of friends and a healthy social life, I hated school. The rote learning bored me, and I rarely felt encouraged to express myself creatively. My provincial teachers and guidance counselors showered praise and attention on students who excelled in math and science (which I did not) and did little to promote literature and writing, even when my short stories won the district fiction award. I credit my twin obsessions—fiction writing and soccer—for keeping me alive during those lean years.

In contrast, I adored my undergraduate experience at the University of Wisconsin–Madison. High school had taught me that my creative production meant nothing, so I never considered that I might enjoy a creative writing class. I majored in English but took courses in history, philosophy, and world literature, including classics, Greek tragedy, Icelandic saga, and some personal favorites in interdisciplinary liberal studies that blended literature, media, history, philosophy, and art. It was not until my junior year that I understood I was intelligent and creative and that my unique way of looking at the world was not a flaw but an asset. At that time, I aspired to become a professor of English literature, but my professors, who were largely trained at the Ivies, said that if I did not get into a top-ten program, I would be wasting my time. Heeding their advice, I only applied to the top ten programs, and, dear reader, I did not get accepted into a single one.

Through sheer good fortune, I lucked into what twenty-two-year-old me considered a dream job at the US Soccer Federation, where I worked as an entry-level administrative assistant paid in pocket change and Nike soccer gear. It was a lot of fun to fly across the country for dozens of meetings scheduled around men's and women's national team games, but it did not take long to realize there was little room for career growth, which prompted a move to Seattle to administer youth soccer programs in Washington State. I gradually grew disillusioned with the politics and pettiness of parents in youth sports, and it was roughly then that I flew back to Green Bay for my ten-year high school reunion. Multiple former classmates asked if I was still writing, and they recalled—with surprising detail—some of the stories I had written for class and the school paper. I felt humbled and had to admit that I had not kept it up.

I decided to move home to Wisconsin and give writing a try, but I learned the hard way that you cannot make a living writing short stories. I attended the 2004 Clarion Writer's Workshop—a training ground famous for graduating many accomplished science fiction, fantasy, and horror writers—and soon saw my work published in competitive venues like the *Magazine of Fantasy & Science Fiction*, *Realms of Fantasy*, *Weird Tales*, and others without making anything remotely close to a survivable salary. So, with my wife's encouragement, I reapplied to graduate school after a decade hiatus to seek a doctorate in English with an emphasis in creative writing. I enrolled at the University of Wisconsin–Milwaukee (the only school that accepted me) in 2006, earning my MA en route to my PhD, graduating in the spring of 2013.

The 2008 global financial meltdown cratered the job market for PhDs, a blow from which higher education has never recovered. As a new dad terrified of going through the stress and expense of graduate school only to wind up jobless, I wanted to increase my prospects by focusing on writing instruction, not just creative writing but professional writing and some rhetoric and composition classes, plus the introduction of digital technologies that would allow for collaboration and the utilization of different forms of media.

Embarking on my literature reviews, I had no problem finding scholarly work on digital writing in the fields of rhetoric and composition and professional writing, but there was practically nothing on digital *creative* writing. In fact, there was a paucity of scholarship in creative writing altogether. When I was finally liberated from teaching only freshman composition, I was assigned my first Introduction to Creative Writing class . . . and I kind of hated it? My students did not read much and showed no interest in crafting literary work. Many of them took it more as a creative outlet or because it was required for education majors, not for the love of language. I was at the midpoint of my graduate years and suddenly wondered if I actually wanted this career at all.

Then, a few curious things happened all at once. Given the lack of scholarship I had found in digital creative writing, one of my advisors suggested I look into the still-nascent field of game studies. I read Noah Wardrip-Fruin and Pat Harrigan's (2006) *First Person: New Media As Story, Performance, and Game*,[9] their (2010) *Second Person: Role-Playing and Story in Games and Playable Media*,[10] and James Paul Gee's seminal (2003) *What Video Games Have to Teach Us About Learning and Literacy*.[11] On the creative writing side, I was reading John Gardner's influential (1984) *The Art of Fiction*[12] and Flannery O'Connor's (1969) *Mystery and Manners: Occasional Prose*,[13] both of which emphasized the importance of creating interesting characters traversing a challenging world. After years of being away from video gaming, I bought an Xbox 360 and tried game genres I had never experienced before, one of which was the (2008) digital role-playing game *Fallout 3*.[14]

To process the stress of school and the transition to fatherhood, I would drink a few beers and play video games late into the night. I became obsessed with exploration in *Fallout 3*, eventually earning a 100 percent completion rate by searching every nook and cranny of that expansive fictional world, and I began thinking about how and why the game had drawn me in. Games scholarship on environmental and emergent storytelling along with essays on role-play not only rekindled my love for tabletop role-playing games but also explained my addiction to the world of *Fallout 3*. In short, it provided an enormous sandbox paired with a set of rules that clarified successful and not-so-successful strategies for overcoming different kinds of challenges. I also found myself pausing to check the Vault, a fan-run wiki site that comprehensively cataloged the world of *Fallout* with separate entries for every person, place, and thing, including locations pinned to an interactive map.

Over a few weeks, these ideas began cohering into a theory: Instead of asking students to write a story from scratch or a single prompt, what if I had them start with a character? The world and the plot would unfold naturally based on the protagonist's decisions as they overcame different types of obstacles. That is how *Fallout 3* and all my favorite tabletop role-playing games pulled me in—a sense of near-infinite possibility constrained by some very specific rules. Why not teach the craft of fiction writing by having students play a role-playing game?

After months of needling the program director, I managed to get a 200-level Introductory Topics in Creative Writing I course titled "Gaming, Worldbuilding, and Narrative" with the theme of postapocalyptic Milwaukee. We started the semester with John Joseph Adams's (2008) short story anthology *Wastelands: Stories of the Apocalypse*,[15] watched the (1985) film *Mad Max Beyond Thunderdome*[16] and the (2009) adaptation of Cormac McCarthy's *The Road*,[17] and played *Fallout 3* with an accompanying assignment that asked students to create a unique character and travel to at least ten unique locations. During class discussion, we discovered that there was no "typical" character build and the ten locations each person found were quite literally all over the map. We spoke about how their characters' traits, statistics, and skills influenced their play strategies and imagined scenarios where we swapped in different protagonists from different stories—how would The Man from *The Road* handle problems differently than *Beyond Thunderdome*'s Max Rockatansky versus what you chose to do with your player character?

We gradually transitioned to coconstructing a postapocalyptic version of Milwaukee, beginning with general features of the world: A superflu had wiped out 80 percent of the population, the "present" was set fifty years postplague, and the remaining infrastructure was steadily collapsing as new social formations took root (complete with raiders, scavengers, and an authoritarian police force protecting the wealthy). From there, twenty students created wiki entries for a total of ten people, places, and things and pinned them to a Google map. I discovered that the volume of their production far outstripped my ability to provide the kind of line-by-line criticism usually employed in creative writing classes, but this was not necessarily a bad thing—the entries added plenty of odd features and interesting characters that made up for imperfect prose with sheer imagination.

Finally, we broke into small groups to run a series of role-playing game sessions with a selection of student volunteers serving as game masters (GMs) for four of the groups and me serving as a GM for a fifth group (plus a sixth made up of student GMs). Those weeks were a chaotic, beautiful mess where I learned about all the advantages and challenges of running tabletop role-playing games in the classroom, something I would continue tinkering with and iterating upon for the next decade and a half. What resonates with me to this day is the level to which the students bought into the project; never had I seen such cooperation, coteaching, and effort to tell their stories in the most compelling ways possible. Furthermore, their fiction was far more interesting than the dull, formulaic stories submitted by students in my traditional Intro to Creative Writing classes.

The student players adored these role-playing sessions because they helped them get into character and collaboratively determine the direction their stories would take. For my part, I became fascinated with their world-building, particularly the assumptions students made about how complex systems interacted. The world lacked a consistent set of social forces—something that students tended to handwave away but left massive gaps in the narrative. To what extent had a functional government risen from the ashes? Was a structured bartering economy in place for scavengers, or was it all ad hoc? What happened to gender and race relations in the years of rebuilding? To what degree was religion present? Or artistic endeavors? I realized that we had bypassed a significant foundational element—namely, which broad social forces were at play and how different characters would have experienced them. This eventually became a central pillar of my research and pedagogy.

Based on this class, I published my first peer-reviewed academic works: a chapter entitled "From Meaning to Experience: Teaching Fiction Writing with Digital RPGs" in the (2012) collection *Dungeons, Dragons, and Digital Denizens: The Digital Role-Playing Game*[18] and a (2011) Games+Learning+Society (GLS) Conference presentation called "Gaming, World Building, and Narrative: Using Role-Playing Games to Teach Fiction Writing."[19]

GLS proved to be a turning point in my academic career, where I transformed from a fiction writer to a scholar and researcher who wrote fiction. There, I met dozens of new colleagues who would become lifelong friends, not least of all a group from the University of Connecticut made up of fellow graduate student Stephen Slota, classics professor Roger Travis, and high school Latin teacher Kevin Ballestrini.

While I continued to stress over my academic job prospects, it felt like a door had opened to a new and spectacular world.

GAMES + LEARNING + SOCIETY

The GLS Conference in Madison, Wisconsin, was, in its time, a mecca for scholars and practitioners of games and learning. The two of us (Trent and Stephen) met at GLS 7 in the summer of 2011 as a pair of first-time attendees. Game-based education was rising in popularity, and we were along for the ride, attending and presenting at every year's conference from our inaugural participation until the final conference held on the University of Wisconsin–Madison campus in August 2017.

Throughout this period, we crossed paths with waves of researchers, graduate students, K–12 educators, and industry experts, many of whom were operating on the cutting edge of games and learning from a diverse set of disciplines and for a wide variety of purposes. Each night after a sumptuous buffet dinner, the conference would move into "play mode" on the terraces of the Wisconsin Union, where attendees sat around tables, drank beer, played games, and networked. Most games featured a meta layer of discussion about the game being played—its mechanics, affordances, and suitability to be adapted for our individual classrooms—that enriched the experience (figure 0.2).

In the conference's twilight years, we perceived subtle changes that affected our understanding of the field more broadly.

First was the emergence of two distinct attendee strands: (1) those who were entirely green to game-based education and (2) those who belonged

FIGURE 0.2
Two examples of collegial play and discussion at the (2015) Games + Learning + Society 11 Conference: Trent and Michael F. Young duking it out in the card-based debate game *CARD-tamen*™ (left); Kevin Ballestrini and Stephen engaged in the fast-paced tabletop role-playing game *Fiasco*™ (right).

to a core group of experienced practitioners. Having long since transitioned from newbies to the latter category, we noted the development of a presentation genre one might call "My First Experience Teaching with Games," which, in most cases, began with an overview of their course design that would ultimately shift into a torrent of challenges and realizations. The veterans among us could predict with exceptional accuracy what the speaker would go on to describe—a failed implementation because they leaped into game-based instruction without understanding the learning theories that underpinned best practices (e.g., aligning instructional objectives with a specific game's play objectives). Although these presentations were no doubt useful for some attendees, they did little to advance the conversation about games and education in new and interesting directions.

Second, and more problematic, was the increasingly prevalent assumption that game-based solutions could be rolled out to entire school districts with little or no teacher training. It often involved digital learning apps installed on student tablets or laptops featuring suites of games aimed at minimizing or replacing the teacher. Contrary to this goal, research suggested that the successful use of instructional games required educators to be *active participants* alongside their students, coaching and encouraging them to think through different strategies while learners externalized the logic behind their decision-making. This only reinforced our belief that the best games for learning were simulations and role-plays, flexible experiences that provided space for students to reflect on their learning—something altogether different than chocolate-covered broccoli.

Contemporaneously, the rapid popularization of digital and tabletop games, as well as expanded tie-ins of large media franchises (e.g., Marvel, Disney, *Pokémon*, *Harry Potter*, *Star Wars*), introduced an intriguing new element; namely, how emergent gameplay narratives (i.e., those resulting from an individual player's experience of a game) could work with or against the "canon" narratives that audiences were receiving across different forms of media—not just films but novels and print fiction, comics, television series, and digital and tabletop games. Because players could now enter their favorite fictional worlds and become active participants in shaping events, we found ourselves wondering what community coauthorship might portend for the future of K–12 schools, universities, and more.

As we pressed into the mid- and late 2010s, Trent's research concentrated on collaborative worldbuilding in creative writing classes as well as the use of role-playing games to drive student fiction writing using *Star Wars* and *Game of Thrones* to leverage students' preexisting knowledge of these worlds into their work in a kind of literary-minded fan fiction. Stephen, meanwhile, busily honed their craft as a learning scientist and educational technologist, serving first as an instructional design specialist and then as an interdisciplinary university professor in educational psychology and digital media design. Our joint synthesis of these domains yielded dozens of academic works over a ten-year period (e.g., the well-cited [2012] *Review of Educational Research* meta-analysis *Our Princess Is in Another Castle: A Review of Trends in Serious Gaming for Education;*[20] the [2017] edited volume *Exploding the Castle: Rethinking How Video Games & Game Mechanics Can Shape the Future of Education;*[21] and the [2018] text *Collaborative Worldbuilding for Writers and Gamers*[22]) as well as a number of educational board, card, and video games for K–12 and higher education (e.g., *VERBA*™, *Underlings of Underwing*™, *Collaborative Worldbuilding Card Deck, EOS-503, Beyond Nuremberg: Courtroom 600*).

THE END OF THE BEGINNING

This book is a product of our continuing collaboration and friendship through guest lectures, conference presentations, roundtable sessions, and more. In that time, we have experienced the games and learning movement maturing and going to seed. We have also seen the United States careen into intense political polarization. We have lamented the spread of pandemic disease and misinformation, the devastation wrought by unchecked capitalism, and the acceleration of climate disaster. We have celebrated the rise in women's, BIPOC, and LGBTQ+ activism; the renewed strength of unions; and the immeasurable ways people have banded together in support of one another. We have borne witness to academic administrators playing Russian roulette with sky-high tuition prices and devastating cuts to courses, programs, and faculty jobs—sequestration and retrenchment rather than visionary expansion into novel, creative approaches to research and instruction.

The forthcoming pages are our way of tilting the wheel in a more favorable direction. Large, complex systems move with all the alacrity of a cruise ship, but we believe that playful pedagogies—including and especially worldbuilding—are the way forward, both for the field of education and the broader challenges now facing humanity. They are tools for practicing empathy, for expanding critical thinking, and for better understanding ourselves and one another. Yes, we may be one raindrop in a monsoon, but alongside other committed innovators, we can bring about the much-needed flood of change that will land us on the sunny shores of something so much better.

We are grateful for your enlistment in our effort and hope you enjoy the adventure ahead.

I FOUNDATION

1 AROUND THE WORLD IN 300 PAGES

"It is the obvious which is so difficult to see most of the time. People say 'It's as plain as the nose on your face.' But how much of the nose on your face can you see, unless someone holds a mirror up to you?"

—Isaac Asimov[1]

Below is a (1902) photograph of the Pemberton Memorial Operating Room in Victoria, British Columbia (figure 1.1).

At the time the photo was taken, the operating room was considered the most advanced of its kind: Outdated kerosene lamps had been replaced by electrical lighting connected to the broader grid, the windows were designed for easy sanitization after each procedure, and the room's layout was organized around antisepsis techniques pioneered by British surgeon and pathologist Joseph Lister. However, viewed through a present-day lens, this setup leaves much to be desired.

Improperly sealed windows created the potential for contaminated air to seep in and out. Lightbulbs dangled loosely overhead. There was a wash basin with no running water. Beside the table sat several unmarked vials, bottles, and containers. No one involved in a surgical procedure wore any kind of personal protective equipment (PPE)—no masks, no gloves, no gowns, and no goggles—even as a patient lay exposed before them.

By contrast, contemporary operating rooms (figure 1.2)[2] house a combination of computers, digital displays, and sterilized equipment. Anyone entering the space is required to fully scrub down and don body-covering PPE. The room is closed to the outside to limit particulate impurities, while an HVAC system maintains airflow and HEPA filtration. Unlike Pemberton, there are fully manipulable light fixtures of varying size and luminosity that allow surgical staff to fully visualize the patient. Surgical procedures can be conducted in person or remotely via microcameras, laparoscopes, and robotics.

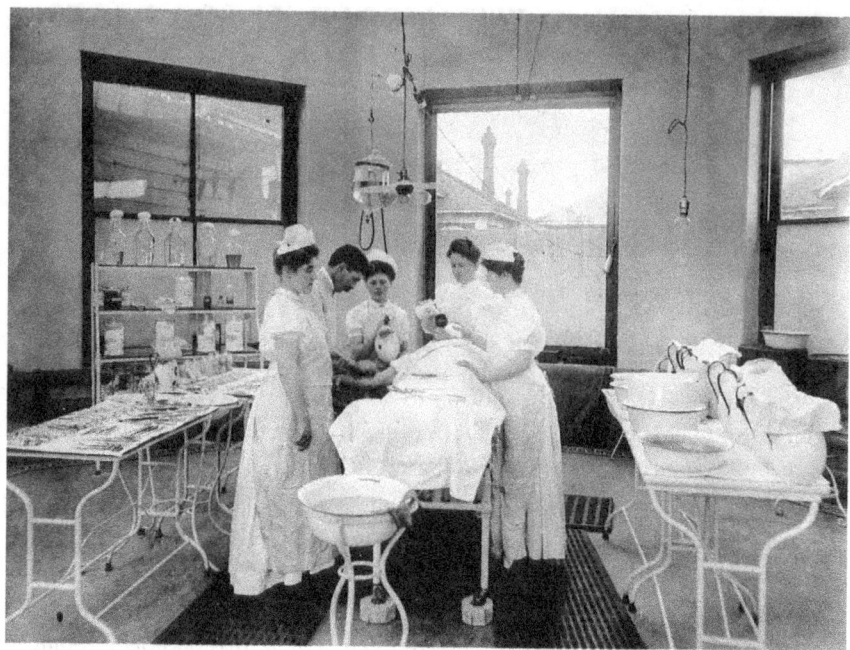

FIGURE 1.1
A (1902) photograph of nurses and a physician operating on a patient in the Pemberton Memorial Operating Room at Royal Jubilee Hospital in Victoria, British Columbia. This space was once the most advanced surgical suite in the world. Source: *The Pemberton Memorial Operating Room at Royal Jubilee Hospital*, 1902, photograph, British Columbia Archives, https://search-bcarchives.royalbcmuseum.bc.ca/pemberton-memorial-operating-room-royal-jubilee-hospital-victoria-2.

If you were scheduled for an appendectomy, would the original Pemberton Memorial Operating Room suffice? Or would you demand something more in line with twenty-first-century standards?

We ask this question to emphasize how strange it is that the field of education has not similarly matured over the last century. Yes, instructional technology has progressed from pen-and-paper exercises to fully online multimedia, and yes, there are decades' worth of scholarship concerning the optimal curricular structure and instructor-learner interaction, but we continue, by and large, to organize classrooms the same way our educational predecessors did (figure 1.3): chalk and whiteboard at the front, learners arranged in rows and columns, and textbooks (or their digital equivalents) used to support retention-oriented activities and assessments.

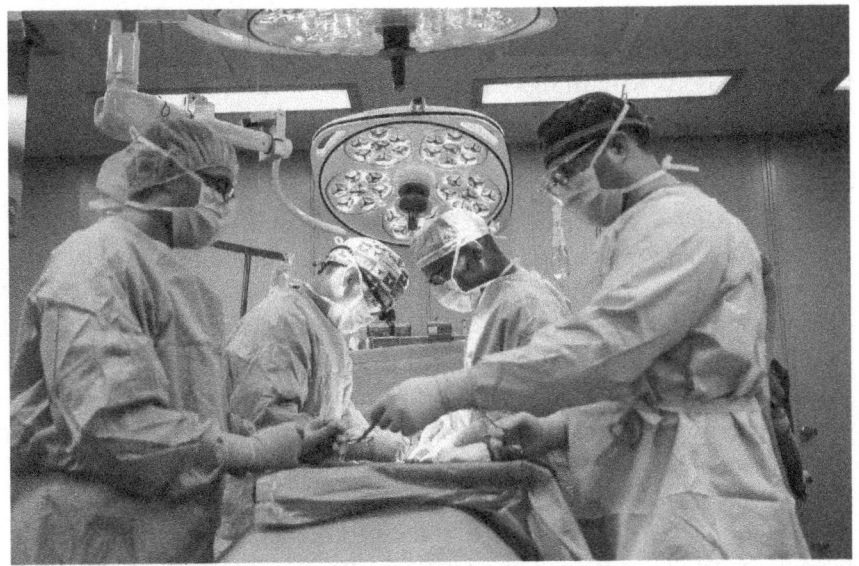

FIGURE 1.2
A (2017) photograph of four sailors aboard the US Military Sealift Command hospital ship USNS Comfort performing surgery on a patient after Hurricane Maria. Source: Petty Officer 2nd Class Stephane Belcher, *Comfort Operation*, 2017, photograph, US Department of Defense, https://www.defense.gov/Multimedia/Photos/igphoto/2002038406/. The appearance of US Department of Defense (DoD) visual information does not imply or constitute DoD endorsement.

FIGURE 1.3
Two schools temporally separated by a century but connected in spirit; a classroom circa 1924 (left) and a classroom circa 2008 (right). Source: Unknown photographer, *Cross Street School Classroom*, 1924, photograph, Flickr CC-BY-4.0, https://www.flickr.com/photos/rich701/albums/72157632322101295/; Allison Meier, Classroom, 2008, Flickr CC-BY-4.0, https://www.flickr.com/photos/astrozombie/3121669013/in/photostream/.

Surgeons in the Pemberton Memorial Operating Room relied on methods that were substantially different than those employed today, and there are good reasons why things changed: We know more about the human body, we have a better grasp of the germ theory of disease, and we invented tools capable of enhancing the way surgeons do their jobs. That type of renewal should not be abnormal in any discipline—in the case of surgery, it ensured that a greater number of patients would survive and thrive. Education could very well be the same. And yet, while surgical suites have undergone a complete transformation over the last one hundred years, educational environments have not.

The problem of education's relative languor is compounded when we consider the speed at which our world now moves and operates. Digital communications fly around the globe in milliseconds, carrying text, audio, and images that can be received by handheld devices with orders of magnitude more computing power than the machines used to land the Apollo spacecraft on the moon. Diseases that ravaged humanity for millennia have been dramatically contained or, as with smallpox and Guinea worm, eradicated. With approximately one hundred thousand flights carrying travelers every day, a human of modest resources can travel to virtually any corner of the earth, and even if they are not able to physically travel, the entire planet can be explored in virtual reality, all of humanity's accumulated knowledge accessible through just a few clicks.

The life of the average human has been inscribed by countless technologies and sophisticated systems that allow us to eat foods from other countries, live comfortably in climate-controlled environments, enjoy globally produced entertainment, and physically transport ourselves at speeds our ancestors could not have comprehended. But how much of the world—full of its modern technological marvels—do we truly understand? How many of us can explain the simple mechanics that power our automobiles, describe the design of our smartphones, or provide rudimentary explanations of the internet's architecture?

If we asked a random passerby to construct a basic outline of US history, we would be fortunate to get a narrative beginning with the Pilgrims' arrival on the Mayflower, the American Revolution, and some uncomfortable silence about the period between the signing of the Constitution and the outbreak of the Civil War. Odds are they would have only the slightest inkling of which Indigenous peoples inhabited American lands before the fifteenth century. We might get something about World War I, World War II, the Civil Rights Movement, and the Vietnam War—oops, we skipped the war in Korea!—before jumping to Watergate, the Gulf War, 9/11, the Great Recession, and ... COVID lockdowns? Whole *centuries* glossed over with a lopsided bias toward today, and we harbor doubts that most American adults could even articulate *this* much without significant coaching.

Now, consider what would happen if you repeated the question with a focus on the history of our North American neighbors, Canada and Mexico. Imagine the blank stare you would get in response. Had the person taken a Western civilization class, they might know something about the culture of the Greeks and Romans, knights and monks in the Middle Ages, Columbus, the discovery and colonization of the New World, and the unconscious adoption of Western cultural norms at the founding of America. But would they know the history of Latin America? Africa? The Middle East, Asia, or Oceania? Yes, Oceania! It is a real geographic region. And yes, humans have lived there for a *very* long time. All of these places and all of these people exist. Each has its own history just as rich and complicated and oft confusing as ours.

In the present, we surf the news and see that Russia has invaded Ukraine. Israel has retaliated against a coordinated set of Hamas-led terrorist attacks. The US Supreme Court has overturned *Roe v. Wade* and ruled that abortion is not constitutionally protected. Iranians protest their government's stream of human rights violations. China rattles its proverbial saber at Taiwan, daring America to intervene. Unprecedented extreme weather events occur around the globe with alarming regularity. A deluge of information pours in from dozens of different authorities—some more credible than others—in a constant blend of fact-reporting, opinionated commentary, and demagogues calling every source they find distasteful "fake news."

Educators (often reluctantly) find themselves on the frontlines of these debates for failing to prepare students for "the real world." Parents, political figures, and industry leaders decry university graduates' inability to solve problems in professional work environments, though rarely do we pin down any parents, political figures, or industry leaders to explain what they mean by problem-solving, what specific job-ready skills graduates lack, or how these criteria should be measured over time. As a society, we choose not to press on more troubling questions, like whether parents, political figures, and industry leaders are better equipped than trained educators to prepare students for the future—not just graduation or the five years postgraduation but the rest of their lives.

We thus offer this book as a humble answer to the question, "What can be done to reconfigure education for the challenges of modernity?" Beyond advocating for the adoption of avant-garde technologies, we believe it vital to help educators at every level and in every discipline revise their *instruction* for critical thinking and its less-talked-about sibling, empathy. As you will see, our strategy is built on deconstructing and analyzing the planet's most mind-bogglingly complex, urgent questions through a combination of collaboration, inquiry, and reflection—a process we call **worldbuilding**.

A SIMPLE CUP OF COFFEE

Before getting down to business, let us collect our thoughts in the same way we do each morning: with a simple cup of coffee.

We—and our students—can often be spotted bustling to class with a digital device clasped in one hand and a cup of joe in the other. The coffee is usually contained in a recyclable cardboard cylinder capped with a plastic lid (figure 1.4). On occasion, the cylinder includes a thin insulator to maintain the coffee's temperature while keeping our hands unscorched. At current prices, a "large" size costs $5 or $6.

When we pass our money on to the barista or drive-thru attendant, it pays for more than just watery bean juice. It pays for each piece of the liquid-containing apparatus. The brand name. The electricity needed to run equipment in the shop. The water to boil. The employee who poured the coffee and served it.

The cleaning staff who ensured the shop was a healthy and safe place for patrons to consume their food and beverages.

It pays for the paper used to create the cup. The lumberer who cut down the trees so they could be sawed and pressed into paper. The ink used to print the logo. The shipping freighter that transported the beans and paper and ink and plastic across an ocean. It pays for the fossil fuels that powered the shipping freighter, the extraction of those fossil fuels, and the various additional industrial and commercial processes that intersect with coffee sales.

While many of us follow a bleary-eyed routine of coffee purchase multiple times per week, rarely do we contemplate the complex systems required to provide us with this fairly mundane aspect of our lives. Our mere existence impels involvement in exceptionally deep and broad chains of production, distribution, and market participation—threads woven first into the creation of an item and then its delivery to our doorsteps.

It is easy to overlook the fact that there are human beings who pick coffee beans, design packaging, manage store locations, take our orders, and serve our coffee. Some of them are our neighbors, while others live halfway

FIGURE 1.4
A freshly brewed cup of Worldbuilder's Choice Coffee™ premium blend—delicious and fictitious!

around the world, speak different languages, and come from different cultures. How the person picking coffee beans feels about their role in the bigger picture of supplying our morning coffee is likely quite different than the corporate brand manager, the food scientist developing new flavors, or the server, the only node in the system with whom we directly interact (even if that interaction is superficial). Some people may take great pride in their role, whereas some participate as a means to an end (i.e., earning a living wage). Others may feel coerced or compelled into participation because they have no better options.

Reflecting on all that goes into satiating our coffee fix is bewildering in and of itself, but the same thought experiment can be repeated with respect to our food, clothing, furniture, electronic devices, modes of transportation, energy sources, toys, and the medium through which you are reading this book. Even worse, the impossible complexity is multiplied across everyone around you; everyone in your city, country, and the world. No set of natural forces would ever produce these things without human intervention. How, then, do we handle the cognitive overload that comes with existing in a seemingly infinite web of causality related to our material culture?

In general, we ignore it.

And understandably so. We have plenty to contend with when it comes to making decisions about our lives in a more immediate sense—our families, our friends, our careers, our pastimes, our physical and emotional health. This is not to say that we *never* think about our positioning in the wider world. We clearly do, particularly when it comes to the overlap of material culture and personal identity, like when we opt for an electric car or energy-saving appliance as a way to minimize our carbon footprint. Conscientious purchases indicate that the consumer understands themselves as part of a broader ecosystem and that their choices have consequences for the environment. On one end of the spectrum, someone might choose to bike or use mass transit, rejecting fossil fuel *and* electric vehicles because both contribute to traffic congestion and threats to pedestrian safety. On the other end, someone might buy the biggest gas-guzzling monster truck on the market as a middle finger to those who care about climate change.

So, beyond the dizzying complexity of our relation to the systems that produce our material culture (or, rather, material cultures, since they vary from place to place), our behaviors are subject to influence from infinite attitudes, beliefs, and values held by individuals and wider society. We just avoid thinking about it.

Wait. How do we identify larger sets of attitudes, beliefs, and values that the "wider" society supposedly holds? And how deeply held are those attitudes, beliefs, and values? How "wide" are we talking? Reasonable people in industrialized countries near-unanimously agree that children should spend their youth being educated in schools rather than working in mines or on factory floors. But ask whether a person should have the right to voluntarily terminate an unwanted pregnancy, and you could not come to a consensus in many *households* much less across wider society. Concerning abortion, specifically, one subset of the population firmly believes in full bodily autonomy and the right to choose under any circumstances. Another believes the unborn fetus has full personhood and must be carried to term. Many more fall between the two dominant poles.

Because the size of each subset fluctuates wildly between cities, regions, and countries over time, we can trace linkages between global systems of attitudes, beliefs, and values just as we do with global systems of material goods. Ergo, when we say "wider society's attitudes, beliefs, and values," we mean the broad swath of attitudes, beliefs, and values observable within specified "fuzzy boundaries" of space and time (we will return to this idea in chapter 6, "Worlds in Space and Time").

Put another way, complex sociocultural systems are not part of some larger immutable reality. They are the product of humans interacting with and regulating their environments. Our day-to-day, moment-to-moment experiences lead us to engage with social forces in myriad ways, and these social forces undergo continuous transformations—large and small—at different rates. It has always been this way, from the first primitive societies right up through today.

Despite the structure of our lives and the ways each of us is affected by reality, we mostly manage to rise from bed, get dressed, and procure our aforementioned blessed cup of coffee to cast off the last vestiges of sleep.

Differences in our individual experiences are subsumed by other "rules" that we uncritically accept as being true for everyone: Without proper nutrition and hydration, your body will wither, sicken, and eventually die; if you dive off a balcony, gravity will cause you to fall downward rather than upward; if you encounter a rabid animal in the wilderness, it will not care about your socioeconomic status, race, gender, or religion. The natural world has no politics.

Things change dramatically when we scrutinize human-constructed systems. For example, anyone can drive their car 35 miles per hour in a 20-mile-per-hour school zone, but whether you are pulled over and ticketed can depend on your race, sex, age, the type of car you drive, and/or the officer's attitude. The same goes for acquiring a bank loan, purchasing property, landing a job, and countless other interactions that are decidedly unequal. A potential employer may not hire a woman for a programming job because they believe men are naturally more logical; a realtor might avoid showing houses to a Black gay couple in the same neighborhood as a white heterosexual couple because of assumptions about which community is best for each set of buyers; an atheist might be denied a job working with children because the hirer assumes atheists lack a well-calibrated moral compass. Many times, people on the losing side of such practices have no idea that they are being discriminated against; moreover, those doing the discriminating frequently fail to realize that implicit biases are influencing their decisions. In the United States, such issues of inequality and redress have become increasingly prominent through the latter half of the twentieth century and the early part of the twenty-first century. While no one has identified a perfect answer, the following sections illustrate how we might hew a novel path forward.

COMPLEXITY, GENERALIZATIONS, AND STEREOTYPES

We collectively navigate our fast-paced, rapidly changing, and endlessly complex world by way of a process called **meaningful generalization**. At the most abstract, we generalize that humans are essentially the same: We require oxygen, hydration, and shelter from the elements to survive; we do not need to debate (nor deeply understand) the basic laws of physics since gravity pulls us to the earth whether we like it or not; we are all susceptible to illness and at times depend on others for care. We also make broad generalizations about acceptable conduct in social interactions, including topics for discussion, public versus private behavior, and styles of dress. For instance, a person traveling to a foreign culture can unintentionally violate local norms if they do not understand the nuances of the culture with which they are interacting or if they mistakenly assume that their home culture's norms are universal—their generalizations about the rules of society can be in some way incorrect, misapplied, or misguided. The ramifications of such errors can range from mild embarrassment to a stern admonition or even a harsh penalty.

These generalizations are not value judgments—they are aspects of society that a reasonable person would recognize as being mostly accurate and true. We often rely on demographics or statistics to support them, including the creation of tentative statements justified by reputable resources and refinement through deeper research. Keep in mind that generalizations are intended to distinguish one place or group from another while leaving room for a nontrivial number of people to resist or defy such categorizations. We do not want generalizing to collapse into lazy sweeping statements or damaging stereotypes (see chapter 8, "Examining Life-Worlds Through Demographics").

Consider the following statement: Residents of Green Bay, Wisconsin, adore the American football team the Green Bay Packers, eat a lot of bratwurst and cheese curds, and drink a lot of beer.

Pushed to support our assertions, we could provide the decades-long waitlist for season tickets to Packers games and per capita food and beverage consumption statistics as compared to other cities in the region and country. We could also clarify that these attributes are *generally* true and differentiate Green Bay, Wisconsin, from Anaheim, California, or Miami, Florida—that is, there are almost certainly more Green Bayans who love the Packers, eat bratwurst and cheese curds, and drink beer than would be found in Anaheim or Miami, each of which has its own sports teams, foods, and drink preferences. However, there are plenty of Green Bayans who do not care for professional sports, eat neither meat nor dairy products, and do not drink alcohol. Although these people belong to the minority in one or more of these categories, their existence is as real and valid as someone who fits our image of an ordinary Green Bay citizen.

We can mitigate the possibility of endorsing a damaging stereotype by using words and phrases that qualify our statements. For instance, we might say *a majority* of Green Bayans self-identify as enthusiastic fans of the Green Bay Packers and that *many* of them regularly consume bratwurst, cheese curds, and beer. We could use terms like *some*, *few*, a *slim minority*, an *overwhelming number*, and others to indicate prevalence without collapsing into a stereotype that pigeonholes people or robs them of agency. The combination of quantitative data and qualifying statements provides us some flexibility in declaring typical factors as distinguishing one place or group from another without descending into totalizing statements.

Our Green Bay example is pretty benign and considered common knowledge for casual American football fans (or a point of local pride for Wisconsinites). We chose it for its minimally controversial subject matter and because one of us (Trent) grew up there. Yet, if we swap out this low-stakes generalization for another, things become uncomfortable very quickly. What traits might we ascribe to political identities like "progressive" or "conservative"? What if we implied that white and Black Americans are intrinsically different? What if we assigned attributes to certain religious affiliations like "Mormon" or "Muslim"? It is not unusual for malicious entities—including those in corporate media—to eschew meaningful generalizations in favor of harmful stereotypes that sow division and resentment.

Consequently, the global community needs to do a better job of understanding that while generalizations are crucial for processing the enormous wave of information continuously flooding our newsfeeds, they are not a blank check to overgeneralize to the point of stereotyping. Generalizations should allow a degree of self-identification (i.e., those aspects of our demographics we wish to define us versus those we actively resist or defy) and hold together our worldviews from moment to moment. Some individuals abuse these lines of variation to claim intergroup conflict is inevitable, but there are clear differences between meaningful generalization and rigid classification.

On the flip side, we must guard against a slide into full cultural relativism lest we platform malevolent voices that seek to undermine diversity and cooperation—white supremacists, child predators, and fascistic authoritarians who demand to have their positions entertained and widely disseminated.

Philosopher of science Karl Popper (1945) identified the problem as a "paradox of tolerance" wherein tacit acceptance of divisive, antisocial perspectives invariably leads to an onslaught of intolerance that can destroy a tolerant society.[3] In the (1987) words of Michel Rosenfeld, "it seems contradictory to extend freedom of speech to extremists who . . . if successful, ruthlessly suppress the speech of those with whom they disagree."[4]

To illustrate this delicate balancing act, recall our morning cup of coffee, this time in the context of the fair-trade movement (i.e., the effort to help developing countries benefit from better trade policies and establish sustainable processes for harvesting crops). Start with the concept of three worlds: the world of coffee production, the world of coffee marketing and distribution, and the world of coffee consumption. First, sketch out the specifics of spatial borders, or the *where* for each of these three worlds. From what regions or countries do coffee beans originate? Who consumes the highest percentages of harvested coffee? Who is responsible for getting the coffee from a plantation to a corner coffee shop?

Some cursory research shows that the top three coffee-producing countries are Brazil, Vietnam, and Colombia, and the top three coffee consumers are the Nordic nations of Finland, Sweden, and Iceland. We next need to draft some quick models of Brazil, Vietnam, and Colombia to compare their cultures and identify similarities and differences in politics, economics, and socioculture. To what extent is the experience of a coffee farmer in Brazil similar to and different from a coffee farmer in Vietnam or Colombia? We can dive deeper to ask whether the experience of all coffee farmers in Brazil is similar, or we can inquire as to whether different coffee-producing regions within Brazil are significantly different from one another. Repeat the process with the top three coffee-consuming countries by asking what they have in common and where they are different. Are their coffee-drinking cultures alike or unrecognizable across borders?

The coffee beans picked by a Vietnamese farmer are eventually converted to hot, brown liquid served in a paper cup in Norway. What happens between those two moments in space and time? How long does it take to move from one place to the other? To answer, we would need to trace the entire process from harvest to final product; learn about drying, milling, and processing; and then study roasting, grinding, brewing, and tasting. Where do each of these steps happen? Who does this work? What are the economics of this labor? Who assumes the costs for each stage? Who profits?

Our explanation will always involve making generalizations, though we should strive to ensure that our generalizations are meaningful and not reductive. Likewise, we must be open to having our preconceptions challenged, modified, or overturned based on what information we uncover. Do we find that working conditions in Brazil, Vietnam, and Colombia are similar, or do some workers have significantly better or worse circumstances? If so, why? Is there a single solution that could improve conditions for *all* workers, or would each nation need solutions tailored to their specific situations? When we consider the profitability and sustainability of this process, how are the profits distributed? What are the most pressing environmental challenges, and where are these challenges geographically experienced? If we tinker with harvesting and distribution, how do we affect end consumers? If café sales fund this enterprise, is there a minimum volume required to keep the system running? Is there a price point for a cup of coffee that coffee drinkers will refuse to pay? Is it possible that they will find it more convenient to grind and brew their own coffee rather than buying it from a local coffee shop?

No matter the domain, we want to account for the human beings involved.

With respect to coffee bean planting, cultivating, and harvesting, do workers in Brazil, Vietnam, and Colombia believe their working conditions are acceptable? Is the coffee processing and distribution business sufficiently profitable for everyone involved? Are consumers satisfied with the product and its price? At this juncture, it is imperative that we stop and think about the primary and secondary sources used to answer these questions. A college student in Toronto might believe that workers in Colombia should be satisfied with their wages or that Scandinavians ought to pay double for their morning cup of coffee, but those opinions fall outside the reality experienced *within* the supply chain. Remaining thoughtful about those most affected depends on our ability to practice critical thinking and empathy, acknowledging that our perspectives are inherently limited by our narrow and subjective bands of existence.

CRITICAL THINKING AND EMPATHY

Since this book argues that critical thinking can be taught, we must define what that term means to us. There are many different opinions on the subject, as described in Jonathan Haber's (2020) *Critical Thinking* and listed on the Foundation for Critical Thinking website.[5] At the (1987) Eighth Annual International Conference on Critical Thinking and Education Reform,

Michael Scriven and Richard Paul offered the following definition: "Critical thinking is the intellectually disciplined process of actively and skillfully conceptualizing, applying, analyzing, synthesizing, and/or evaluating information gathered from, or generated by, observation, experience, reflection, reasoning, or communication, as a guide to belief and action. In its exemplary form, it is based on universal intellectual values that transcend subject matter divisions: clarity, accuracy, precision, consistency, relevance, sound evidence, good reasons, depth, breadth, and fairness."[6]

While different articulations have their merits, we like the succinctness of Scriven and Paul's definition, and, to us, it covers three essential points:

- It describes the process as being disciplined (in the sense that someone who thinks critically does so in a thorough—not necessarily linear—way).
- It includes multiple parallel means by which we understand different kinds of information.
- The end goal of critical thinking is to shape beliefs and take action.

This distinguishes critical thinking from problem-solving, the latter of which we see as being related to developing solutions to well-defined challenges. A good problem solver will usually be a good critical thinker, but we see critical thinking as being composed of a broader set of skills that include a question's ethical dimensions and human considerations. For instance, calculating the velocity of a comet a million light-years away is a sophisticated question that has a definitive, mathematical answer. However, there is no single, definitive answer as to why statistically fewer physicists are women or people of color. The first involves problem-solving without any ethical or human considerations—the comet will continue on its way regardless of what we do. The second involves critical thinking about how humans develop career aspirations and who on our planet might have one or more advantages (or disadvantages) when it comes to realizing their goals. The system by which someone becomes a physicist is designed and administered by us; we cannot do much to alter a comet's velocity, but we can certainly affect the trajectory of human-created institutions.

Like critical thinking, empathy has many different definitions, the most basic being the ability to understand and appreciate another person's feelings, emotions, and viewpoints. While we might interrogate what it means to "understand" or "appreciate" someone else's perspective, we find the general definition sufficient for our purpose in this book. When we say "worldbuilding helps develop empathy," we mean that the process positions learners to consider the perspectives of different people who exist in the world and reflect on the roles that they play. We couple this with the question, How would you feel about a given situation if you traded places with someone else in the world you are examining?

This question has no correct answer and relies on learners tapping into their imaginations, traversing time and space to jettison the reality that they inhabit and explore a different (possibly alien) one. That means temporarily shelving their own beliefs to adopt those of other human beings who may view things quite differently. Can we accurately imagine what it would have been like to exist as a peasant man or a noblewoman living in the sixteenth-century Aztec Empire? Probably not. However, with some research and critical thinking, we can approximate it.

What were the relationships between the different classes in this world? Did people expect to have any social mobility? How did gender affect an individual's role in society? We can debate the plausibility of different answers based on what historians, anthropologists, and descendants of the culture have said or written. We can also apply basic logic to draw conclusions about likely events and perspectives, such as assuming that a merchant would enjoy a more comfortable life than someone who was enslaved, acknowledging how agency, autonomy, and liberty affect everyone in a society.

We should briefly note the difference between empathy (the ability to understand another person's perspective) and sympathy (showing compassion for their circumstances and desiring to mitigate their suffering). We can, for example, *empathize* with communities in economically depressed rural areas of the United States who feel abandoned by their government and confused by rapid social change without *sympathizing* with the minority who adopt bigotry and white nationalism as an outlet for their dissatisfaction. Two things can be simultaneously true: White nationalism can be abhorrent, and there can be a legitimate need to dispassionately evaluate its underlying causes for the purpose of positing potential solutions. Hence, we recommend leveraging empathy as a tool for *understanding* rather than relying on sympathy, which may be employed to justify or excuse beliefs that have no place being elevated. We hope that you will continue thinking about how these concepts interface with the development and implementation of instructional activities as you read on.

WHAT IS WORLDBUILDING (AND WHAT CAN WE DO WITH IT)?

As signaled throughout the preceding pages, worldbuilding is an effort to represent daily life in a given world as accurately and from as many perspectives as possible. This involves evaluating interrelated governmental, economic, social, and cultural forces to

- characterize these forces at a specific moment in history;
- account for why these forces came to be in the first place; and
- examine how different people experience(d) these forces differently based on their socioeconomic and sociocultural contexts.

The process can be subdivided into six stages:

1. Locating the world in both space and time by defining its scope and sequence
2. Modeling the social forces at play in a world based on its structures and substructures
3. Writing a metanarrative lead that broadly describes different aspects of the world, accounting for different perspectives and lived experiences
4. Populating a catalog with entries of People, Places, Things, Events, and Groups that are relevant to the world
5. Working with different analyses, simulations, and role-play scenarios based on the worldbuilding project
6. Concluding with a debrief and critical reflection

When well implemented, these stages comprise a rigorous yet playful venture that can be adapted for many different purposes. It is not like a board game with physical pieces, an established set of written rules, and a well-defined win condition but a loose skeleton that can be adjusted to meet the wants and needs of users with varying goals.

Importantly, worldbuilding does not depend on prior knowledge of game-based learning scholarship, and this book does not retread or relitigate those ideas. We view it as a separate interdisciplinary pedagogy with a distinct setup and function. If you would like a detailed explanation and dissection of games in education, we suggest reviewing James Paul Gee's (2003) *What Video Games Have to Teach Us About Learning and Literacy* as well as more recent works from scholars such as Sasha Barab, Anna Arici, Kurt Squire, Constance Steinkuehler, Douglas Clark, Valerie Schute, Fengfeng Ke, Yasmin Kafai, Deborah Fields, Matthew Farber, and Kat Schrier.

Notwithstanding the above, worldbuilding and game-based learning *are* grounded in the same educational theories and principles, and we have found the former to be an effective vehicle for discussing "why" and "how" high-quality instructional design and teaching unfold. Many K–12 educators get just a passing glimpse of learning theory as they pursue their certifications, and faculty in higher education usually default to the same methods with which they were taught (e.g., information delivery through didactic lectures and knowledge reproduction via quizzes, papers, and short answer or multiple-choice exams). We aim to highlight the explicit relationship between theory and practice so that *all* educators can better unify the two and develop more substantive, defensible instructional practices, worldbuilding-related or not.

We have therefore organized the forthcoming chapters into four complementary segments that connect learning science, instructional planning, practical concerns, and lived examples:

- Part I, "Foundation," reflects on the history of education and the evolution of different learning theories that support worldbuilding-based pedagogy. It also describes frameworks for understanding community-building and assessment strategies to accompany worldbuilding curricula.
- Part II, "Concepts," targets the application of theory to develop worldbuilding units of different lengths and for different purposes, including guidelines and best practices for different stages of a worldbuilding project.
- Part III, "World Modeling," explains the process by which a worldbuilding project proceeds in the classroom, templatizing it for the reader's use.
- The final portion, part IV, "Case Studies," provides real-world cases from instructors who delivered units on world modeling, simulation, and play as part of their classes. They report on their goals, personalized activities, and conclusions.

The order in which you engage with these segments will differ based on your experience and proficiency with their content. For instance, a veteran educator or designer who has long studied the ins and outs of learning science may find it useful to skip ahead to parts II and III or part IV while using part I as a reference guide. A corporate trainer seeking vertical slices of instructional worldbuilding might jump to the case studies in part IV while working through parts I, II, and III. A casual reader with no formal training in education or design should probably follow a linear path from part I to part IV. We deliberately authored the text as a reader-driven choose-your-own-adventure whose chapters can stand independently *and* as a cohesive whole, thereby addressing multiple constituencies with diverse instructional and design objectives. Use the following summaries to determine which route is right for you:

- Chapter 1, "Around the World in 300 Pages," initiates part I and provides a general overview of how the authors understand complex systems, their analysis, and the politics of worldbuilding.
- Chapter 2, "Road to Contemporary Learning Theory," chronicles the history of public education in the United States, the relationship between educational psychology and philosophy, and the evolution of learning theory.
- Chapter 3, "Theory to Practice," applies contemporary learning theory to instructional practice, demonstrating how and why different theoretical foundations lead to different teaching methods (including and especially worldbuilding).
- Chapter 4, "Collaboration and Community," introduces Communities of Practice as a framework for cultivating productive collaborative worldbuilding environments.
- Chapter 5, "Assessment," compares and contrasts approaches to evaluation and characterizes their implementation as part of worldbuilding curricula and activities.
- Chapter 6, "Worlds in Space and Time," inaugurates part II and outlines relevant terminology for worldbuilding projects, beginning with the "fuzzy borders" that define worlds in space and time.
- Chapter 7, "Structures and Substructures," describes how to tease out a world's structures and substructures—Governance, Economics, Social Relations, and Cultural Influences—to analyze how these interconnected systems create opportunities and disadvantages for different people.
- Chapter 8, "Examining Life-Worlds Through Demographics," discusses the need to account for all people in a world—including outsiders, the politically marginalized, the socially ostracized—and considers how individual lives are shaped by that world's social forces.
- Chapter 9, "Class Preparations," transitions to more practical concerns, covering the materials an instructor should gather and ideas they should consider when electing to incorporate worldbuilding into a lesson, class, workshop, or program.
- Chapter 10, "Wikipedia as a Model for Worldbuilding," analyzes wiki organization and entry construction to facilitate the development of straightforward, nonjudgmental "neutral" articles.

- Chapter 11, "Constructing the World Narrative," opens part III, providing guidance on how to help students put a nebulous concept like "social forces" into language by identifying concrete examples and data that accurately describe the world.
- Chapter 12, "Cataloging People, Places, and Things," explains how to write articles describing the People, Places, and Things that exist in a given world. This is the last stage of the world modeling process and may be the conclusion of your project should you choose not to incorporate simulations and role-play.
- Chapter 13, "Simulations," explores thought experiments where the instructor changes the worldbuilding project in some way, perhaps moving forward or backward in time or introducing a seismic sociocultural, economic, political, or natural disruption.
- Chapter 14, "Role-Play," explains how to run role-play sessions wherein learners adopt the identities of characters in the world your class has collaboratively created. Because role-plays can be counterproductive or even harmful if the subject deals with traumatic moments in history, we describe how to avoid such mishaps and plan for role-play sessions that safely encourage learning.
- Chapter 15, "Wrap-Up and Critical Reflection," covers the denouement of a worldbuilding project as well as debrief methods that cement student learning from the process. We advise carving out time for both group and individual reflections so learners can express—in their own words—which parts of the project most resonated with them and how it differed from work or activities in their other classes.
- Last, "Epilogue: Notes from the End of the World," meditates on worldbuilding as a whole, the field of education, and this particular moment in the United States.

2 ROAD TO CONTEMPORARY LEARNING THEORY

"Not having heard something is not as good as having heard it; having heard it is not as good as having seen it; having seen it is not as good as knowing it; knowing it is not as good as putting it into practice."

—Xun Kuang[1]

When consulting with curious educators, we are frequently asked whether worldbuilding is instructionally sound or just another form of edutainment. Their worry is understandable—after all, there are countless grifters shilling meaningless buzzwords and contrived programs that have no substantive justification for their implementation in either schools or corporate environments, and anyone seeking to integrate new methods as part of their practice should want evidence that what they are investing time and money into is not a house of cards waiting to be blown over by a skeptical parent, administrator, or learner. Between strained budgets, exorbitantly priced technologies, and the legitimate need for improved academic performance in an increasingly competitive world, there is much to lose if and when resources go to waste.

Accordingly, we want to assuage any potential fears by explaining why and how worldbuilding fits into the broader context of human cognition and learning. This chapter details how contemporary theories came to be and connects them to our approach for educators of all ages and disciplines.

WHERE DID YOU COME FROM, WHERE DID YOU GO?

During the seventeenth and eighteenth centuries, education in the thirteen American colonies was organized around highly localized one-room schoolhouses, especially in Puritan New England. The Puritans' belief that a godly society depended on its citizens' ability to read and communicate about the Bible led to the passage of the nation's first School

Laws, which, among other things, required that any town of fifty or more homes have at least one elementary school teacher and those of one hundred or more homes have a full grammar school. These schools emphasized classical languages like Latin, Greek, and Hebrew, and they were treated as a pathway to further study in ministry, philosophy, and law. Being controlled by selectmen of the colony rather than the clergy, they laid a foundation for what would eventually become compulsory, publicly funded education.

Educational expansion did not happen equally quickly for all colonies and peoples—in fact, it took until 1918 for every part of the United States to offer compulsory elementary schooling, another thirty-six years until the landmark (1954) Supreme Court decision in *Brown v. Board of Education* (establishing that school segregation was unconstitutional),[2] and a further four decades until the (1996) Supreme Court decision in *Sheff v. O'Neill* (establishing that inequitable state expenditures on schools in majority Black/Latino communities were unconstitutional).[3] These cases paralleled legislative action meant to establish parity between different subgroups, including Title IX (a provision in the 1972 Education Amendments prohibiting sex-based discrimination in any school or education program that receives funding from the federal government);[4] the (1975) Individuals with Disabilities Education Act;[5] the Rehabilitation Act of 1973, Section 504;[6] and the (1990) Americans with Disabilities Act.[7] But even with those guardrails in place, constructs like race, gender, (dis)ability, and class remained substantially determinative of which students were apportioned access to particular resources across localities, owing to the persistence of institutional and structural racism, sexism, ableism, and classism.

This emphasizes how our definition of "school" is inherently interwoven with a broader, more complex economic, political, and sociocultural ecosystem—the degree to which different people have been empowered to access education has always been tethered to a combination of money, political representation, and governing philosophy. One-room schoolhouses in Massachusetts Bay Colony existed in the context of particular religious conceptions about good citizenship, and *Brown v. Board of Education* occurred due to a confluence of environmental factors and incentives that shaped the thinking and behavior of the people and institutions involved. We should not take for granted that American education was inevitably destined for its current form; rather, it is a product of deliberate and incidental decision-making over the course of three centuries. Changing our trajectory to better support an idealized pluralistic, fully accessible public education system requires reflection on the conditions that made ubiquitous teaching and learning desirable in the first place, dislodging capitalist fan fiction about K–12 schools and universities as workforce training facilities built for compliance, conformity, and efficiency rather than creativity and critical thinking.

ONE FATEFUL DAY

At the same time public education was being popularized throughout the United States, philosophy and psychology emerged as correspondent domains that would eventually codefine the underlying rationale for (and structure of) schooling.

The two fields began as a singular discipline aimed at understanding consciousness through reason. They deviated from one another toward the start of the Enlightenment era—between René Descartes's (1637) proclamation that "Je pense, donc je suis" ("I think, therefore I am"; "cogito, ergo sum")[8] and German physician Franz Joseph Gall's (1796) development of the pseudoscientific practice of phrenology (measuring skull bumps and grooves to "diagnose" emotional states, behaviors, and characteristics)[9]—with one peculiar nineteenth-century accident changing our collective understanding of body and mind.

On the afternoon of September 13, 1848, twenty-five-year-old American railroad foreman Phineas Gage went to work doing the same task he had completed many times: clearing rocks for the Rutland and Burlington Railroad company. Fatefully, Gage neglected to pour sand on top of an explosive charge before pressing it into the ground, and his tamping rod struck a spark that detonated the blasting powder beneath it. The resulting explosion fired the thirteen-pound, meter-long iron dowel straight upward through Gage's left cheek and out the top of his skull (figure 2.1).

Gage's unlikely survival and subsequent recovery (he suffered no loss of language use or motor control) swiftly became a case study illustrating the relationship between a person's brain and their behavior. Prior to his injury, Gage was an amicable, even-tempered colleague, but upon losing his left frontal lobe, he morphed into an angrier, more restless, and unreliable version of himself (though it remains unclear whether this change was permanent; records of his temperament pre- and postaccident are limited). Importantly, his condition offered direct evidence of the frontal lobes' role in manifesting emotions and personality, answered longstanding questions

FIGURE 2.1
An illustration of Phineas Gage holding the iron tamping rod that pierced his skull (left); an illustration of Gage's skull at the moment the iron tamping rod launched through his face (adapted from Van Horn, Irimia, Torgerson, Chambers, Kikinis, and Toga) (right). Source: John Darrell Van Horn, Andrei Irimia, Carina M. Torgerson, Micah C. Chambers, Ron Kikinis, and Arthur W. Toga, "Mapping Connectivity Damage in the Case of Phineas Gage," *PLoS ONE* 7, no. 5 (2012): e37454, https://doi.org/10.1371/journal.pone.0037454.

about the brain's function, and provided key insights as to what further research might yield.

Thus was born an early bifurcation between psychology and philosophy—the former seeking to answer the "what" and "how" of human cognition, while the latter addressed the "why." The two would continue intersecting as scientists sought to contextualize relationships between behavior and thought, but they would maintain distinct orientations toward capital-T "Truth" concerning life's big questions.

ROOTS OF EDUCATIONAL PSYCHOLOGY

Not long before Phineas Gage's legendarily bad day at the office, a young naturalist on the opposite side of the Atlantic set sail for a small volcanic archipelago off the west coast of South America. It took four years for him to reach his destination—the Galapagos Islands—but Charles Darwin would eventually spend thirty-four days in 1835 traversing San Cristobal, Floreana, Isabela, and Santiago to collect species and survey the landscape. Those findings would later form the basis of his theory of evolution by natural selection and (1859) *On the Origin of Species*, forever altering the landscape of biology and human history.[10]

Darwin's work, paired with a rich legacy of philosophical history and early research on the brain, led scientists like German physician Wilhelm Wundt to suggest a new, more scientifically rigorous means of understanding the nature of consciousness. His (1873) *Principles of Physiological Psychology* argued for studying the constituent elements of cognition through a process he called "internal perception" (introspection), where an individual would articulate their conscious experience as objectively as possible while external observers noted any discernible invocation of subjective thought or belief.[11] The effort ultimately proved too subjective even with external observation—participants could not divorce themselves from their preexisting biases, nor did observers agree about what they were witnessing—but Wundt's first-in-the-world psychology laboratory was successful in experimenting with reaction time and other directly measurable functions of the brain and body.

Likewise, American scientist William James understood Darwin's explanation of evolution by natural selection to mean that human cognition could be explained as a consequence of physiology. What set James apart from Wundt, however, was the strongly held belief that internal states directly caused external behaviors (i.e., emotions as a physiological response to environmental stimuli; later branded functionalism). In 1875, he offered Harvard University's first psychology course, The Relations Between Physiology and Psychology, and went on to grant the institution's first doctorate of psychology in 1878 as well as publish a pair of highly influential (1890) psychological research summaries titled *The Principles of Psychology*.[12]

In subsequent decades, Wundt and James laid the understructure for behaviorists such as Ivan Pavlov and John Watson, a famous dyad of late nineteenth- and early twentieth-century scholars of **classical conditioning.** Pavlov, a Russian physiologist and neurologist, is best known for his salivating dog experiments, where he paired food (an unconditioned stimulus) with a ringing bell (neutral response) to induce involuntary salivation whenever a bell rings (conditioned response), while Watson is remembered for "Little Albert," an infant who Watson conditioned to fear innocuous fuzzy, white objects through the use of terrifying paired stimuli like loud banging noises and scary images. Their findings ultimately inspired Edward Thorndike, an American comparative psychologist whose study of conditioning manifested as the (1905) law of effect (i.e., responses that produce a desired effect are more likely to reoccur, and those that produce an unpleasant effect are less likely to reoccur).[13]

Coincident with Thorndike advancing his law of effect at Columbia University, two young men in neighboring Vermont and Massachusetts—John Dewey and W. E. B. Du Bois—emerged as preeminent reformers whose scholarship would bridge the realms of psychology, philosophy, and education. Their progressive interpretations of education's sociocultural function (as described in Du Bois's [1913] *The Souls of Black Folk*,[14] Dewey's [1916] *Democracy and Education: An Introduction to the Philosophy of Education*,[15] and Dewey's [1938] *Experience and Education*[16]) aimed to foster more equitable, student-centered approaches to understanding the world by empowering learners of all backgrounds, providing a robust liberal arts education, and supporting democratic ideals. This bucked anti-Reconstructionist notions that Black and white students were not equally capable of academic achievement as well as contrasted the regressive attitudes of segregationists and eugenicists. Thorndike himself was a eugenicist, arguing that "selective breeding can alter man's capacity to learn, to keep sane, to cherish justice or to be happy; there is no more certain and economical a way to improve man's environment as to improve his nature."[17]

Hence, our historical journey wraps back around to philosophy and establishes the infrastructure for modern education and psychology. Enter the learning theorists.

THE LEARNING THEORISTS

As Europe lurched from the darkness of World War I toward the darkness of World War II, Swiss psychologist Jean Piaget's study of childhood development opened a new window into human cognition, memory, and psychosocial maturation. His American contemporary B. F. Skinner spent that same period transitioning from aspiring novelist to expert psychologist, experimenting with pigeons, rats, and puzzle boxes to better understand reinforcement as a means of shaping behavior. The two had dramatically different notions of how thinking and learning unfolded in situ: Piaget believed that mental processes were cultivated through experience with the world and organized into **schema** (i.e., mental maps of an individual's knowledge, memories, and skills), while Skinner—a staunch opponent of the metaphysical[18]—believed that learning was a by-product of **operant conditioning** (i.e., behavioral training via the application of rewards and punishments) measurable only through observable, external behaviors formed through environmental interaction.

Ever the provocateur, Skinner vociferously championed his theory of "radical behaviorism" as the best explanation for how and why individuals' behaviors would change over time. If the environment responded to an individual's behaviors with positive reinforcement, that individual would re-perform the associated behaviors more frequently. Conversely, if the environment responded with punishment and/or reinforcement became less frequent, the individual's use of those behaviors would diminish and, eventually, extinguish.

This model was particularly attractive through the mid-twentieth century as it neatly complemented concurrent structuralist philosophy and rejected the need for a disembodied mind (circumventing the homunculus problem[19]).

Piaget was reluctant to treat learning so mechanically as Skinner, preferring the investigation of young children's thinking (including that of his own offspring) as a means to catalog fluid phases of cognitive development (i.e., sensorimotor stage, preoperational stage, concrete operational stage, and formal operational stage). These phases traced a progression from hands-on exploration and verbal representation to logical thinking and applied reasoning wherein children would interact with the environment, discover mismatches between their preexisting judgments and real-world outcomes, and then modify their understanding through assimilation (i.e., fitting new information into a preexisting mental map) and accommodation (i.e., restructuring a preexisting mental map based on new information). Departing from Skinnerian behaviorism, Piaget's model suggested a cyclical relationship between an individual and their environment that emphasized the brain as a tool for information gathering and processing (i.e., memorization, contextualization, and problem-solving; cognitivism).

By the late 1950s, Skinner's behaviorism had ascended to become the predominant psychological framework for human learning, though his reasoning on questions of complex causality remained opaque and, to some, nonsensical.

For example, linguist Noam Chomsky's (1959) critique of Skinner's (1957) *Verbal Behavior* panned Skinner's handling of language acquisition as reductive and obfuscated behind hand-wavy explanations.[20,21] It was this vaguery that prompted Canadian American psychologist Albert Bandura to explore interconnections between behavior and social interaction, eventually arguing for a holistic **social cognitive model**.

Bandura garnered substantial attention between the 1960s and 1980s, owing to his research on self-efficacy (i.e., understanding of one's own ability vis-à-vis accomplishing target goals) and so-called Bobo doll studies. During these experiments, young children watched adults aggressively interact with a round-bottomed inflatable clown (e.g., punching, kicking, throwing, and hitting it with a hammer) before being allowed to interact with the doll themselves. In initial iterations, no direct reinforcement nor punishment was used to manipulate the children's behavior; they were simply provided with equivalent environmental conditions and tools (though later versions examined the role of vicarious reinforcement [i.e., reinforcement and punishment of the adult models] as a means of encouraging or discouraging aggressive behavior). Generally speaking, those who witnessed adult aggression toward the doll demonstrated a much higher likelihood of assaulting it themselves, while those who were shown prosocial behaviors tended to engage in neutral or prosocial behaviors. Repeated replication of these outcomes led Bandura to believe that behavioral modeling was the primary means by which learning occurred, and a model's relatability to its audience was largely determinative of whether an observer would imitate the behavior (i.e., model and observer being the same sex, gender, race, ethnicity, etc.). These findings were threaded together in a (1977) treatise titled *Social Learning Theory* through which he defined four factors responsible for observational learning: Attention, Retention, Motivation, and Reproduction.[22]

Notably, Bandura bridged observable external behaviors with unobservable internal thoughts, which neither Piaget nor Skinner had been able to do. Although he lacked a biological mechanism, his work made it apparent that seeing and processing the behavior (and reinforcement) of others could change an individual's understanding of their own thoughts and conditioning. This resolved one of the biggest criticisms of Skinnerian behaviorism insofar as it established that learning could occur without a direct change in behavior (i.e., a person could learn from observation without necessarily *acting* on that learning), but it did not explain why and how sociocultural contexts yielded widespread effects on long timescales for large numbers of people. Thus, we turn to the work of Soviet psychologist Lev Vygotsky.

Perhaps counterintuitively, Vygotsky's **social constructivist** framework for human cognitive development came years before Piaget, Skinner, and Bandura—his manuscripts were initially published between 1920 and 1934, and it was not until 1962 that they were translated and popularized as part of the Western psychological canon (leaving aside the fact that initial versions were rough and incomplete; a full translation was not finished until 1978).[23] Yet even without Bandura's social learning theory to lean on, he observed that social relationships, environmental conditions, and culture were deeply influential on children's learning, which suggested that cognition was not immutable from birth but variably defined by factors that could change over time. To him, learning was an internalization of culture, and education (both formal and informal) occurred via progression through **zones of proximal development** wherein learners gradually developed understanding and skills by collaborating with more knowledgeable others, known as cognitive apprenticeship.

Given the breadth of his contributions to the field (as well as the somewhat unusual chronology of events), learning theorists tend to uphold Vygotsky as the pioneer of multiple foundational psychological concepts. Of course, Piaget, Skinner, and Bandura deduced many crucial "big picture" concepts related to cognitive development and function, but Vygotsky's particular sociocultural flavor proved an essential ingredient in the collective psychology stew. Social constructivism, specifically, revolutionized the way we coordinate classroom teaching—from sage on the stage to guide on the side—and it is cited in teacher education programs as best practice for small group and team-based pedagogy.

Here we arrive at the critical junction of learning theory and classroom teaching. It would yet be a half-century until schools took these ideas to heart (with some exceptions), but there was finally a means to translate philosophical abstractions of the ivory tower into practicable blueprints for empirically testable instruction and assessment methods.

TO THE INFORMATION AGE AND BEYOND

The brain has long been likened to whichever advanced technology was available to scholars of the respective era, including clockwork machinery (1749),[24] the telegraph (1875),[25] and the telephone switchboard (1911).[26] However, the mid-twentieth century introduced an on-the-nose-perfect analogy for neuronal electrical signaling: the computer.

Just as Vygotsky's suppositions were being compared, contrasted, and synthesized with those of his scholarly descendants, a wave of poststructuralists and postmodernists busily unraveled long-established theories of language, philosophy, and psychology. Their nouveau perspective—aptly named **cognitive information processing** (CIP) theory—connected Piaget's schema theory with aspects of Bandura's social learning theory and wrapped them in the broader zeitgeist of the Information Age. At its core, CIP implied that the brain was an information management device responsible for storing, recalling, and problem-solving by virtue of short-term, long-term, and working memory. Moreover, brains were purpose-built (or evolved, more accurately) to process data inputs into logic-based outputs. Although the earliest computers were not sophisticated enough to mimic cognition, psychologists and computer scientists alike expected that the boxy number crunchers would eventually catch up to and surpass human intelligence (e.g., the "Turing test" imitation game[27]).

This shift in thinking would prove transformational for K–12 schools. Mathematician and computer scientist Seymour Papert, for instance, spent the 1960s, 1970s, and 1980s leveraging computational thinking as a new framework for elementary and middle school education. A South African-born American Piagetian protégé, Papert was intensely interested in how programming languages could serve as instructional tools for young learners, and he expanded upon Piaget's conceptualization of constructivism to rethink math education in terms of experiential learning. More narrowly tailored than its older sibling, Papert's constructionism was defined by hands-on discovery through which learners manufactured tangible objects as evidence of their growth. His (1980) *Mindstorms* elaborated:

> I take from Jean Piaget a model of children as builders of their own intellectual structures. Children seem to be innately gifted learners, acquiring long before they go to school a vast quantity of knowledge by a process I call "Piagetian learning," or "learning without being taught." For example, children learn to speak, learn the intuitive geometry needed to get around in space, and learn enough of logic and rhetorics to get around parents—all this without being "taught." We must ask why some learning takes place so early and spontaneously while some is delayed many years or does not happen at all without deliberately imposed formal instruction.[28]

In agreement with Vygotsky, Papert suspected that learning was an effect of enculturation and wanted to introduce richly authentic problem-solving opportunities as a natural part of the classroom. This meant replacing direct instruction and abstract word problems (*disassociated* learning) with exploration and deduction mapped to students' lived experiences (*syntonic learning*). In an ideal world, students would tell personalized stories about their learning rather than regurgitate memorized facts; they would construct schema through active engagement with the environment instead of passively waiting for a teacher to fill them with knowledge.

Papert's theory was grounded in real-world examples emergent from the instructional use of a mobile robot called the Logo Turtle. The device was so named for two reasons: First, the programming language used to input commands was itself titled Logo, and second, the device's plastic, hemispheric body bore a strong resemblance to a turtle's shell. Once unleashed in a classroom, children were encouraged to experiment with inputs (commands to move forward, backward, and rotationally: FD 50, BK 100, RT 90, etc.) to draw geometric shapes via a pen equipped on the turtle's underside. There was no singularly correct way to do this—learners would self-define what their end product should look like and leverage their understanding of the programming language and the turtle's corresponding movements to complete the task. For instance, if asked to outline a square, students would experiment with commands until deducing which combination yielded the desired end state (e.g., FD 50, RT 90, FD 50, RT 90, FD 50, RT 90, FD 50), applying creativity and problem-solving skills to concretize often abstract logic and mathematical concepts.

Constructionism helped reinforce John Dewey's contention that play- and inquiry-driven instruction are necessary for robust student learning: Classrooms that offer little or no direct interaction do not lead to student ownership or deep understanding of content, but those where students engage in richly authentic hands-on experiences quite effectively lead to academic achievement. Regrettably, there remained an inconvenient homunculus problem. Sure, CIP laid a foundation for conceptualizing brain function, but the computational metaphor lacked any biological explanation for how or why a brain would internalize and process environmental information. Where did memory reside? How did the processing mechanism evolve? What was managing the organization and navigation of schema?

Fortunately, a married duo of American psychologists would soon uncover answers that had been hiding in plain sight.

SITUATING COGNITION

Throughout their careers, James and Eleanor Gibson were motivated by the deceptively simple question "why do we see the world as we do?"—not as a figurative matter but a literal one. James became interested in the subject of

FIGURE 2.2
A mother calls to her infant from the far side of a visual cliff; there is a plexiglass surface capable of supporting the child's weight, but the illusion of a potential fall causes reluctance to cross. Adapted from Eleanor J. Gibson and Richard D. Walk, "The 'Visual Cliff,'" *Scientific American* 202, no. 4 (1960): 64–71.

optic flow during his time in the US Air Force, and he went on to specialize in ocular physiology to better understand the eye's perception of and reaction to light. His wife Eleanor, similarly intrigued by vision and the relationship between individuals and their surrounding environments, worked alongside James to explain how children developed perceptual awareness (one such experiment involved mothers coaxing their infants to crawl over a visual cliff; see figure 2.2).

Over four decades and multiple publications—including *The Perception of the Visual World* (1950),[29] *The Senses Considered as Perceptual Systems* (1966),[30] *Principles of Perceptual Learning and Development* (1969),[31] and *The Ecological Approach to Visual Perception* (1979)[32]—the couple argued that cognition was not a metaphysical phenomenon but an entirely ecological one. Organisms (including humans) directly perceived their environments and responded by acting on affordances of available objects, information, and relationships (i.e., possibilities for action to solve in-the-moment problems). For example, the ontological descent from hunger to satiation might unfold as follows:

1. A hungry person surveys the environment for sources of nourishment using their physiological effectivities (e.g., sight, hearing, touch, taste, proprioception, and balance).
2. A combination of visual and olfactory stimuli lead them to detect a nearby slice of pizza.
3. The brain recognizes pizza as having an affordance for satiating hunger based on prior exposure to pizza and/or its constituent elements.
4. The body engages in ballistic grasp to reach, grab, and move the pizza into the person's mouth.
5. The body's digestive system activates to break down and absorb fats, carbohydrates, and proteins to refuel metabolic processes.
6. Having released neurochemicals to lower hunger signaling, the person transitions to other tasks in their hierarchy of goals.

Unlike CIP, this perspective extended from the epistemology of rationalism (i.e., the act of knowing through reason rather than intuition or gut instinct) and sidestepped the homunculus problem by framing consciousness as an incidental side effect of biological perception and action. It therefore presented a very different conception of cognition than CIP or social learning theory, particularly regarding where and how knowledge exists. While an information processing theorist might say "the world is in my head," an ecological psychologist would counter that "our heads are in the world." There is no amorphous set of pictures and words locked inside the human skull, nor do we conjure image files when asked to imagine or remember. Everything we "know" is a matter of direct experience, and the abstraction we call "memory" is the manifestation of continuous dialogue between an individual and their surrounding environment. To an ecological psychologist, "remembering" is better described as "reexperiencing," "thinking" as "perceiving," and "knowledge" as "action."

All of this is to say ecological psychology grew out of a completely different worldview than the learning theories that preceded it. The vocabulary distinctions may seem superficial because so much terminology associated with CIP also exists in the ecological framework, but ecological psychology challenges definitions presented by information processing theory. It dismisses the possibility of an unfalsifiable, undetectable force responsible for cognition by characterizing identity and problem-solving as inevitable products of interaction between one's genetics, physiology, social relationships, culture, and environmental context. Nature and nurture, inseparable and enduring.

It should come as no surprise that the Gibsonian lens drew a great deal of interest from fellow CIP skeptics—and ire from the (much larger) information processing community. Notwithstanding its potential benefits, psychologists, philosophers, and educators had invested substantial time and resources into developing institutions and norms that assumed mind and memory were defining features of the brain. This new perspective would require a wholesale reinvention of instruction and assessment activities to target directly observable learner actions (e.g., student-driven inquiry, project-based learning) as opposed to indirect measures of rote knowledge (e.g., direct instruction, standardized multiple-choice tests).

Invigorated by the possibilities, many researchers took steps to translate the Gibsons' ecological psychology into a practicable framework for K–12 and university education. Robert Shaw and Michael Turvey founded the Center for the Ecological Study of Perception & Action to bring an ecological worldview into the domain of experimental psychology, while John Bransford, leader of the Cognition and Technology Group at Vanderbilt, pursued the application of ecological psychology as anchored instruction (for more on this topic, see chapter 3, "Theory to Practice"). Undergirding their efforts were three fundamental ideas advocated in John Seely Brown, Allan Collins, and Paul Duguid's (1989) *Situated Cognition and the Culture of Learning*:[33]

1. Learning is the education of <u>in</u>tention and <u>at</u>tention—an educator's job is to induce learners to adopt new goals related to target content/skills.
2. Teaching is the act of tuning learner perception toward critical information, behaviors, and similarities/difference between relevant contexts.
3. Knowledge is situated (i.e., like language, knowledge is inextricable from the activities and situations in which it is produced; to know is to perceive and act).

Meanwhile, social anthropologist Jean Lave and educational theorist Étienne Wenger expanded ecological thinking to observational psychology research. The pair distilled social interactivity into a theory of Communities of Practice that treated learning and doing as synonymous with perception, apprenticeship, and shared expertise. Their (1991) book *Situated Learning: Legitimate Peripheral Participation* proposed that richly authentic learning environments were critical for knowledge and skill transfer from one activity to another, while impoverished environments (i.e., those lacking opportunities for cognitive apprenticeship and direct perception) were destined to fail (for more on this topic, see chapter 4, "Collaboration and Community").[34] Further, they touted the value of problem-based instructional approaches reminiscent of Dewey's, Papert's, and the Cognition and Technology Group at Vanderbilt, all of which pushed for inquiry, problem-solving, and critical thinking over memorization and recitation.

Parallel to these efforts, a separate collection of learning scientists turned their attention to the unique dynamics of adult learning. Malcolm Knowles's (1975) *Self-Directed Learning*[35] and (1984) *Andragogy in Action*[36] introduced the subdomain of adult learning theory (i.e., andragogy) and specified four principles for successful curriculum implementation:

1. Adult learners benefit from involvement in the planning and evaluation of their learning.
2. Practical experience (including mistakes) should be the basis for learning activities.
3. Adult learners are most inclined to engage with subjects that have immediate relevance to them (i.e., directly impact their personal and/or professional lives).
4. Adult learning should be problem centric rather than content centric (i.e., focused on solving real-world problems as encountered in personal/professional life).

Knowles's peer, American sociologist Jack Mezirow, posited a similar series of best practices for adult learners under the broader umbrella of **life-transformative education**. According to Mezirow, life-transformative education is a constructivist approach "which holds that the way learners interpret and reinterpret their sense experience is central to making meaning and hence learning."[37] It follows in the footsteps of philosopher Paulo Freire's (1970) critical pedagogy and establishes distinct stages through which learners undergo the transformation process:[38,39]

1. The learner faces a disorienting dilemma.
2. They self-examine feelings of guilt or shame, sometimes turning to religion for support.
3. The learner conducts a critical assessment of their assumptions.
4. They recognize that their discontent and the process of transformation are shared (and that others have negotiated a similar change).

5. They begin exploring options for new roles, relationships, and actions.
6. The learner plans a course of action.
7. They acquire knowledge and skills for implementing their plans.
8. They provisionally try out new roles.
9. The learner renegotiates existing relationships and negotiates new relationships.
10. They build competence and self-confidence in new roles and relationships.
11. They reintegrate into their life based on conditions dictated by their new perspective.

The combination of situated cognition and adult learning theory proved deeply consequential for educational psychology into the twenty-first century. Not only did the two provide a more parsimonious explanation for human cognition than CIP (i.e., matter over mind), but they complemented rising digital technologies like the internet, social media, and smartphones—superb tools for inquiry-driven, student-centered instructional methods.

WHAT ABOUT WORLDBUILDING?

Rapid technological breakthroughs over just fifteen years turned the early 2000s into a veritable treasure trove for constructivists and constructionists determined to introduce situated pedagogy in K–12 and higher education classrooms. The internet (and by extension smart tools, digital media, online games, etc.) offered the first scalable replacement for outdated didactic instruction, and it paved the way for a kind of student-centered "playful" learning proposed a century earlier.

During the 1930s, Dewey and Vygotsky independently wrote about the necessity of play for children to interpret, understand, and mimic adult behaviors (e.g., a child using a stick to pretend they are riding it to mimic the way an adult would actually ride a horse; playing "house" or "war" to emulate role models around them). However, their brand of inquiry-based exploratory learning was so difficult to achieve in industrial-style, lecture-dominated environments that it failed to gain traction outside a small group of devotees (e.g., Italian physician and educator Maria Montessori). A shift began once computers introduced new ways to interact with complex datasets, but hands-on, play-based instruction mostly remained a creature of the military (e.g., training simulations), healthcare (e.g., medical role-playing exercises at McMaster University School of Medicine circa

1969), engineering, business, diplomacy, and other professional environments until the latter portion of the twentieth century. Papert's Logo did not emerge until the 1970s, and Bransford's Cognition and Technology Group at Vanderbilt did not publish its studies on anchored instruction until the 1980s and 1990s: a very long-arc transition from the older CIP model of education to a contemporary situated model of education.

The most important linkage through all of this was student action—learners directing their own learning through narrative frameworks that facilitated transfer from one context (e.g., school) to another (e.g., the workplace). In his (1986) book *Actual Minds, Possible Worlds*, American cognitive psychologist Jerome Bruner insisted that weaving stories through instruction was the key to helping learners understand core ideas in a meaningful, richly authentic way (rather than impoverished abstraction, which would lead to misunderstanding and a failure to transfer).[40] A series of similar publications in the early 2000s energized this perspective and led instructors to investigate how play might be adopted from higher education and professional training to inform K–12 instruction, fueled in large part by James Paul Gee's (2003) *What Video Games Have to Teach Us About Learning and Literacy*.[41]

Gee, an American psycholinguist and literacy specialist, noticed that when his young son interacted with video games, he developed skills that cross-applied in both game worlds and the real world. Logically, the games must have been designed to teach players how to play them, so it was not incidental that his son would pick up a controller and figure out what to do; for him to "win," games had to teach him how and why. These observations received a boost from game designer Jane McGonigal's (2010) *Reality Is Broken: Why Games Make Us Better and How They Can Change the World*, which asked pertinent questions about game affordances and ways in which play can address complex societal needs (e.g., happiness, belonging).[42]

Between 2010 and 2012, intensive efforts to research playful learning fed a positive consensus judgment about their utility for education. Sigmund Tobias and J. D. Fletcher's (2011) edited volume *Computer Games and Instruction* became the first long-form documentation of gaming integration in classroom environments,[43] and Michael Young et al.'s (2012) *Review of Educational Research* meta-analytic review *Our Princess Is in Another Castle: A Review of Trends in Serious Gaming for Education* cataloged more than three hundred quantitative and qualitative studies of game-based learning across a range of domains—science, language arts, mathematics, social studies, and physical education.[44] Young and his colleagues cautioned against overly reductive questions about play-based instruction (i.e., "are games 'good' or 'bad' for learning") given the complexity of individual learner-environment interactions, proposing instead that play- and game-based research focus on interrelationships between individuals and their learning contexts to determine whether particular games could facilitate particular outcomes in particular teaching and learning environments for particular groups of learners. A third treatise on games in education, Pieter Wouters et al.'s (2013) *A Meta-Analysis of the Cognitive and Motivational Effects of Serious Games*, examined non-discipline-specific affordances of games for learning (e.g., motivation) and made suggestions for ongoing development processes that could leverage game structure and function to support more effective teaching practices.[45]

In 2016, Douglas Clark, Emily Tanner-Smith, and Stephen Killingsworth offered the first true meta-analysis of games for academic disciplines in their *Review of Educational Research* publication *Digital Games, Design, and Learning: A Systematic Review and Meta-Analysis*, which looked across the breadth of all available games literature to characterize affordances common to every discipline.[46] The extremely challenging process of pinning down these affordances introduced several new questions that formed the basis for Michael Young and Stephen Slota's (2017) edited volume *Exploding the Castle: Rethinking How Video Games & Game Mechanics Can Shape the Future of Education*, a dozen interconnected essays arguing that games research should be evaluated through specific theory-based lenses to understand their usefulness for teaching and learning (e.g., data exhaust, log files, badging systems, virtual/alternate reality, play-based social interactions).[47]

And with that, we arrive at the present: worldbuilding and its relevance for twenty-first-century instructional environments.

ONWARD AND UPWARD

The next three chapters will connect theories of teaching and learning with concepts drawn from the realm of game- and play-based education. By the time you finish, you should be well equipped to tackle the processes described in part II, "Concepts," and begin work on worldbuilding and world modeling activities for your own instructional environment.

Before making the leap forward, though, we want to clarify a few definitions that will ease your transition into the worldbuilding process.

You may have some familiarity with terms like "serious games," "gamification," "playful learning," "game-based learning," and/or "instructional games"—we have already invoked a few thus far. Understand that this terminology is still maturing, so many words and their definitions remain in flux as emergent scholarship informs how we think about playful instruction and assessment. We believe the following will be particularly handy as you read on:

- We will use "playful learning" as a nonspecific means of describing activities that are playful but not necessarily organized in a formal capacity (e.g., lesson plans).
- Although some of the activities we describe can be quite serious (e.g., deconstructing military conflicts, discussing historical injustices), we generally avoid the term "serious games" because it too narrowly constrains the possibility space, which may be playful, lighthearted, and/or unserious depending on the context.
- The terms "instructional game" and "game-based learning" will be used as two sides of the same coin—anyone utilizing games in an educational context is either an instructor (i.e., employing an instructional game) or a learner (i.e., engaged in game-based learning).
- "Gamification," the term most often applied by journalistic outlets to describe game- or play-based instructional activities, is used only when discussing very specific operant conditioning-driven tools that take the form of badges, points, or other types of proficiency credentials.
- "Worldbuilding" and "world modeling" will refer to the process of (de)constructing complex systems to better understand how and why worlds operate as they do (i.e., evaluating the perspectives of individuals who occupy those worlds and critically interrogating interrelationships between cultures, economic systems, governments, etc.).

3 THEORY TO PRACTICE

"The purpose of a storyteller is not to tell you how to think, but to give you questions to think upon."

—Brandon Sanderson[1]

Learning theory serves as a mediator between educational philosophies, target instructional goals, pedagogical approaches, and assessment measures, which is the reason it is one of the first subjects that preservice educators are required to study in pursuit of teacher certification. Different theories define different constraints and affordances for different design pathways, and they dictate how different philosophies should be translated from abstraction to implementation.

Unfortunately, leading with learning theory poses something of a "chicken and egg" problem: It is difficult to grasp the relevance of different theories without prior classroom and curricular design experience, but postponing the exploration of different theories until after student teaching hinders curriculum development and the creation of content-related activities. The situation is even bleaker for university faculty, most of whom do not receive *any* training in learning theory or pedagogical design during graduate school—although they may be familiar with general philosophies of education, they do not necessarily know how to translate philosophy into pedagogy.

To address that disconnect, the following chapter tackles theory to practice head-on: translating research on teaching and learning into practicable, evidence-supported instructional methods that we know can "work" for a wide range of educational environments. Not all methods will necessarily fit all classrooms, instructors, and personalities equally, but we believe they provide a strong foundation for developing your own student-driven, inquiry-based worldbuilding and world modeling activities capable of inducing learner goal adoption and transfer.

Even if this sort of thing is not your usual cup of tea (or coffee), bear with us! There is real utility in drawing a line from your conceptualization of how and why learning happens to how and why you implement instruction for a particular audience of learners.

TARGETING TRANSFER

There are myriad ways in which instructors (and their worldviews) differ, yet the desire for transfer is one quality they have in common. It is the justification for all courses, programs, training sessions, workshops, and professional development seminars. It undergirds every learning objective we write, every story we tell, and every discussion we facilitate. It is the raison d'être for education.

So, what *is* it? And why is it so important?

In short, transfer is the application of knowledge, skills, and information learned in one context to another, different context. We should care about it because it sits at the heart of curriculum development and implementation, orienting learners to identify when and how their learning can be applied to solve real-world problems. It also answers the age-old question "why do I need to know this?"—not "because it's good for you" or "because I said so" but because situations will inevitably emerge where prior experience with an idea or strategy will be the difference between generating a solution or burning precious energy and resources rediscovering something that was already known or knowable.

From the National Research Council's (1999) text *How People Learn*:

> Organizing information into a conceptual framework allows for greater "transfer"; that is, it allows the student to apply what was learned in new situations and to learn related information more quickly (see Box 1.3). The student who has learned geographical information for the Americas in a conceptual framework approaches the task of learning the geography of another part of the globe with questions, ideas, and expectations that help guide acquisition of the new information. Understanding the geographical importance of the Mississippi River sets the stage for the student's understanding of the geographical importance of the Nile. And as concepts are reinforced, the student will transfer learning beyond the classroom, observing and inquiring, for example, about the geographic features of a visited city that help explain its location and size (Holyoak, 1984; Novick and Holyoak, 1991).[2]

The notion of transfer grew out of Edward Thorndike and Robert Woodworth's (1901) contention that learning is defined by an individual's ability to recognize and act on common elements shared between two environments.³ When a learner observes that elements from one environment can be cross-applied in another, they can be said to have transferred their learning. Notably, because we cannot dissociate ourselves from our experiential backgrounds, this happens all the time in all contexts, but schools are explicitly designed to induce transfer as a means of learner preparation for other scenarios where knowledge, skills, and information might be relevant.

The problem, though, is that transfer is notoriously difficult to achieve and even more challenging to measure. Douglas Detterman and Robert Sternberg's (1993) book *Transfer on Trial: Intelligence, Cognition, and Instruction* argued that even if the phenomenon exists, it is nearly impossible to prove because of how indirectly and unpredictably it occurs, particularly on longitudinal scales that fall well outside the bounds of traditional teaching and learning (e.g., a single semester or school year).[4] And while assessing near transfer (e.g., applying knowledge of how to use a fork to using a bigger or smaller fork) can be fairly straightforward, assessing far transfer (e.g., applying knowledge of how to use a fork to using chopsticks) is much more difficult because it is a complex process influenced by multiple factors that parallel, overwrite, and interact with one another over time. This is especially true of transfer occurring across months, years, or decades, like a middle school lesson about Upton Sinclair's (1906) *The Jungle* informing a learner's sociopolitical decision-making during adult life[5]—there is simply no way to demonstrate that a specific interaction with an idea or skill in one context can or will influence critical thinking and problem solving in another.

Consider Mary Gick and Keith Holyoak's (1980) research article *Analogical Problem Solving*,[6] which grappled with learner transfer between multiple versions of Karl Duncker's (1945) radiation problem.[7,8] Half of the study participants were presented with the following (analogous) story before being presented with Duncker's problem:

> A small country was ruled from a strong fortress by a dictator. The fortress was situated in the middle of the country, surrounded by farms and villages. Many roads led to the fortress through the countryside. A rebel general vowed to capture the fortress. The general knew that an attack by his entire army would capture the fortress. He gathered his army at the head of one of the roads, ready to launch a full-scale direct attack. However, the general then learned that the dictator had planted mines on each of the roads. The mines were set so that small bodies of men could pass over them safely, since the dictator needed to move his troops and workers to and from the fortress. However, any large force would detonate the mines. Not only would this blow up the road, but it would also

destroy many neighbouring villages. It therefore seemed impossible to capture the fortress. However, the general devised a simple plan. He divided his army into small groups and dispatched each group to the head of a different road. When all was ready, he gave the signal and each group marched down a different road. Each group continued down its road to the fortress so that the entire army arrived together at the fortress at the same time. In this way, the general captured the fortress and overthrew the dictator.

Only 10 percent of learners managed to spontaneously generate a solution *without* exposure to the aforementioned story. Exposure to the story led to a slightly (though not much) higher proportion of learners identifying convergence as the potential answer—about 30 percent. When given a hint that the story might be of use in solving the radiation problem (but without making explicit reference to a possible analogy), the solution rate jumped to 92 percent. Solutions were further facilitated by asking participants to read two stories rather than just one, which increased the likelihood that they would transfer their learning to solve the underlying problem.

We mention this to establish the following:

1. Although transfer is desirable enough that we have collectively built our entire education system based on the assumption it happens, it remains extremely rare unless or until contrasting stories (or cases, narratives, etc.) are employed to ground learner comprehension.
2. The theoretical foundations we use to scaffold our instructional methods are not arbitrary; they truly *do* matter.
3. While the worldbuilding methods described in this book cannot *guarantee* transfer, they have explicit affordances for improving the probability of transfer based on a robust body of learning science research.

Hence why we regard instructional worldbuilding as much more than a bunch of aspirational, buzzword-y fluff—it is a theory- and evidence-based methodology with real potential to shape teaching practices, restructure teaching and learning environments, and maximize critical thinking, problem-solving, and transfer among learners.

The forthcoming section will expand on this idea by introducing an exemplar subject and guiding you through its evolution from the hypothetical to the actionable. Then, we will apply two instructional design frameworks to inform the pedagogical approaches, instructional technologies, and assessment measures used to craft thematically and strategically coherent lessons, units, courses, and programs of study.

Now hurry up and pack your bags! We're kicking things off with a quick trip to twentieth-century Eastern Europe.

WELCOME TO PRIPYAT

The breadth and depth of content that educators and learners cover through lessons, units, courses, and programs demands different design frameworks tailored for different disciplines—it would be challenging, for instance, to leverage the world of Michael Crichton's (1990) hit science fiction novel *Jurassic Park* as the foundation for teaching middle school home economics as opposed to high school or university-level biology.[9] But curricular activities that are designed for one isolated learning objective can be less instructionally useful than those with broad, ill-defined goals spanning multiple objectives, like using the (1975) comedy *Monty Python and the Holy Grail* to teach a lesson about witchcraft, specifically, versus a lesson about absurdist satire, generally.[10] As a result, curriculum development must be flexible if it is to properly inform learners about the world as it actually exists (many interconnected, interdependent domains) rather than how it is often presented (a series of siloed, mutually exclusive disciplines).

By virtue of its structure, worldbuilding is a great way to achieve flexibility in parallel with content progression.

Imagine that you are developing a new engineering ethics curriculum intended to improve learner engagement and induce content transfer to the outside world. Because you are seeking to introduce interdisciplinary discussion, you choose an example that you expect learners will find more interesting and relevant across multiple domains: the Chernobyl nuclear disaster.

In April 1986, one of the Ukrainian Soviet Socialist Republic's reactors failed during a steam test at the Chernobyl nuclear power plant. The explosion precipitated a meltdown that exposed the surrounding region to a plethora of airborne radioactive contaminants and killed as many as nine thousand people, including long-term, cancer-related fatalities in modern Ukraine, Belarus, and Russia.[11] Driven by a combination of problematic reactor design and human carelessness, the event catalyzed the Soviet Union's collapse thanks to the communist government's stringent control of the information ecosystem and refusal to openly admit what happened, plus the material cost of containment (estimated to be 18 billion rubles [inflation adjusted to US$81 billion in 2024]). A number of resources speak to the broad, intersectional challenges posed by this catastrophe (e.g., Svetlana Alexievich's [2006] book *Voices from Chernobyl*,[12] HBO's [2019] *Chernobyl* television miniseries[13]), and a savvy educator could use it as a case study to encourage exploration of ethical decision-making, chemistry, geopolitics, physics, mis/disinformation, and other topics.

Precisely how one would incorporate this information—and the broader worldbuilding associated with Chernobyl—depends on the selected theoretical framework (e.g., behaviorism, cognitive information processing, situated cognition, social constructivism), but the bizarre and disarming narrative would be an effective vehicle for knowledge construction and reflection. Learners could use this as a starting point to interrogate what happens when different aspects of different disciplines come into contact with one another, and instructors could use it to facilitate a deconstruction of complex systems that can be difficult to achieve using traditional pedagogical methods.

Below, we outline the process for fusing the story of Chernobyl with theory, pedagogy, content objectives, and instructional resources to create a comprehensive engineering ethics curriculum development plan. This will require circling back to a handful of concepts we have previously discussed, but the bigger picture is easier to grasp when mapped to contemporary theory and instructional design practices that support worldbuilding for teaching and learning.

PHILOSOPHY AND PSYCHOLOGY

As illustrated throughout chapter 2, "Road to Contemporary Learning Theory," psychology and philosophy are a bit like fraternal twins—they emerged from the same parent discipline, and they share many characteristics despite being distinct entities. Their origin stories include many of the same individuals, but the goals and intellectual trajectories of those individuals regularly diverge and reconnect over time.

The wending and winding of educational psychology history has thus led us to organize teaching and learning environments around varied belief structures that beget different rationales for why "school" should exist in the first place, as well as who should control curricula, under what circumstances, and toward what ends (table 3.1).

These perspectives are roughly defined by their respective relationships with economic institutions, civic institutions, and sociocultural norms. When extended to curricular design, they give rise to dramatically different instructional and assessment methods, such as:

- **Economic Equalization:**
  - Education is meant to create an equitable economic playing field by preparing learners for the workforce.
  - All learners are entitled to equal opportunities.
  - The system is meant to protect and enable those who lack economic resources.

Table 3.1. A list of example educational philosophies, each of which specifies a particular purpose for schools and community they should serve

Philosophy	Description	Theorist
Perennialism	There are persistent truths based on the assumption that the natural world does not change; because humans are rational beings, their minds must be developed through familiarization with great ideas of Western civilization.	Robert Maynard Hutchins
Essentialism	Certain knowledge must be passed on through each generation's familiarization with the Western canon, but unlike Perennialism, the curriculum should be updated over time; emphasis is placed on the value of hard work and deference to authority.	William Bagley
Romanticism	Knowledge comes from intuition rather than deduction, so education should be organized around student self-actualization and emotional self-awareness to bring about societal improvement; the greatest emphasis is placed on creativity, exploration, and responsibility for one's own learning.	Maria Montessori
Progressivism	Education is a holistic endeavor that focuses on a human's well-being and personal growth rather than specific curricular content or hierarchies of authority; learning should be inquiry-driven and based on student questions or interests rather than a prescribed curriculum.	John Dewey
Marxism	Any formal education system in a capitalist society is fundamentally rooted in exploitation and oppression (i.e., knowledge is gatekept); class consciousness cannot be achieved so long as schools are designed to teach efficiency and obedience in service of the capitalist ruling class.	Karl Marx
Conservatism	Education should be grounded in tradition and used as a vehicle to communicate sociocultural norms and expectations; individualism is frowned upon and emphasis is placed on learner assimilation; it is not the job of educators to engage in custodial or nonacademic functions.	Edmund Burke

- **Democratization:**
  - Education exists to foster a functional democracy with informed citizens.
  - All learners should be taught to understand one another's needs.
  - The system is meant to facilitate intellectual preparedness as a foundation for democratic governance.

- **Self-Actualization:**
  - Education exists to enhance critical thinking and problem-solving on both individual and social levels.
  - All learners are taught to ask and answer "big questions" (e.g., the meaning of life, the universe, and everything).
  - The system is meant to support self-actualization for the purposes of making society better for all.

A classroom built for Self-Actualization tends to look quite different from one built for Economic Equalization, and although there can be overlaps (e.g., emphasizing Democratization by way of Self-Actualization [Progressivism] or Economic Equalization [Marxism]), applying all at once can generate internal conflict between principles that are inherently incompatible (e.g., pragmatism versus idealism). This is why choosing the "right" philosophy for classroom and curricular design is so important—misalignment between the core philosophy and methodologies leads to ineffective instruction and minimal transfer.

This speaks to the need for educators to understand the direct connection between learning theory and instruction, treating theory as an essential part of curriculum design rather than a frivolous distraction. Doing so integrates instruction with contemporary psychology rather than theory as history (e.g., memorizing the perspectives of Horace Mann, W. E. B. Du Bois, Benjamin Bloom, Jean Piaget, Lev Vygotsky, John Dewey, Maria Montessori, and others), and it improves the possibility that students' learning will stick with them and be applied outside the classroom context.

Of course, there is no "correct" learning theory to connect each educational philosophy with a particular instructional approach or context, but as previously noted, specific theories tend to be associated with specific instructional goals, pedagogical approaches, and assessment measures that are "better" or "worse" depending on the instructional environment and audience of learners. It can help to think of the theories as different pairs of tinted sunglasses, each making certain colors pop or fade depending on their tint—green causes grass to fade but the sun to be more visible; blue causes the sky to fade but flowers to be more visible—the same instructional environment can be understood using any/every learning theory, and the optimal approach to pedagogical design and assessment will change depending on the environment's "color" as seen through the chosen learning theory "lens."

For instance, in our engineering ethics classroom, a cognitivist who believes in developing schematic webs and relying on student memorization to codify/internalize knowledge might teach ethical decision-making as a rote exercise with worksheets and diagrams. By contrast, a behaviorist who believes in reinforcement to shape thinking and behavior could look at the same classroom and determine that the best approach is to train learners to recognize (un)ethical decisions using tickets, points, candy, or other reinforcers. A social learning theorist who believes that learning occurs via modeling and social construction of knowledge would ask students to observe a video of a professional demonstrating their ethical decision-making process as a rocket scientist, while a situated cognitivist who believes learning is context dependent and rooted in "doing" would have students engage in a series of hands-on role-playing sessions anchored in real-world case narratives.

Consider whether and how each of the learning theory "lenses" in table 3.2 matches your particular instructional environment and audience of learners.

To facilitate your reflection, imagine that you want a group of students to showcase their "knowledge" of engineering ethics. Which of the following most appeals to you?

- Developing a reinforcement system to shape engineering student behavior over time (e.g., awarding a prize each time a student engineer correctly identifies an [un]ethical decision or situation; punishing the student engineer each time they misidentify an [un]ethical decision or situation)
- Giving a quiz where the correct response involves writing a bulleted list of procedural steps associated with ethical decision-making
- Encouraging student engineers to work in teams, share expertise, and collaborate to draft their own set of engineering ethics standards
- Requesting that student engineers directly demonstrate their understanding by engaging in a simulation and/or role-play experience where they must make (un)ethical decisions for themselves

Table 3.2. A list of major learning theories, their definitions, relevant keywords, and relevant theorists

Theory	Definition	Keywords	Theorist(s)
Behaviorism	The application of reinforcement and punishment to shape learner behaviors, gradually moving them toward/away from particular kinds of thinking and action	Reinforcement; operant/classical conditioning; rewards; punishment	Ivan Pavlov; Edward Thorndike; B. F. Skinner
Cognitivism	The development of knowledge maps (i.e., schematic webs) that assume the brain behaves like a computer (i.e., storing and retrieving information to solve future problems via memory)	Computer information processing; encoding; memory; knowledge; memorization; schema; mind; accommodation; assimilation; automaticity	Jean Piaget; Lawrence Kohlberg; Carol Gilligan
Social Learning Theory	The use of observation and role models to demonstrate important knowledge, attitudes, and behaviors within a particular domain (i.e., Attention, Retention, Reproduction, Motivation)	Role models; leadership; expertise; demonstration; motivation; imitation	Albert Bandura
Constructivism	The gradual construction of knowledge (i.e., abstract concepts and ideas) through activities that organize piece-by-piece organization of new and old information	Collaboration; coconstruction; interaction; culture; zones of proximal development; meaning-making; scaffolding	Lev Vygotsky; John Dewey
Constructionism	The demonstration of domain knowledge through literal construction of tangible objects or other work products that showcase understanding of important concepts and principles	Building; construction; projects; hands-on; models; creation; artifacts	Seymour Papert

Theory	Definition	Keywords	Theorist(s)
Situated Cognition	The belief that "knowledge is doing" and learners must engage in legitimate peripheral participation (i.e., apprenticeship) to develop experience as members of richly authentic contexts/ Communities of Practice (minimizing barriers to transfer as much as possible)	Anchored instruction; apprenticeship; ecological psychology; legitimate peripheral participation; Communities of Practice; goal adoption; perception-action; situation; context; environment	John Seely Brown; John Bransford; Jean Lave; Étienne Wenger
Andragogy	The fostering of self-guided reflection among adult learners through individually determined goals (e.g., career or otherwise) and life-transformative experiences; information provided on an as-needed, "on-time" basis	Life-transformative education; reflection; self-direction	Malcolm Knowles; Jack Mezirow

Again, none of these approaches is "right" or "wrong"—they simply represent different kinds of "knowing." And while it is *technically* possible to teach someone about engineering ethics by giving them a text-based manual and written exam or sending them to a live nuclear reactor to learn via trial and error, there are trade-offs that different educators need to gauge based on their instructional goals, time and resources, potential outcomes, and other factors (e.g., safety, practicality).

The trick to balancing affordances and constraints is tracking whether and how different aspects of a lesson, unit, course, or program act as complements or antagonists, not just the content and pedagogy but also the theoretical framework and any supporting technologies (i.e., materials and tools used to implement instruction).

This is the underlying theme of Punya Mishra and Matthew Koehler's (2006) Technology, Pedagogy, and Content Knowledge (TPACK) framework for teacher knowledge (figure 3.1).

Instructors, they argued, must weigh disciplinary material against technological availability and instructional approaches.[14,15] No individual

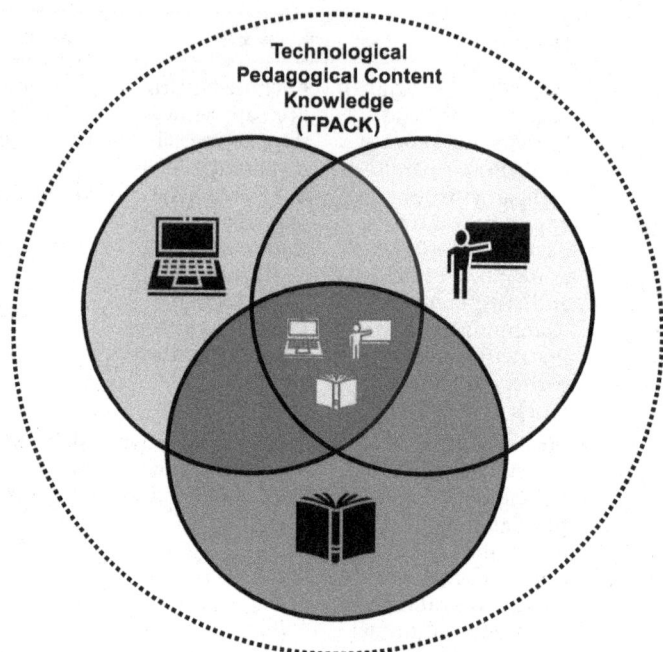

FIGURE 3.1
A triple Venn diagram adaptation of Mishra and Koehler's (2006) Technology, Pedagogy, and Content Knowledge (TPACK) framework. Source: Punya Mishra and Matthew J. Koehler, "Technological Pedagogical Content Knowledge: A Framework for Teacher Knowledge," *Teachers College Record* 108, no. 6 (2006): 1017–1054, https://doi.org/10.1111/j.1467-9620.2006.00684.x.

element is arbitrary; content reinforces pedagogy reinforces technology, and every possible combination of the three. The "sweet spot" occurs when all pieces function in tandem to support transfer, meaningfully incorporating technology to convey how and why professionals engage in discipline-specific practices.

Referring to this framework throughout the curricular development process better positions educators to create activities and assessments capable of surviving implementation; consider the "sweet spot" a constant reminder that high-quality instruction comes from the wise integration of particular technologies with particular domain content based on contemporary learning theories. Take our engineering ethics exemplar: The instructor could pair Bethesda Game Studios' (2008) video game *Fallout 3* (Technology) with a content-oriented learning objective (Content Knowledge; "Learners will describe [un]ethical decision-making in the context of the Chernobyl nuclear disaster") to support a student-led worldbuilding project (Pedagogy) that compares scientific and political (un)ethical decision-making in the fictional world of *Fallout* with that of pre- and post-Chernobyl Ukraine and Russia. Here, TPACK grounds designer, instructor, and learner understanding about activity and assessment goals to facilitate the teaching of individuals whose intentions may be orthogonal to those of the instructor.

It can be easy to write off TPACK as disconnected from the goings-on of live teaching and learning environments, especially given the impact of uncontrollable, externally imposed facets of education—administrative initiatives, mandatory testing, and so on—but it is our best option for cross-checking the internal consistency of lessons, units, courses, and programs. When instructors accidentally shift from one theoretical foundation to another during curriculum development and implementation, there are real costs borne by learners and the instructor: Pedagogy becomes misaligned with learning objectives, time/resources are lost, and transfer diminishes. Rather than being prescriptive, TPACK is a tool to determine whether and how misalignment has crept into our planning—helping us see the difference between each piece of the instructional puzzle acting in conjunction with its peers versus each acting individually and, potentially, incomprehensibly.

The next section will elaborate on how we can apply TPACK to scale curricular design for individual activities and lessons all the way up to entire courses and programs of study.

INTRODUCING ADDIE

Curriculum development is a lot like preparing a meal: Learning theory is the recipe, pedagogy is the cooking method, technology is the kitchen equipment, content is the assortment of ingredients, and the lesson/activity (as implemented) is the completed dish. You cannot devise a process or choose appropriate foodstuffs without knowing what you are attempting to produce, and the meal will taste different depending on which recipe you choose as a template. A behaviorist's lesson and evaluation measures will look substantially different than a social learning theorist's lesson and evaluation measures because they are working toward very different goals based on very different views of how and why people learn. In other words, you need to decide what is being baked, broiled, or sautéed based on the texture and flavor profile you seek to evoke (i.e., your learning objectives).

This is not to say educators can only ever incorporate practices espoused by their primary learning theory—a situated cognitivist can use points/

grades to get graduate students to do their work, and information processing theorists can use marble jars/tickets to induce sharing among elementary schoolers. The question is which theory and associated pedagogies/assessment strategies best support your instructional design writ large. Just because you incorporate behavioral reinforcement as a schema theorist, social constructivist, or situated cognitivist does not mean behaviorism is *the* theory governing your overarching course design, assignments, activities, and so forth (i.e., it can function as an add-on rather than the driving mechanism for your teaching/learning).

To determine which theory (and subsequent practices) you should apply in your particular teaching and learning environment, we recommend coupling TPACK with the widely used Analysis Design Development Implementation Evaluation (ADDIE) instructional design model. The acronym—popularized in 1975 by Florida State University—refers to a cyclical process by which designers determine which learning objectives to target, which instructional and assessment methods to employ, and how to revise their product(s) based on user feedback:

- **Analysis:** Clarification of learning objectives via surveys, interviews, focus groups, pretests, and reviews of existing curricula; thorough analyses save time, resources, and energy by ensuring the curriculum and assessment measures are properly aligned with the live implementation context/needs. Relevant questions include:
    - Who are the end users (learners), and what are their goals?
    - Who is implementing the curriculum (instructors), and what are their goals?
    - What knowledge, skills, and behaviors should be taught/learned through this curriculum?
    - What constraints exist within the teaching/learning environment?
    - What is the project timeline, and which project elements are absolutely necessary versus "nice to have but not mandatory"?
    - What assessment measures are practicable and relevant given the learning objectives?
    - Which learning theory and consequent pedagogical approach best fit the given context, learners, instructor, and learning objectives?
- **Design:** Initial construction of wireframes, storyboards, and other guiding documents that outline a logical curricular progression for learners and instructors to follow during implementation; this also includes

assessment measures, media (videos, instructional activities), and other instructional resources.
- **Development**: Integration of materials created during the Design phase; this involves constructing the course hub, resource pages, discussion board, wiki, and other physical and/or digital materials for pilot testing.
- **Implementation**: Enacting the designed curriculum with end users (i.e., learners) in the target instructional environment/context; this includes enrollment, instructional activities, assessment and evaluation, and follow-up.
- **Evaluation**: Collecting feedback and assessment results to determine whether and how learners are engaged with target content, skills, and behaviors; although it is positioned at the end of the ADDIE model, the Evaluation phase is continuous throughout the entire process and used to refine, revise, and tweak materials generated during every other phase of analysis and development.

The designer (or design team) engages in a needs analysis to capture relevant information before drafting wireframes and storyboards; then, they use draft documents to build out a vertical slice (i.e., a representative sample version of the product) for focus groups to review. If user assessment data suggest that learners are successfully applying the content knowledge and skills being taught, full implementation can begin.

We favor this approach because it is discipline agnostic and any educator can apply it within their domain for their specific audience without burdensome extra steps, content, or materials—a perfect scaffold for K–12, higher education, corporate training, and other teaching and learning environments. Although it is typically associated with multimember instructional design projects, it can easily be pared down to accommodate a single designer—a classroom teacher, professor, corporate trainer—who is writing objectives, planning instructional activities, or determining which technologies to integrate with instruction.

Follow along as we unpack ADDIE and TPACK to develop a methodological framework and sample learning objective.

DESIGNING INSTRUCTION

Instructional designers compose their target learning objectives by synthesizing Needs Analysis findings (i.e., surveys, focus groups, and interviews with various stakeholders) into brief statements that convey context, desired behavior, assessment, and target goal (taking the form of "Given

[X Resources], learners will . . ."). Each objective is typically written as a single sentence that indicates:

1. **Context**: The given resources/learning context
2. *Behavior*: The desired action the learner will take (i.e., Bloom's taxonomy verbiage)
3. *Assessment*: The means by which learners will be evaluated
4. Goal: The conditions expected for learners to meet proficiency

For example, "**Given an internet-connected device and novice to mid-level typing proficiency**, *learners will demonstrate collaboration in a shared Google Doc* **by writing one four-sentence paragraph that describes an engineering-based ethical dilemma** using a single voice and containing zero grammatical or spelling errors."

We want learning objectives to be this clear so both instructors and learners will know precisely what is expected of them and how each step of teaching and learning is meant to unfold. We similarly want to ensure that learning objectives are hierarchical in nature and feed into one another over time.

Taking things a step further, we can check for coherence and internal consistency by extending our learning objectives into scientific-style research questions that connect the context, behavior, assessment, and goal in terms of TPACK. In so doing, it is perfectly acceptable to move beyond simple binaries (e.g., "Does pedagogical method X succeed in instructional environment Y, yes or no?") and traditional scientific controls (i.e., null conditions for comparison) to qualify underlying conditions and learner circumstances.

For instance, it is much less useful to ask "does worldbuilding lead students to achieve higher scores when given a multiple-choice test about engineering ethics?" than to ask "how does worldbuilding for engineering ethics compare to traditional ethics training, and what are the possible benefits/challenges of employing worldbuilding in a university engineering course?"

By posing questions with the latter framing, we establish *how* and *why* a particular instructional method will help a particular group of learners improve along a particular variable in a particular learning and application environment. Most instructors do not strive to publish generalizable, statistically valid, and reliable research about their teaching, so the primary focus should remain on (1) achieving best practice for the instructional method of interest and (2) considering how that instructional method can be leveraged in different environments and/or for different purposes (i.e., creative cross-application).

This may seem counterintuitive or uncomfortable for individuals accustomed to standard laboratory research—chemists, physicists, and other STEM faculty typically maintain a combination of positive/negative control conditions that can be used to compare one or more experimental conditions. However, this is impossible to do in educational contexts because we cannot control for human behavior, environmental interactions, and many other facets of the complex systems governing how "school" happens. Our best bet is to plan for instructional methods to be implemented under sets of similar-but-not-the-same conditions where we minimize differences between implementation sessions as much as possible (e.g., the same instructor teaching the same learners with the given method over the course of multiple content units).

Approaching our instructional methods this way—qualitative, fluid, and dynamic—is often more useful than treating them as quantitative, replicable, and context independent. We could, for example, attempt to quantify worldbuilding's effectiveness for improving learner engagement by implementing it opposite traditional direct instruction and comparing learners' end-of-unit exam performance (i.e., an ABAB implementation; Worldbuilding → Direct Instruction → Worldbuilding → Direct Instruction), but a qualitative investigation of worldbuilding's effects on learner engagement (thereby providing each learner the opportunity to blend their creative/practical strengths in multiple ways) would yield a much richer understanding of the instructional method's affordances and drawbacks. Both examine the same variable—engagement—but the second steps outside a narrow definition of "success" and into the realm of optimizing instructor and learner experience (i.e., TPACK).

A THEORY OF WORLDBUILDING

You may be wondering why so much of a book dedicated to worldbuilding has been spent explaining learning theory, educational philosophy, and instructional design rather than worldbuilding itself.

The truth is, it can be intimidating to run a worldbuilding unit or project under the best circumstances, and instructor knowledge of high-quality, effective teaching and assessment practices is a make-or-break contributor to how smoothly the process unfolds (especially given the number and type of ways it challenges learner and instructor critical thinking, problem-solving, and creativity). You deserve a full suite of tools at your disposal before being sent into the wild blue yonder.

There are a small number of learning theories that we believe are particularly well suited for worldbuilding—not only do they streamline the planning process, but they also better maintain alignment between learning and activity objectives than the alternatives. Below, we synthesize the most effective of the bunch into a broader theory of worldbuilding for use in your own instructional context.

Analyzing Life-Worlds

As described in chapter 1, "Around the World in 300 Pages," the world is extremely complicated, and our individual experiences with its constituent parts are deeply situated in the contexts where they occur. Accordingly, our identity and positioning are enormously consequential for how we thread together knowledge, organize our thoughts into beginning-middle-end structures, and set them against a backdrop of personalized goals influenced by and dependent on our individual life-worlds.[16] That makes a person's life-world the ideal frame of reference for interrogating their identity and positioning as part of the worldbuilding process.

Simply put, a life-world is the totality of an individual's experiences with the lived-in world; the aggregate of their physiology, emotions, cognitive states, environment, goals, social relationships, and behaviors. Although two people can occupy the same room, have similar relationships, or even share DNA (e.g., identical twins), they *cannot*, by definition, share a life-world. We all carry unique experiential luggage from moment to moment, and our luggage is uniquely defined by objects, social interactions, and material phenomena that are salient only to us as individuals. From the (2019) book chapter "Una Vita: Exploring the Relationship Between Play, Learning Science, and Cultural Competency,"

> Humans are unique collections of information with unique understandings of the environment based on unique genes running through unique sets of lived circumstances. No two individuals can live the same life or have the same thoughts or experience the same social relations with their peers. Even experiences we return to at a later time in the same place with the same people doing the same thing are shaped and reshaped by the in-between periods during which we are individually exploring the world and making our own judgments about people, places and things. We are biological storybooks with pages printed upon by the external world; continuous narratives that tie together existence across the space-time we occupy. Each one of us is one life through which questions are asked and ideas are explored to define who we are and where we belong and what story we ultimately leave behind.[17]

Because situativity is fundamental to worldbuilding, we can use life-worlds to deconstruct how individuals perceive and act based on the confluence of their genetic predispositions, physiological effectivities (e.g., the senses: sight, smell, hearing, touch, proprioception, balance, etc.), prior experience with the world, and a vast array of wants and needs (e.g., biological [thirst, hunger], social, context specific). This directly parallels two key points about situated cognition covered in chapter 2, "Road to Contemporary Learning Theory":

1. **Learning is the education of *in*tention and *at*tention.** Worldbuilding instruction is meant to induce goal adoption related to target content/skills and then tune audience perception to important elements of the content/skills to be learned.
2. **Knowing is doing.** Learners engaged in a worldbuilding project only "know" something if they are able to perform a particular behavior or skill, not just list steps in a procedure or succeed on a multiple-choice test.

It follows that a holistic life-world analysis can introduce an opportunity for learners to contextualize their preexisting knowledge, confront their biases, and interrogate different perspectives.

Keep in mind that reflection on identity and positioning is precisely what enables meaningful (de)construction of complex, interrelated systems. When we discuss divergent goals, motivations, perspectives, experiences, and attitudes, we inevitably train ourselves to be more empathetic and better comprehend how macro and micro systems shape the world across space and time. There is no way to fake that kind of understanding either; it is self-evident in our behaviors, attitudes, and language. If the goal is to manifest new generations of thoughtful, self-actualized, emotionally mature learners ready to grapple with civilization-level problems, worldbuilding should be a go-to.

Note that life-world (de)construction and analysis also applies to the instructor—the information and resources we choose to adopt in our lessons, units, courses, and programs are wholly dependent on the experiential luggage we carry into curriculum development and teaching practice. Whether we invite and incorporate different student perspectives (i.e., on-the-fly modification of assignments, discussion questions, readings, activities, etc.) hinges on how we understand the (mis)match between instructor and learner conceptions about what is being taught or learned. So, we are all just as responsible for taking stock of potential biases and preconceived belief structures as our students, especially given how those biases and preconceived beliefs might influence our receptiveness to alternative student opinions and points of view.

Anchoring Instruction

The term "anchored instruction" refers to the use of stories or case studies as a means of organizing learning objectives and curricular content into comprehensible beginning-middle-end structures. Much like moorings in a marina that tether boats to prevent them from floating away, narratives *anchor* learning to facilitate (1) recognition of context(s) where knowledge and skills are directly pertinent and (2) transfer of knowledge and skills to new and different contexts.

This approach grew in popularity through the 1980s and 1990s as John Bransford and his twenty-five-member Cognition and Technology Group at Vanderbilt (CTGV) applied principles of situated cognition to the earlier work of John Dewey (discovery learning), Lev Vygotsky (constructivism), Seymour Papert (constructionism), and Jerome Bruner (narrative psychology).[18] Specifically, the team produced a dozen laserdisc-based videos under the series title *The Adventures of Jasper Woodbury*, each of which depicted the titular character and his friends engaged in real-world applications of mathematics, economics, social studies, and literature.[19] Unlike traditional word problems that are typically implemented as summative assessments such as quiz or exam questions, CTGV's videos were introduced to middle school students at the start of a unit and shown multiple times to support identification of the underlying problem(s), questioning of the given scenario, definition of goals/constraints, exploration of embedded data, derivation of relevant algorithms, and collaborative problem-solving.[20] Addressing these narrativized challenges often required complex, multistep deduction, and the dilemmas presented in each episode were intentionally ill-defined such that learners could develop and propose entirely unique solutions based on their individual interpretations and creative strengths (i.e., leveraging their life-worlds toward reflection, connection, and cross-context application).[21]

We view worldbuilding as a form of anchored instruction not unlike CTGV's *Jasper* series:

1. Both are inquiry driven and require learners to interrogate how different elements of complex systems interact.
2. They incorporate multiple stories, narratives, and/or cases to be compared and contrasted (i.e., learners identify invariant elements of stories, narratives, and/or cases to understand how and why target knowledge and skills apply across contexts).
3. They encourage learners to connect their identities to ideas and skills discovered through inquiry.

4. They are situated in richly authentic real-world events, scenarios, ideas, contexts, and resources.
5. They are inherently interdisciplinary and treat knowledge and skills as intrinsically linked across domains.
6. Every implementation yields different outcomes and work products depending on the individual learners (and instructors) engaged in the process.

Importantly, it will not work if learners are not provided the opportunity to engage in student-led inquiry and deduction—they must construct understanding for themselves by grappling with central ideas, conducting research, collaboratively generating summaries of their findings, and developing personalized solutions. The moment a narrative anchor becomes an end-unit word problem, it falls apart; learner-driven inquiry comes to a halt, ownership of the content/skills deteriorates, and transfer becomes much less likely.

Instructors planning to use anchor-based pedagogies like worldbuilding should think very carefully about how they can best build their target lesson, unit, course, or program on top of the narrative anchor so students will generate questions, ideas, and solutions without explicit direction from the instructor (i.e., leaning on TPACK and ADDIE to ensure one-to-one alignment between learning objectives and pedagogical activities). As stipulated above, this is a necessarily ill-defined process, so it is normal (and expected) for learners to feel awash in possibility when they begin. The instructor's job is to act as a guide on the side rather than a sage on the stage, helping learners remain in their respective zones of proximal development and tuning their perception to ideas and information that will help them discover, and take ownership of, core content and skills.

Actualizing Andragogy
One of the most valuable features of worldbuilding is its direct alignment with the fundamental tenets of andragogy.

The term "andragogy" refers to the practice of teaching *adult learners* as opposed to the more general practice of "pedagogy," which speaks to teaching *all* learners (both children and adults). It is differentiable from other forms of instruction based on its specific tilt toward self-direction, practicability in work environments, and problem-based learning, though this leaves the line between andragogical techniques and other instructional approaches—like anchored instruction—somewhat blurry. The primary distinction is that andragogical teaching and learning environments directly link activities, readings, discussions, and assessments with particular career pathways and practices, imbuing instruction with immediacy that is often absent from K–12 education (i.e., on-demand and on time versus abstract and distant; e.g., corporate workplace seminars concerning supervisor-subordinate power dynamics versus high school cell biology with no in-the-moment application).

This immediacy prompts learners to consider the potential life-transformative effects of their learning, including and especially how content and skills apply to their personal and professional lives. If that rings a bell, you have been paying close attention: It returns us to the affordances of life-world analysis for bridging what happens in the learning environment with what happens outside of it (transfer), inducing learner ownership of critical ideas, and inspiring the trial and adoption of new perspectives. It also neatly maps to a situated cognition worldview by contextualizing learning in the environment(s) where it pertains rather than assuming that learners will automatically recognize when, why, and how the concepts they are taught are relevant to in-the-moment problem-solving.

Applying andragogical curricular design to our engineering ethics example, we might focus on the relationships between learners' lived experiences in engineering environments as compared to the thinking and behaviors of engineers involved with Chernobyl and/or other engineering disasters (Three Mile Island, Fukushima, the Space Shuttle Challenger explosion, Apollo 13, the Great Molasses Flood). We could further connect learner life-worlds with ethical decision-making in the context of fictional engineering ethics-related environments like *Fallout 3* as a means of extending thinking into the hypothetical. Such case comparisons would promote reflection on similarities and differences between student engineers and professionals as well as underscore how contextual elements (such as obligations to friends and family, desire for prestige, financial incentives) affect ethical decision-making in ways that are seldom perceptible or acknowledged when evaluating one's ethics in a decontextualized, and often impoverished, learning environment, like a professional development workshop or college course. Moreover, it would better prepare learners to actualize their ethics training when confronted with legitimate ethical challenges in the workplace by reducing barriers to transfer than traditional direct instruction and multiple-choice tests (e.g., the Engineering Ethics Reasoning Instrument).

Worldbuilding involves precisely this kind of critical thinking and problem-solving: deconstruction of individual and communal motivations, examination of how interlocking parts in a complex system exert influence over one another, and informed speculation about possible futures. Although it can be done with all age groups, disciplines, and learning communities, it is foundationally andragogical, and it is designed to connect the personal with the impersonal: what happens to me (at a micro scale) and what happens to society (at a macro scale). Consequently, the fact that much of the learning science research referenced throughout this chapter was originally conducted with school-aged children does not in any way negate the utility of worldbuilding and anchored instruction, generally, for adult learners. To the contrary, it is a flexible approach capable of catering to all levels, disciplines, and audiences if wisely tailored using the instructional design frameworks characterized in prior sections.

PULLING IT ALL TOGETHER

The broad dimensions of learning theory and instructional design can be a lot to absorb, especially when it is compressed into just a few dozen pages, but we wanted to spell out precisely how tightly tied worldbuilding as pedagogy is to a long legacy of empirically demonstrated concepts and methods. Unlike the proverbial silver bullets offered by many other texts on the pedagogy bookshelf, there is meat on these bones—and, crucially, all of it is directly *actionable*.

Let us pull things together with one last stop in northern Ukraine's Kyiv oblast and our engineering ethics classroom.

We opened with the idea of creating an engineering ethics curriculum that would engage learners and induce transfer, accomplished in part through the incorporation of the Chernobyl disaster as a real-world case study. To structure our content objectives, pedagogical methods, and assessment measures, we took stock of potential theoretical foundations, considered which would be the best "lens" for evaluating (un)ethical decision-making, and used TPACK to weigh the collective internal consistency of our learning goals, planned activities, and instructional resources (i.e., technologies).

Employing ADDIE to organize our curriculum development process, we landed on a situated approach that incorporated the use of popular media (*Fallout 3*, HBO's [2019] *Chernobyl*, and Svetlana Alexievich's [1997] *Voices from Chernobyl*) to anchor our content objectives and tune learner perception to important elements of (un)ethical decision-making. We also integrated collaborative writing with student life-world analysis so learners could compare and contrast their own (un)ethical decision-making experiences with those of both fictional and real engineers. Our worldbuilding centered on de- and reconstructing the world of *Fallout 3* in relation to pre- and post-Chernobyl Ukraine to trace how and why different (un)ethical decisions led to particular outcomes. This was followed by the introduction of additional real-world cases (Three Mile Island, Fukushima, etc.) that learners could investigate to triangulate their findings and propose personalized criteria for making ethical choices in engineering contexts (anchored instruction and ill-defined problem-solving).

Everything in our engineering ethics curriculum exists in service of encouraging learner reflection and application. Not only do we want these learners to recognize when and how ethical decisions are made, but they need to be able to exercise their knowledge and skills if and when they find themselves in the midst of real-world ethical quandaries. To improve the possibility of that transfer occurring, we could add simulation and role-playing activities (see chapter 13, "Simulations," and chapter 14, "Role-Play") as well as a longitudinal portfolio of self-evaluations and other work products that substantiate each learner's growth throughout the course (see chapter 5, "Assessment"). Taken together, these activities should yield greater learner self-awareness about (un)ethical decision-making and, hopefully, lead to a transformation in how student engineers view their respective identities, career trajectories, and work-related roles.

With sufficient resources and a flexible instructional context, it may be possible to expand this curriculum into a fully interdisciplinary program of study. Simply scale our plan one level higher—an overarching narrative structure supported by multiple courses with interconnected learning objectives, worldbuilding activities, and cross-context applications of learning:

- **Science:** Laboratory practices, safety procedures, engineering-specific skills
- **Math:** Relationships between theoretical and practical aspects of engineering, economics of ethical decision-making in engineering environments, statistics and probability in risk assessment
- **Language Arts:** Stories and literature grounded in ethical decision-making, philosophy of ethics, sociocultural structures and their relationship to (un)ethical decision-making
- **Social Studies:** Global communities and relationships with (un)ethical decision-making, the intersection of trade economics, safety, ethics, and culture (i.e., geopolitics of engineering ethics)
- **World Language:** Communicating about (un)ethical decision-making in cross-cultural contexts, standardization of ethical processes and norms across geopolitical boundaries

- **Fine Arts**: Multi- and transmedia depictions of (un)ethical decision-making, making practical and philosophical ethics concerns approachable to pre- and in-service engineers
- **Interdisciplinary Project(s)**: Collaboratively constructed worldbuilding wikis that establish how and why ethical frameworks function (or fail) in different contexts and for different communities; depictions of historical events related to engineering ethics; scholarly workshops, presentations, and/or poster sessions that communicate principles and/or processes of ethical decision-making to authentic audiences (i.e., practicing engineers)

Under this umbrella, learning objectives and activities would naturally vary from day to day and course to course, but the holistic endeavor would center on student inquiry and offer something more memorable, richly informative, and authentic than traditional university programs. It is a wholly different archetype for higher education than learners typically experience, and it would be an asset for preparing learners to participate in a world governed by interdisciplinary systems rather than multiple discrete, mutually exclusive domains.

WHAT'S NEXT?

The coming chapters will detail the nuts and bolts of collaboration and assessment as they relate to the worldbuilding process. Although both are deeply interconnected with learning theory and instructional design, we anticipate that a bit of breathing room will make them easier to understand and implement as part of your worldbuilding lesson, unit, course, or program.

4 COLLABORATION AND COMMUNITY

"Yes, but Marge, you're not . . . you're missing the point! The **individual** doesn't matter—it was a **team** effort! And **I'm** the one who came up with the whole team idea! Me!"

—Homer Simpson, *The Simpsons*[1]

You no doubt noticed that the previous chapter's translation of theory to practice only briefly touched on the dynamics of collaboration and community. Fret not—there is a method to our madness. Giving these ideas special treatment in their own chapter allows us to emphasize their unique role in the worldbuilding process, defining precisely how and why social constructivist teaching and learning can be organized for richly authentic problem-solving and transfer.

Sharing reflections—on our identities, problems, and worldviews—helps paint a more comprehensive picture of how different situations and contexts are perceived by different individuals acting from different life-worlds. It likewise provides a chance to fine-tune our interpretation of heuristics and adjust our behavior. Individual perspectives are inescapably subjective, but social constructivism and situated cognition are ideal for building redundancy, thoroughness, and precision into our shared knowledge base, as well as debating the accuracy, utility, and flexibility of what we believe.

The coming pages bring together personal and communal learning as a way to facilitate the development of worldbuilding lessons, units, courses, and programs. After all, this type of instruction can only succeed if instructors understand how their learners form goals, act in unison (or dis-unison), and contribute to (or draw on) the broader learning community. By zooming in and out of individual and group instruction strategies, we will establish best practices for recognizing and optimizing community-based critical thinking as well as provide insight into distributed knowledge and expertise.

IDENTITY, POSITIONING, AND SOCIAL CONSTRUCTIVISM

In figure 4.1, two brains perceive the same object (represented by the letter D). However, the left-hand brain interprets the shape as a square, while the right-hand brain interprets it as a circle. The two are influenced by their relative positioning and experience sets, only able to understand the shape from their respective point of view. This is not a failure of either brain but a product of comprehension from distinct viewpoints.

It may seem obvious that the "correct" interpretation of this shape is the letter D, but there is no impartial referee who can pass such a judgment. The best we can do is formulate asymptotic approximations based on many interpretations over an extended period, falsifying our hypotheses through empirical study (or, for topics that cannot be falsified [e.g., philosophy, religion, art], the most internally consistent, logical reasoning available to us). Whatever we agree on ultimately becomes "truth."

As a result, we need to set guideposts for truth-seeking, especially with respect to

- whose interpretations and perspectives are being centered and
- why those interpretations and perspectives are being centered.

Our subjectivity and limited time/resources demand deliberation over positioning and capacity to uplift others' voices. Expanding on Hong Kong dissident Bao Pu's suggestion that "the 20th century was a century of ideology; the 21st century is a century of identity," we need to appreciate how communication and decision-making have traditionally been limited to a select few highly influential individuals and institutions operating with top-down ideological valencing.[2] The twenty-first century has brought us social media and decentralization of knowledge (e.g., online wikis, discussion boards) that have dramatically shifted who can amplify and direct attention

FIGURE 4.1
Two brains diverged in a yellow wood, and I—I took the path dictated by my subjective, highly contextualized experiential background.

to an array of belief structures, actions, and information. We should consequently ask whether the content we produce represents nuanced, multiperspective analysis or reductive, antisocial speculation; a deconstruction of worldviews through which individuals and communities evaluate their environments and push for change.

Although we seldom think about it, the continuous reconstitution of our identities from moment to moment is shaped and reshaped by events that unfold in between our interactions with various people and circumstances. We even collaborate across dozens of versions of *ourselves*, and whatever actions we take bear a range of identity fingerprints based on what we are thinking, feeling, and experiencing up to the second we act. The range of perspectives that influence us grows exponentially as we account for all other individuals—who themselves possess multiple identities, biases, and experiences—that we encounter in our daily lives.

Because identity and positioning inform our perspectives (and vice versa; our perspectives inform our identity and positioning), the act of worldbuilding is inherently inseparable from ourselves, our biases, and our worldviews. This is a net positive so long as we understand worldbuilding to be a social enterprise that necessitates the incorporation of diverse viewpoints with which we lack intimate, personal familiarity (i.e., a space to coconstruct knowledge) (see chapter 8, "Examining Life-Worlds Through Demographics").

Coaction, then, is the name of the game—figuring out how to navigate the world in coordination with others whose perspectives fill in our blanks.

OF TERMITES AND MEN

Termites and humans have few physiological characteristics in common, but the coaction of termites toward shared objectives is analogous to the coaction of human learners toward shared objectives. To fully appreciate this commonality (i.e., termite brood behaviors as a simplified model of agent-environment interaction and human behaviors as a more complex model of agent-environment interaction), consider how either set of organisms acts in their respective environments to achieve individual and community goals.

Peter Kugler and colleagues' (1991) ecological psychology research described the creation of large termite mounds (figure 4.2) to demonstrate how many individuals acting together can achieve more than any individual ever could.[3] Although each termite in the brood has individual intents and effectivities (i.e., sensory abilities), their moment-to-moment movements

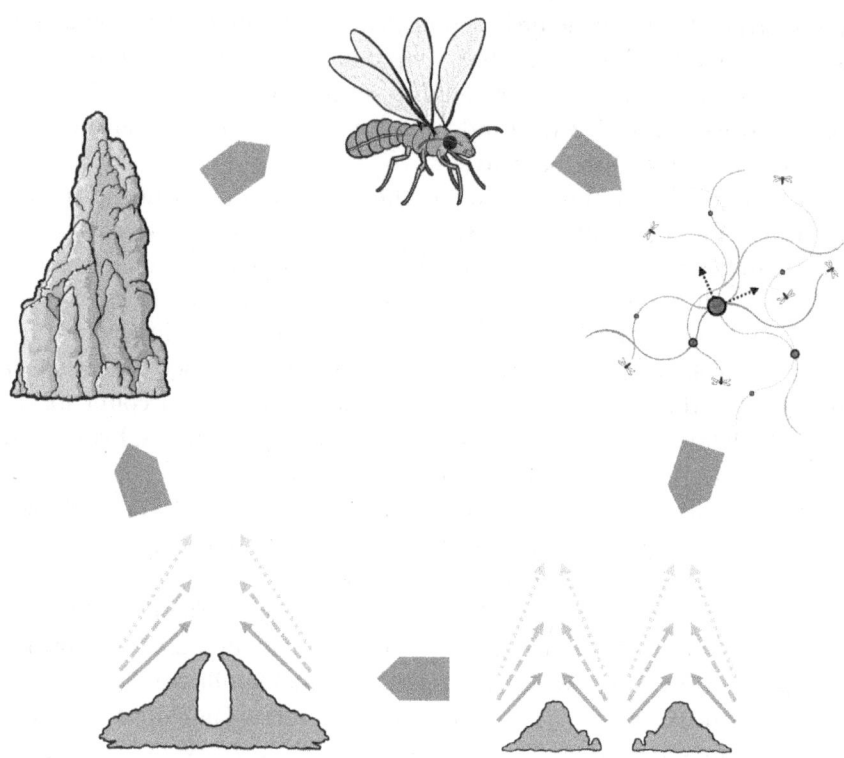

FIGURE 4.2
An illustrated depiction of Peter Kugler and Michael T. Turvey's (1987) scholarship on nonlinear → linear insect behaviors. In the words of the (1993) *Jurassic Park* character Ian Malcolm, "That is one big pile of shit." Source: Peter N. Kugler and Michael T. Turvey, *Information, Natural Law, and the Self-Assembly of Rhythmic Movements* (LEA, 1987); *Jurassic Park*, directed by Steven Spielberg (Universal Pictures, 1993).

and behaviors (dictated by their individual life-worlds) add to the efforts of other individuals across the system (i.e., the full termite community). There are no long-winded town hall and zoning meetings to conduct their coordinated work; instead, the termites release pheromones with their excrement (the same material used to build the mounds) that amasses around each individual termite's worksite. The mounds are quite small early on, but as additional termites detect the pheromones and migrate closer to their source, a macro pattern emerges wherein more and more termites converge at the same location until they collectively (and not explicitly "consciously") excrete a tower of waste under which they live, reproduce, and find protection from the elements—a whole greater than the sum of its Isoptera parts (i.e., a supraorganism[4]).

Correspondingly, when humans enter a shared environment, they tend to self-organize into community groups and orient toward some shared intention (e.g., constructing a project, solving a problem). The ways they intend and act to achieve their goal(s) naturally varies from person to person, so it takes a substantial organization (as well as prolonged interaction) to shift the group from individual to collective behavior (i.e., an intentional system of coordinated coactors). This is why effective leaders thoughtfully cluster community members around social dynamics that minimize conflict and maximize cooperation—the more cohesive the community, the more likely individual goals and behaviors will synergize, and the greater the synergy, the greater the probability that the target objective(s) will be fulfilled.

There are, of course, important distinctions between the collective actions of humans and termites. For one thing, humans have the benefit of tools like language, whereas termites are limited to mechanisms of biochemical reinforcement; humans have complex sociocultural norms that mediate our interactions, while termites belong to a literal hivemind; and humans engage in a variety of collaborative projects (e.g., orchestral performance, hospital management, geopolitics), but termites are limited to shoveling around their own waste (though, in fairness to our termite friends, the same could be said of Wall Street bankers, venture capitalists, and Silicon Valley billionaires).

Thankfully, there exists a broad body of academic research concerning human collective action that both expands beyond excrement-based construction and provides a comprehensive conceptual framework for how and why different types of communities thrive or collapse. In the next section, we explain this framework—as well as its implications for instruction, specifically—to ground the organization of your teaching and learning environment and foster a worldbuilding-based Community of Practice.

COMMUNITIES OF PRACTICE

For as long as there have been humans, we have self-organized into highly social, co-oriented groups of individuals in service of overcoming mutual challenges. Jean Lave and Étienne Wenger's (1991) *Situated Learning: Legitimate Peripheral Participation* observed that such groups, which they called

Communities of Practice (CoPs), share several essential characteristics,[5] including

- a common domain of interest,
- criteria that define group membership,
- common objectives established by group members,
- fluid roles that members adopt based on group needs,
- expertise distributed across multiple community members, and
- shared behavior patterns, practices, and knowledge.

It may be tempting to assume that any and all social environments possess these characteristics, but there are important distinctions that separate different kinds of collaborative groups (formal and informal) from true CoPs.

Lave and Wenger pointed to member relationships and interactions as the primary point of divergence, with CoPs (versus other socially collaborative groups) featuring individuals who (1) explicitly opted in (i.e., were not coerced or forced into participation) and (2) engaged in acts of legitimate peripheral participation (LPP). A butcher shop, they suggested, might have multiple individuals adopt interrelated roles within the butchering process, yet those individuals seldom act in the same space and time as their peers. Instead, they are isolated into different parts of the building and, for the most part, do not directly witness what others are doing—the job of a slicer is distinct from that of a custodian, which is distinct from that of the sales clerk. They do have the shared overarching goal of butchering and selling meat; they do not engage with most parts of the process or the broader community. Therefore, a butcher shop would not qualify as a CoP, nor could it be said to afford LPP.

Liberian Vai and Gola tailors, on the other hand, share an overarching goal and engage in LPP throughout fabrication. Cutters, sewers, steamers, ironers, and sellers work within the same physical environment, and all participants can watch and interact with their peers from the beginning of the process to the end. Novices are not sequestered from experts—they are directly integrated into the community, and as they master one role (e.g., ironing), their newfound expertise qualifies them to shift from the community's outer periphery toward the center. This is where the words "legitimate," "peripheral," and "participation" fuse together: Task completion is richly authentic and meaningfully contributes to the larger group (legitimate); tasks are completed in conjunction with the work of others (peripheral); and every individual is an active community member, not simply an observer (participation). In Lave and Wenger's (1991) words, "learning is an integral part of generative social practice in the lived-in world,"[6] and social practices are more important to the adoption of ideas, perspectives, and skills than the internalization of rote knowledge.

It may help to think of a CoP as being one of many different socially collaborative spheres to which we belong: personal and professional, large and small, local and distant, face-to-face and virtual. We contribute to them in a variety of ways, and our expertise and social standing within a particular CoP codetermine our centrality to that community at any given time. Because CoPs often overlap or are nested within one another, we simultaneously exist on the periphery of some while being central to others, and our positioning changes as our knowledge, skills, interests, and relationships shift in different directions.

Figure 4.3 illustrates how an individual educator (represented by the black dot) might interact with four different but interrelated CoPs (a faculty advisory group [A], a local political party [B], their labor union [C], a hobby organization [D]) at four different points in time (T_1, T_2, T_3, and T_4). Their position within each CoP fluctuates from T_1 to T_4, demonstrating how they move from the periphery to the center (or vice versa) depending on the

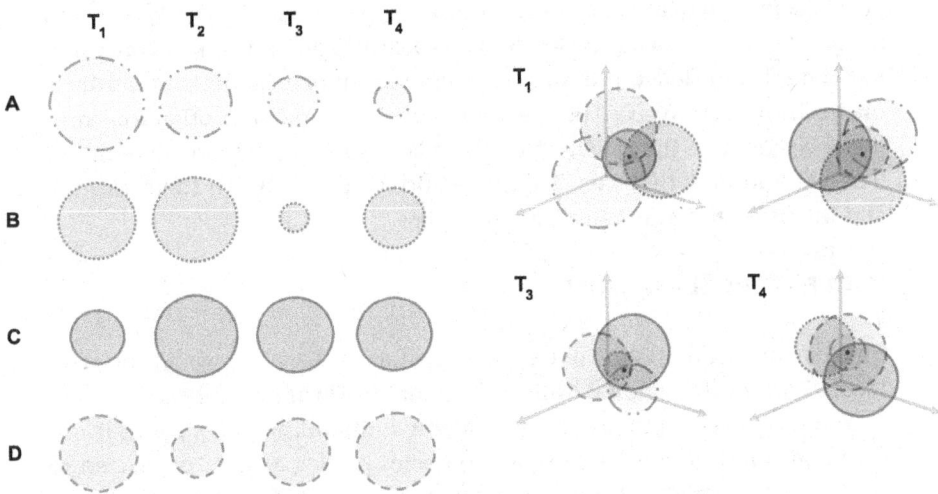

FIGURE 4.3

Visualization of overlapping Communities of Practice (adapted from Cochran, Slota, and Young). An educator (represented by the black dot) grows/reduces their participation and centrality in various communities (A, B, C, and D) as those communities fluctuate in size/importance over time (T_1, T_2, T_3, and T_4). Source: Andrew Cochran, Stephen T. Slota, and Michael F. Young, "League of Legends: The Case for Nested & Braided Communities of Practice" in *The Literacies of the Esports Ecosystem*, ed. Hannah R. Gerber (Brill Sense, 2024).

development of new skills, increased or decreased interest, social dynamics, and/or other factors.

Because of the way CoPs dynamically interact with one another, they can be a useful vehicle for educators seeking to induce transfer among learners—they provide a natural interdisciplinary bridge between topics, skills, and social relationships, and they allow individuals from disparate backgrounds to identify commonalities between their own worldviews and those of other people.

However, the emergence of CoPs in traditional teaching and learning environments is not automatic or inevitable. Some CoP characteristics apply to schools, classrooms, and training contexts, but it is extremely difficult to cultivate a true CoP so long as learning is compulsory and/or group members lack social cohesion. Any instructor seeking to develop a CoP should be prepared to flatten the superior-inferior relationship between the instructor and learners as well as orient the community toward a shared goal. Learners must understand that it is both valid and desirable for their relative levels of expertise with different tasks to differ from their peers, and they should be given the opportunity to watch and "do" as the group completes tasks, develops proficiencies, and continuously reorganizes itself. This goes a step beyond plain, old social constructivism—learners are not simply constructing shared knowledge but shared *identity* grounded in the community's overarching objective(s). They are as much reliant on one another for learning and growth as they are the instructor, and social interaction determines whether and how they perceive the relationship(s) between their learning and the broader context in which it applies.

CoPs FOR THE CLASSROOM

Imagine you are designing a twentieth-century history unit about the post-World War II International Military Tribunal (IMT) at Nuremberg.

You have decided to use instructional worldbuilding to help your learners understand how different constituencies participated in or reacted to the 1945–1946 trials. Ideally, you want them to come away with comprehensive knowledge of the affected parties, the inauguration of an international justice system, and a definition of crimes against humanity. They should also be able to articulate how Nuremberg continues to resonate long after the final verdicts were delivered (i.e., "Learners will summarize the IMT's historical legacy and evaluate its influence on subsequent events through the present").

Rather than relying on traditional stand-and-deliver methods, you aim to establish a CoP grounded in collaborative research and presentation skills. This includes splitting students into small but interconnected work groups; welcoming external community members into the CoP to share their knowledge, skills, and experiences with the topic(s) at hand (e.g., historians, archivists, legal professionals, museum curators, Holocaust survivors); and ensuring all members of the CoP are privy to the work being done by other members (i.e., maintaining visibility and transparency across individuals and groups to achieve LPP). In pursuit of these objectives, you introduce a wide array of primary and secondary resources, highlight multiple perspectives, encourage information sharing and collaboration, and plan activities that will grow relationships between different constituencies within the CoP (e.g., museum field trips, guest lectures, hands-on investigations, library visits, cross-group discussions).

Constraints like mandatory attendance, standardized testing, seclusion from different parts of the system, and overly structured objectives imposed by external authorities make it difficult to cultivate a CoP in relatively inflexible spaces like K–12 schools, university classrooms, corporate workshops, and military retreats. Yet, we can roughly capture their structure and function by adhering to the tenets outlined by Lave and Wenger, at least insofar as we can invite learners into the teaching and learning environment as peers rather than subordinates. That means the larger group's research topic(s), the process by which subgroups or teams are formed, the nature of presentations, and the final work product should not be set in stone by the instructor—they should be codetermined by all community members via cooperation and discussion.

Put another way, the instructor is never *the* authority in the room; they are one colearner among many, and each colearner is a relative expert on different aspects of the project. Everyone, regardless of their formal status as "teacher" or "learner," directly participates in brainstorming, research, collaborative writing, and publication (e.g., wikis, multimedia, individual/group stories). Akin to termites in a hive,[7] the cells in a slime mold,[8] and naval quartermasters on a submarine,[9] everyone is an information/skill node within a broader network, and their individual behaviors occur alongside and in response to environmental feedback. They come to anticipate how others will comport themselves under shifting conditions (i.e., prospective perception) and transition from siloed action to collective action without the need for explicit direction by some central authority.

In the case of our Nuremberg example, learners' coconstructed knowledge about the IMT would improve as their self-generated objectives and project contributions come into alignment with the broader CoP, thereby allowing the instructor to focus on (1) introducing new resources that suit different community member specializations (e.g., prosecution, defense, evidence, historical context), (2) facilitating goal adoption and fulfillment among community members (acting as the guide on the side), and (3) pushing community members to the edge of their respective zones of proximal development. Each learner's centrality to the CoP would necessarily change on a moment-to-moment, as-needed basis, so everyone is simultaneously a novice testing their abilities against novel challenges and an expert leading others to mature within the domain of interest. It is egalitarian, distributed, and discovery driven, more accurately reflecting the dynamics of real-world social learning and skill application than prescriptive, didactic lecture.

It may help to think of CoP-based learning as being a subset of social constructivism: The latter emphasizes learners working in pairs or groups to develop understanding, generally, but the former more specifically asserts that understanding is mediated by community membership and interaction at a particular place and time—*it is not static*. It requires a deep, long-term commitment to connecting new members with existing or former members, and the community will grow, shrink, and gain or lose knowledge as its membership ebbs and flows. Thus, CoPs are not simply small groups of learners working on a shared slideshow or document for two weeks; they are more complex (and rewarding) efforts that unite many people around a shared "big picture" goal and draw on each person's unique identity, perspective, and relationships to grow the community as a functional whole.

FROM HERE TO THERE

CoP cultivation can seem like an unwieldy beast, but it boils down to a few core ideas: forming strong relationships, creating opportunities for LPP, and regularly deploying socially constructive activities such as journaling, wiki creation, presentation development, and online communication. What matters most is that the instructor is prepared to support colearners if/when disagreements arise, point them toward relevant resources, and foster connections between disparate portions of the community.

Part II, "Concepts," and part III, "World Modeling," will detail several preparatory steps that can make community-oriented worldbuilding simpler and smoother than it sounds in the abstract—we even provide a template with specific directions to make it more accessible for anyone new to the process. For the time being, though, we will shift to assessment methods that you can directly port into your instructional environment. This should put you on track to practically apply the theories described over the last few chapters and help you incorporate worldbuilding into your classes as intentionally and effectively as possible.

5 ASSESSMENT

"Miss Wormwood, I protest this 'C' grade! That's saying I only did an 'Average' job! I got 75% of the answers correct, and in today's society, doing something 75% right is outstanding! If government and industry were 75% competent, we'd be ecstatic! I won't stand for this artificial standard of performance! I demand an 'A' for this kind of work!"

—Calvin, *Calvin and Hobbes*[1]

Traditional assessment measures like tests, quizzes, and essays tend to be suboptimal for evaluating student achievement in collaborative worldbuilding environments—who gets credit for which contributions? How can quality be weighed against quantity? Should learners be evaluated as a group, or should each individual be evaluated independently?

This chapter introduces acute and longitudinal assessment strategies to gauge learner growth without defaulting to decontextualized points and scores. We discuss alphanumeric versus standards-based grading, self- and coassessment, the usefulness of one-on-one conferencing, and applications of "ungrading" to foster learners' metacognitive skills. Together, these methods form a configuration for highly personalized evaluations that support the kind of student-centered, inquiry-driven learning and transfer needed for learners to extend curricula into their personal and professional lives.

ALPHANUMERIC GRADING

The practice of alphanumeric grading (i.e., assigning a letter or number to represent student achievement, e.g., A, B, C, D, F or 1–100 percent) is a fairly recent innovation popularized in the late nineteenth and early twentieth centuries as a mechanism for universities to compare the students they graduated.[2] It has some obvious merits—simple to interpret, efficient for large groups, and easy to calculate—but it comes with some caveats grounded in how behavioral reinforcement shapes learner understanding and goal adoption.

Consider your own experiences with grades: the frustration, the inequity, the anxiety. Pressure to outperform peers. Lost sleep. Those feelings, any one of which can be completely debilitating, are conditioned through years of treating success and failure as binary outcomes. Growth over time is seldom the primary objective, and individual assignments are treated as mutually exclusive of one another.

From a learner's perspective, it makes sense to focus on grades given their relationship to college admissions, participation in extracurricular activities, and potential career paths. Yet, on the instructor's side of the desk, grades assigned for homework, exams, or full courses increase perverse incentives within the education system by (falsely) equating intellectual risk-taking with abstract letters and numbers. In a perfect world, the two would be one and the same, but in our lived reality, they are not—grades are distinct from and distantly correlated with critical thinking, problem-solving, and creativity.

Take a moment to reflect on the following questions:

- Does an A from the same instructor in two different class sections mean the same thing? What about an A from two different instructors in the same school teaching the same subject? Or an A from two instructors in the same state teaching the same subject? Or an A from two different instructors in different parts of the country?
- If two learners in the same class take the same test, does the learner who receives an 87 percent know 3 percent more than the learner who receives an 84 percent?
- What conditions lead to learners valuing grades? How is the way learners view grading reinforced by instructors, other learners, parents, employers, and the education system itself?

Given the situated nature of teaching and learning, there is no way to achieve parity across instructors, learners, and contexts; each is equipped with their own life-world and objectives. But it is not enough to acknowledge the flaws in alphanumeric grading—we need a solution.

Thus, we propose standards-based assessment as the go-to methodology for every worldbuilding educator.

STANDARDS-BASED ASSESSMENT

In standards-based assessment, attention shifts from the quantitative value associated with a final product to the process a learner undergoes to create it—that is, the use of standards (by way of detailed learning objectives and a corresponding rubric) emphasizes a combination of growth over time and reflection. Our own course syllabi state that "grades are not a terribly great indicator of learning; in fact, they are often an obstacle to idea sharing and other critical elements of discussion. Consequently, you will not receive number or letter grades on posts or assignments in this course. Emphasis will instead be placed on what you learn and how you apply it to your own lives. Try to think of your discussion posts, instructor-learner conferences, and assignments as portfolio artifacts demonstrating how you have grown over the semester, not boxes you need to check to receive an A."

Educators have a responsibility to help learners value learning over the external behavioral reinforcement of grading. As efficient as letters and percentage scales are, they do not provide insight as to the conditions that led to a student's understanding, what specific knowledge and skills the student possesses, nor how the student's thinking changes over time. With rubrics and reflection-driven assessments, we have a chance to positively reinforce behaviors we want our students to carry into adulthood and the workforce (e.g., critical thinking, reflection, creativity, and problem-solving versus memorization and regurgitation of information on traditional assessments).

There are a few different ways to integrate standards-based assessment measures into a teaching and learning environment, the most straightforward of which is to adopt rubrics that evaluate performance along a series of particularized learning objectives.

Let us imagine we are developing a course centered on the sociology of healthcare. As with the engineering ethics example in chapter 3, " Theory to Practice," we need to craft a series of learning objectives organized into course-, unit-, lesson-, and activity-level goals. All levels of the goal hierarchy should target a primary objective that is achieved via the cumulative completion of each activity, lesson, and unit. For example, we can structure the course objectives at different levels as follows:

- **Course**: Learners will evaluate political, economic, sociological, and cultural factors that define healthcare systems and the practice of medicine.
- **Unit**: Learners will compare and contrast social causes of health disparities across geopolitical, sociocultural, and economic borders.
- **Lesson**: Learners will characterize different populations' experiences with healthcare systems and medical treatment.
- **Activity**: Learners will review quantitative and qualitative data about individuals' experiences with local and state healthcare systems.

We can further specify any number of behavioral and resource expectations that define our teaching and assessment strategy:

- **Course:** Given a fourteen-week course including [course texts] and [additional resources], learners will evaluate political, economic, sociological, and cultural factors that define healthcare systems and the practice of medicine by proposing three model trajectories for the future of healthcare using statistical evidence, experiential accounts, and worldbuilding deconstruction to support those models.
- **Unit:** Given a two-week unit that incorporates [readings] and [resources], learners will compare and contrast social causes of health disparities across geopolitical, sociocultural, and economic borders by selecting and researching the healthcare systems of three distinct global regions.
- **Lesson:** Given access to regional healthcare data, learners will characterize different populations' experiences with healthcare systems by creating archetypes of different individuals who interact with or work within those systems.
- **Activity:** Given an internet-connected device and prior experience applying common research skills, learners will review quantitative and qualitative data about individuals' experiences with local and state healthcare systems by developing five online wiki pages summarizing those experiences (including hyperlinks to a minimum of five sources per page).

Next, we use our objectives to develop rubrics that delineate precisely what criteria the instructor will use to evaluate learner proficiency. Table 5.1 illustrates what this might look like as part of a sociology of healthcare task where learners are asked to share their initial research findings and perspectives in an online discussion board.

Similarly, table 5.2 depicts a rubric that could be used to evaluate final projects in our full fourteen-week sociology of healthcare course (i.e., a long-term endeavor versus a short-term discussion assignment).

Under this assessment paradigm, the highest rubric category is equated with "exceeds standards," which is not quite the same thing as an A or A+; it instead refers to particularly noteworthy syntheses of learning goals, work products, and reflections. Not everyone can or will exceed standards, and learners should not panic if they do not reach this benchmark. None of us should expect to be exceptional in all categories at all times, which is why it should be reserved for situations where a learner *far exceeds* general proficiency (i.e., in a category separate from and beyond other acceptable

Table 5.1. Sample standards-based assessment tool for a discussion forum in a sociology of healthcare course

	Below Standards	Meets Standards	Exceeds Standards
Expression of Ideas	Addresses the prompt inadequately or inappropriately. Response may be off-topic or incomplete. Response demonstrates little or no awareness of audience.	Addresses the prompt adequately. Responds in a general manner. Response may demonstrate limited awareness of audience.	Addresses the prompt appropriately and completely. Responds to prompt knowledgeably and accurately. Response consistently demonstrates awareness of audience.
Elaboration	Provides few or no appropriate details, or may not attempt to elaborate at all. Shows no evidence of support.	Elaborates occasionally with some appropriate details in a generally coherent manner. Shows some evidence of support.	Elaborates consistently with appropriate and precise details in a coherent manner. Shows clear evidence of support.
Competence	Identification of significant ideas and theories is weak or lacking. Provides few or no appropriate connections between attitudes, values, and ideas held by the sociology community.	Identifies significant ideas and theories. Identifies appropriate connections between attitudes, values, and ideas held by the sociology community.	Identifies and describes significant ideas and theories. Explains how theories and worldviews relate to attitudes, values, and ideas held by the sociology community.
Vocabulary	Uses inadequate vocabulary. Language inhibits communication throughout response.	Uses adequate vocabulary. Language may noticeably negatively affect communication at times.	Uses extensive, appropriate, and accurate design terminology.
Risk-Taking	Deals with unstructured situations. Experiments or guesses only with assistance and/or prompting.	Deals with unstructured situations; predicts, guesses, and experiments on occasion.	Demonstrates a high degree of willingness to take chances. Defends ideas, experiments, and predictions. Puts plans into action.

Table 5.2. Sample standards-based assessment tool for a final course project in a sociology of healthcare course

	Unacceptable	Below Standards	Meets Standards	Exceeds Standards
Communication Quality	Regularly occurring errors in spelling, grammar, punctuation, and/or communication; errors render content incomprehensible and/or difficult to understand.	Spelling, grammar, punctuation errors, and/or communication errors are common and distracting, but content is still comprehensible.	Few spelling, grammar, punctuation, and/or communication errors; errors that occur do not distract from content.	No errors in composition and/or communication.
Organization	Submission is poorly organized; disjointed; lacks cohesion.	Somewhat organized but quality is inconsistent, and/or supporting materials conflict with target objectives.	Mostly well organized with occasional instances of distracting and/or unclear structuring.	Well-organized submission with a clear, well-thought-out foundation; comprehensive, consistent, and thorough.
Alignment of Objectives	Sociological factors affecting healthcare systems and medical treatment are not explicitly discussed and/or only discussed in extremely vague terms.	The project incorporates few sociological factors affecting healthcare systems and medical treatment, resulting in an unclear and/or misinformed presentation.	The project proficiently articulates the relationship(s) between sociological, economic, political, and cultural factors that affect healthcare systems and medical treatment; includes evidence to support claims.	The project draws a clear connection between sociological, economic, political, and cultural factors that affect healthcare systems and medical treatment; it is well referenced and creatively exemplified; uses appropriate terminology and demonstrates expert understanding.
Theoretical Understanding	Absence and/or apparent misunderstanding of relevant principles, skills, and/or concepts.	Limited use and/or understanding of one or more core principles; principles, concepts, and/or skills are erroneously applied.	Sufficient use and proficient understanding of core principles; thoughtful attempt at applying principles, concepts, and skills.	High level of understanding is apparent; demonstrates clear, concrete, and appropriate application of core principles, concepts, and skills.

	Unacceptable	Below Standards	Meets Standards	Exceeds Standards
Theory to Practice	Practical applications of core ideas are erroneous and/or altogether absent.	Minimal practical application of core principles; limited explanation of how sociological research can affect healthcare systems and practices.	Proficient application of core principles; ideas presented in the project are logical, practical, and consistent with generally accepted sociological practices.	Expert application of core principles; not only is the project logical, practical, and consistent with sociological practices, but it also creatively conveys those ideas and expands beyond the course objectives.
Forward-Thinking	Description of how the project could be further refined and implemented is extremely vague or absent.	Plans for refinement and implementation are present but inconsistent, impractical, and/or conflict with core sociological practices.	Plans for refinement and implementation demonstrate an understanding of relevant sociological practices and consideration of relevant theories and resources.	Plans for refinement and implementation are exceptionally well-thought-out and reflect a deep understanding of relevant theories and resources; opportunities for growth/expansion are obvious.

demonstrations of learning). In general, this includes well-constructed responses, outputs, and interactions that showcase intellectual risk-taking on top of completeness, logical reasoning, and evidence-based argumentation. It may also include artistry, creativity, and problem-solving that accurately capture the thinking and behavior of real-world professionals engaged in domain-relevant tasks.

Standards-based evaluation cannot fully replace alphanumeric grading without system-wide efforts to enact such a shift, so grades *can* be calculated by applying rubric categories to the percentages associated with each assignment. Assuming a typical rubric format, this would mean:

- **Below Standards** ≈ < C−/B [< 70–85]
- **Meets Standards** ≈ B+/A [86–95]
- **Exceeds Standards** ≈ A+ [96–100]
- **Distinction** ≈ Special Denotation [100+]

Notably, these boundaries are not immovable—like the (1998) improv comedy television show *Whose Line Is It Anyway?*, it's all made up and the points don't matter.[3] Standards-based frameworks are meant to offer wiggle room for instructors to assess learners on a case-by-case basis, and we strongly recommend maintaining that flexibility to avoid mutating rubrics into just another quantification of student achievement. The instructor should prioritize how and why different learners perform at different levels within each rubric category and treat knowledge and skill development as grounded in the life-world of each individual learner (as described in the sections "Self-Assessment" and "One-on-One Conferencing"). That means conditions meriting an A for one student may not, in fact, be identical to those meriting an A for another, and the instructor must exercise discretion when weighing different aspects of different learners' progression through the lesson, unit, course, or program (as constrained by course and assignment rubrics).

To the extent that "grades" are calculated, their value is determined as a function of quality, not quantity, of learner participation. This serves two purposes: (1) allowing learners to showcase individual skills (as overlapping with course content) and (2) acting as a longitudinal demonstration of learning across all course activities (e.g., class participation, discussions). It also actualizes constructivist principles by encouraging learners to focus on inter- and cross-disciplinary synthesis that is not necessarily predictable by the instructor. The individual life-world of each learner becomes a fulcrum for sharing expertise and growing the knowledge base of the entire learning community (i.e., everyone in the learning environment, including both learners and the instructor, takes the role of novice *and* expert depending on what content is being discussed and in what context).

UNGRADING

Resources, assessments, and other artifacts have long been adapted for face-to-face, hybrid, and online instruction with varied levels of success, and there are several challenges that must be addressed before K–12 schools, universities, and corporate training environments achieve genuinely equitable, accessible, and effective standards across courses and programs. As argued at the opening of this chapter, alphanumeric grading systems are particularly ill-equipped for the task—especially in the context of artificial intelligence (large language model) text generators, social media, and collaborative writing software—which has necessitated a reevaluation of what assessment is and should be.

Thankfully, standards-based assessment practices provide a framework for project-based and life-transformative assessments grounded in equity, accessibility, and effectiveness. As a bonus, they require student-instructor interactions that cannot be manufactured, cheated, or faked via contemporary technologies: an approach called ungrading.

Ungrading—popularized by Jesse Stommel's (2021) "Ungrading"—is an instructional and evaluation practice wherein points, scores, and letter grades are eliminated in favor of proficiency-based reflection activities, self-assessments, and one-on-one conferences.[4] This is *not* the same as not grading; it is a qualitative, portfolio-based process that crosswalks learning objectives with activity objectives so learners can easily track what they are learning/doing and why they are learning/doing it. Course, program, and department-wide rubrics outline the chronology and reasoning behind all aspects of the learning process, and transcripts note specific learning objectives alongside information about a given student's corresponding ability level. This has been common in high-ranking graduate programs for decades but can (and should) be exported to other instructional environments as well.

Like anchored and inquiry-based instruction, ungrading centers students as the subjects of learning rather than objects of it—whether learning occurs is a question of how the learning environment is constructed around the interrogation of learners' life-worlds and their relationship(s) with content. It derives from Paulo Freire's (1970) critical pedagogy (in which learners examine what they know, the systems and contexts from which knowledge emerges, and how that knowledge is actualized in the real world) and serves the dialogic deconstruction of social, cultural, political, economic, and other structures to facilitate learner self-actualization.[5] It is, in keeping with our theory of worldbuilding, a deeply situated, personal, and context-dependent form of assessment.

Below, we examine two major components of ungrading that are directly applicable to instructional worldbuilding: self-assessment and one-on-one conferencing.

Self-Assessment

One of the most effective and clear-cut ways to evaluate learner understanding is to have learners externalize their thinking through reflection, also known as "going meta." Rather than prescribing assessment activities like essays or exams, they can tell us—in their own words—what engaging with new ideas or perspectives has meant to them and how they foresee content or skills informing their thinking and behavior in the future. We can also ask that they co-evaluate their prior work, thinking, and performance as a way to exercise ownership of learned material.

In a fourteen-week (semester-long) course, we recommend arranging *at least* two opportunities for learners to reflect and share. This allows the instructor to adapt course content, introduce scaffolding that targets areas of weakness, and differentiate resources or activities based on each individual learner's needs. Such self-assessments need not be overly complicated, nor should they be treated as "gotcha" moments that put learners on their heels; they should offer space to provide honest observations about student problem-solving and critical thinking faculties.

For example, a midsemester self-assessment might include the following questions:

- How would you rate your overall engagement in the course thus far (i.e., class participation, assignment completion, contributions to group work, asking thoughtful questions, etc.)?
- Please rate your agreement with the statements listed below (from 1 for "strongly disagree" to 5 for "strongly agree"). These pertain to your participation, production, critique, and incorporation of feedback throughout the course.
  - "I positively contributed to the group discussion for all (or nearly all) modules."
  - "I completed all requested work in a timely fashion and shared it with peers to solicit feedback."
  - "I provided clear, thoughtful feedback to my peers about their respective ideas."
  - "I earnestly considered and incorporated peer feedback into my thinking."
- What are your goals for the rest of the semester?
- Which topic(s) would you like more detail about?
- What topic(s) have you found confusing and/or challenging?
- What topic(s) have you found most fascinating and/or compelling?
- What has been the most valuable takeaway from the course thus far?
- If you were to evaluate yourself for this course, what would your conclusion be? What evidence would you cite to showcase your learning/growth over time?
- Are there any other thoughts, questions, ideas, or emotions you would like to share?

Again, the goal is not to ask pointed questions about memorized course content but to center the learner's understanding of their own thinking and behavior so the instructor can meet them where they are. Not only is this something that cannot be faked (because large language model chatbots and other cheating tools/options lack the direct experience of an individual learner responding to the survey), but it provides a chance to build trust with the instructor and develop a sense of belonging (i.e., legitimate participation in the Community of Practice; see chapter 4, "Collaboration and Community").

The end-of-semester self-assessment has a similar function but emphasizes growth and reflection on a longer, more comprehensive timescale:

- How would you rate your overall engagement in the course (i.e., class participation, assignment completion, contributions to group work, asking thoughtful questions, etc.)?
- Please rate your agreement with the statements listed below (from 1 for "strongly disagree" to 5 for "strongly agree"). These pertain to your participation, production, critique, and incorporation of feedback throughout the course:
    - "I positively contributed to the group discussion for all (or nearly all) modules."
    - "I completed all requested work in a timely fashion and shared it with peers to solicit feedback."
    - "I provided clear, thoughtful feedback to my peers about their respective ideas."
    - "I earnestly considered and incorporated peer feedback into my thinking."
- How has your understanding of complex systems changed since the beginning of the semester?
- How has your personal relationship with interdisciplinary, individual, and community narratives (e.g., articles, books, films, television, games, cartoons, graphic novels) changed since the beginning of the semester?
- How do you foresee incorporating ideas/skills learned in this course as part of your longer-term career?
- What topic(s) have you found confusing and/or challenging?
- What topic(s) have you found most fascinating and/or compelling?

- If you were to grade your participation in/contributions to your worldbuilding group, what grade would you assign?
    - How would you characterize your group contributions and justify your self-assessment?
- If you were to grade your peers' participation in/contributions to your worldbuilding group (as a whole), what grade would you assign?
    - How would you characterize your group members' contributions and justify your assessment of them?
- How would you describe your group's collective efforts and/or interpersonal dynamics?
- If you were to evaluate yourself for this course, what would your conclusion be? What evidence would you cite to showcase your learning/growth over time?
- Overall, would you say you gave this course your best possible effort? (It is totally reasonable for activity level and effort to fluctuate—this is an opportunity to explain how you have been adapting and if/whether there are externalities you would like the instructor to know about.)
- In one sentence, what was your most valuable or important takeaway from this course?
- Is there anything else you would like the instructor to know about your experience (e.g., favorite/least favorite modules, readings with the greatest/least practical value, activities that were especially helpful/could use improvement)?

Once learners complete their self-assessments, the instructor can use them as a foundation for further questioning and feedback. This can be done asynchronously (e.g., written comments, annotations) or synchronously (e.g., one-on-one conferences), and it can be paired with one or more rubrics detailing which direction the instructor suggests the learner travel in future units, courses, or their career.

However, because self-assessment questions are open-ended, so too is their interpretation, and different individuals may perceive growth or progress differently. For instance, a learner may overestimate their abilities and understanding of one or more topics, which underscores the importance of clarity and honesty in instructor feedback (see the below section "Feedback"). Self-assessment should not be a stand-in for critique—ungrading depends on good-faith consensus building where the instructor leverages their comparably greater experience with domain knowledge and skills to help learners understand what they know, what they do not know, and what they do not know they do not know.

One-On-One Conferencing

Self-assessment is frequently paired with one-on-one conferencing in standards-based ungrading teaching and learning environments. The underlying rationale follows from the same principles as anchored and inquiry-based instruction, both of which are built to emphasize student inquiry and ill-defined problem-solving. Conferencing, specifically, allows the instructor to engage with individual learners and ask follow-up questions about their work products, reflections, and self-assessments. It also allows the learner to expand on comments provided in their self-assessments and demonstrate familiarity with course content and skills.

We recommend allocating approximately thirty to sixty minutes for each one-on-one conference, though the actual time needed to speak with each learner will vary based on several factors, such as student familiarity with the content, depth of reflections, responses to follow-up questions, completeness of the self-assessment, and the number of previous meetings. Sessions can be hosted either face-to-face or virtually via video communication platforms and distributed throughout the week or bunched during specific hours. The purpose, as with the self-assessment, is not to badger learners about memorized content (e.g., names, dates, textbook information) but rather to develop a broad awareness of how they conceptualize content and foresee applying their learning in their other courses, careers, and/or day-to-day lives. This helps learners refine their goals, track their growth, and more capably transfer their learning from the educational context to real-world situations in which it applies.

Conferences can be treated as graded evaluations of learner knowledge and skills (i.e., contributing to an alphanumeric course grade), but they should prioritize intellectual risk-taking and content fluency. For instance, learners should be prepared to discuss

- the intersection of ideas, concepts, and information learned through the course and other areas of life (i.e., detecting invariance between contexts, applying knowledge outside the classroom);
- individual aims and plans to achieve them in the short, medium, and long term (i.e., expectation setting); and
- how course resources have informed their understanding of the discipline (i.e., describing valuable readings, activities, and discussions that shaped their worldview or changed their mind).

Questions about specific course objectives can be seeded into the conference, but it should remain as conversational as possible—you do not want the meeting to become a highly constrained interview or oral exam. There are a few reasons for this: (1) we want learners to feel comfortable sharing their genuine thoughts, feelings, and reflections rather than assume there are "correct" answers; (2) anchored instruction (and worldbuilding, specifically) are collaborative enterprises where the instructor is a colearner and coproducer, not a superior; and (3) flowing conversation allows for a more authentic debate over ideas than is possible with a preordained script. "Grades" should not dominate the discussion, and to whatever extent possible, growth, change, and practical application should be the focus of inquiry.

To be candid, conferencing is not inherently easier or more efficient than traditional assessment measures, though it does yield a sharper picture of who our learners are and what matters to them. It is more comprehensive than an exam or essay, and it affords learners the chance to differentiate themselves from their peers (i.e., directly connecting course content, skills, and ideas to their respective life-worlds). On a practical level, one-on-one conferences take about the same amount of time as reading, commenting on, and grading traditional assessments, but they have the advantage of increasing student-instructor rapport and reinforcing community cohesion.

Neither self-assessment nor conferencing is meant to supersede the use of other assignments to determine whether and how students have learned—they simply provide a way to drill down on details that may be excluded or overlooked without interpersonal exchange. By all means, delegate project responsibilities and tasks that facilitate growth and change; just do not overrely on quantitative evaluation measures that strip out context and attempt to standardize the learner experience.

FEEDBACK

Instructor feedback in an ungrading environment should be direct, thorough, and relevant. Its form will change depending on the presentation context, but clarity and directionality are essential for learners to accept and act on whatever critiques they receive. Below are some general strategies that can be employed throughout the worldbuilding process:

- **Individuals:** Impart comments that speak to the learner's specific life-world and background experiences; draw on the learner's self-assessment responses to ask follow-up questions; explore connections between the individual's work/growth and their topics of greatest interest (e.g., career

pathways or roles); introduce supplemental resources that map to the learner's specific abilities, needs, and goals.
- **Groups**: Do not single out individuals; speak to the group's collective work product(s); provide feedback that can be digested and acted upon by the entire group (via delegation); organize peer feedback sessions (e.g., writer workshops) so learners can share their work and receive critiques from groupmates or other groups; organize blind peer review opportunities so learners can provide anonymous critiques about one another's work.
- **Face-to-Face**: Allow learners to guide the conversation; take advantage of "teachable moments" or those spaces in discussion where the instructor can ask leading or follow-up questions to tune learner perception in new and different ways; avoid putting individual learners on the spot by offering multiple methods to contribute (e.g., verbal, webchat, digital polls); use frequent breakouts to allow learners the opportunity to hear from one another before sharing with the larger group or instructor; if possible, maintain a live chat during lectures or presentations so learners can provide in-the-moment feedback to the instructor and their peers.
- **Online**: Elicit learner questions and comments through both oral and text-based discussion (i.e., maintain a live chat through presentations and activities); split learners into discrete, independent groups and target feedback to three to five individuals at a time (rather than the larger class); invite learners to participate in polls, surveys, or other live interactions during presentations, discussions, and activities; encourage the use of emojis/emoticons during discussion as a way to register ideas, feelings, and responses; record sessions and provide annotated video to denote particularly important content, questions, and/or ideas.

In all cases, feedback should be timely and substantive as well as oriented toward growth rather than alphanumeric grades. Learners should not be pitted against one another nor have their work compared to that of their peers; it should be evaluated on its own terms within the context of the individual learner's particular strengths, weaknesses, and skills.

Although it can be challenging to maintain open lines of communication, know that frank and honest discussion can go a long way to deepening learners' sense of belonging within the Community of Practice. We do not want self-assessments and related feelings about the course experience to be sent into the void without recognition lest we lose the trust needed for our feedback to be taken seriously. By acknowledging learner questions and concerns without obfuscation or insult, we more effectively cultivate the mutual respect needed for a socially healthy teaching and learning environment as well as reduce the probability of acrimony and conflict between the learner and instructor.

SCALING ASSESSMENT

The assessment strategies we have described are typically scaled for individual instructors working with small- or medium-sized groups of learners (i.e., class sizes of twenty to twenty-four, maximum). But what would happen if we used worldbuilding as part of a large lecture? An entire program? A massive open online course?

Anchored instruction and other inquiry-driven pedagogical methods *can* be scaled so long as there is adequate resourcing and careful modification of the assessment framework. Even though this comes with some risks—especially concerning adherence to the core theoretical foundation—the overarching implementation process looks more or less the same with a dozen learners as it does with 120 learners.

For instance, if we were to scale the sociology of healthcare course described earlier in the chapter, we would need to develop hybrid activities that merged large- and small-group course methods (e.g., polls, multiple-choice evaluations, and direct instruction versus breakout groups, peer review workshops, and collaborative writing) with corresponding broad and granular feedback. We might incorporate an overarching, democratically governed choose-your-own-adventure story where individual learners vote on different narrative pathways for the entire class to follow. Some personalization would be lost, yet the spirit of anchored instruction would remain intact—inquiry and exploration leading to the production of portfolio artifacts and reflections that capture a snapshot of each learner's growth. Self-assessment could continue, though one-on-one conferencing would be subject to dramatic change, including making conferences optional, providing feedback through asynchronous annotation of learners' self-assessments, and/or mediating small-group discussions focused on general areas of weakness and growth. It may also be necessary to blend self-assessments with more traditional assessments like exams and term papers or to have learners submit personal "artist statements" that connect the dots between portfolio artifacts, reflections, and course objectives so the instructor can see exactly how and why relevant knowledge and skills were applied throughout the semester and/or within particular assignments.

ON THE HORIZON

Now that we have connected instructional design, anchored instruction, collaborative learning, and assessment, we are prepared to press on to the worldbuilding process itself. The next chapter will transition to part II, "Concepts"—beginning with scope and sequence—and facilitate the application of your objectives, activities, and assessments to our template.

II CONCEPTS

6 WORLDS IN SPACE AND TIME

"The truth about the world is that anything is possible. Had you not seen it all from birth and thereby bled it of its strangeness, it would appear to you for what it is, a hat trick in a medicine show, a fevered dream, a trance bepopulate with chimeras having neither analog nor precedent, an itinerant carnival, a migratory tent show whose ultimate destination after many a pitch in many a mudded field is unspeakable and calamitous beyond reckoning."

—Cormac McCarthy[1]

As outlined in chapter 1, "Around the World in 300 Pages," the world is a veritable Gordian knot of codefined systems where even the act of acquiring a morning cup of coffee is ensnared in a massive web of global supply chains and human labor—and that is just one small, relatively insignificant example among truly awe- and horror-inspiring alternatives (e.g., addiction to fossil fuels and cheap disposable goods, poverty, malnutrition, the rise of authoritarianism, climate change, threat of nuclear war). Further complicating matters, every facet of the world operates, shifts, and changes in parallel every minute of every day. How can we possibly hope to get our heads around any of it, much less *all* of it?

Let us disabuse you of the notion: We cannot, on an individual level, get our heads around all of it. The planet is too large, diverse, and transitional for that goal to be anything other than a fool's errand. Yet, with perseverance and care, we *can* get our heads around quite a lot, including the experiences of people we have never met and the nature of places we have never visited. Doing so requires that we partition off specific portions of the planet—freezing them in space and time—to examine the lived conditions of individuals, societies, cultures, economies, and governments. These spatially and temporally frozen slices of life can help us construct more accurate, useful, and responsible models of complex systems that capture how they have interacted in the past, how they interact in the present, and how they might interact in the future. The aim here is not to uncover some objective, capital-T "Truth" but to establish a well-reasoned representation from which we can draw tentative conclusions and refine our collective understanding of reality.

This process brings a measure of order to chaos, particularly within the context of teaching and learning environments like classrooms, workshops, and other spaces where we seek to explore why things work the way they do. We call it worldbuilding, or the practice of capturing the social forces and lived experiences contained within a world (i.e., a place bound by spatial and temporal boundaries).

Take, for instance, the world of the American Revolution. We can distinguish the American Revolution from other worlds using some fairly straightforward spatial and temporal boundaries—the space consists of a geographic region delineated by the political borders of the Thirteen Colonies, and the time is set between the Stamp Act of 1765 and the Treaty of Paris in 1783; the Thirteen Colonies are a single, contiguous territory with borders consisting of New France to the north, New Spain to the south, the Atlantic Ocean to the east, and wilderness beyond the Appalachian Mountains to the west. This is largely how school-age children in the United States are taught to think about the subject (i.e., a self-contained period leading up to and including the Thirteen Colonies' war with Britain).

However, as a matter of worldbuilding, our interrogation must go a step further to specify the social forces at play in the Thirteen Colonies and how those social forces shaped the experiences of individuals living in this geopolitical region during the relevant eighteen-year period (e.g., the political, economic, social relations, and cultural influences of the Thirteen Colonies and the worlds next door). If we accept that political borders provide the region's boundaries, we need to ask how life in the Thirteen Colonies differed from life in New France and New Spain. What did people living in the northern colony of Massachusetts have in common with people living in Georgia, the southernmost colony? How did their experiences compare to those of their geographically closer neighbors across the borders of New France or New Spain, respectively?

Different colonies (defined by political borders) exhibited differences in language, religion, cultural customs, cuisine, and laws prescribed by the various powers exerted by England, France, and Spain, but each geographic region (not necessarily defined by political borders) shared climate conditions, commercial interests, and dealings with Indigenous tribes. So, individuals living in the Thirteen Colonies frequently had more in common with their neighbors in New France or New Spain than their colonial partners (e.g., the northeast versus the southeast). By enumerating similarities and differences between the *worlds* of the Thirteen Colonies, New France, and New Spain, we gain insight into daily life and can theorize what it might have felt like to experience that particular space and time.

Put another way, although we can make some useful generalizations about commonalities that united the Thirteen Colonies, it is important to think about the world of each colony (e.g., the world of the Province of Massachusetts Bay, the world of the Province of New Hampshire) as interconnected with but independent of its peers. In so doing, it becomes clear that there was a wide range of experiences (i.e., life-worlds; see chapter 3, "Theory to Practice," and chapter 8, "Examining Life-Worlds Through Demographics") even within an individual province—the lived experience of a Bostonian as compared with that of a settler on the western border of Massachusetts. This process enables a scaling up or down of scope that introduces less or more granularity as needed by the worldbuilder (e.g., examining the urban world of eighteenth-century Boston versus the rural world of Berkshire County).

Considering the politics of the age, it is just as important to pan away from the "microworld" of Boston's urban streets to perform a similar analysis of England, comparing its political scene, economic conditions, social relations, and cultural influences over the same time period. Again, the wider the lens, the broader our generalizations about life in late eighteenth-century England and its peers (e.g., France, the Netherlands, Spain) necessarily become; for a clearer and more accurate picture, we should compare and contrast at all possible social, cultural, economic, and political levels, from life at Buckingham Palace to life a few miles east in Whitechapel.

SCOPE: WORLDS IN SPACE

Thus far, we have emphasized the spatial, geographic borders of a world fixed in time—that is, the world's *scope*. Scope can be as broad as the continent of North America or as narrow as a single neighborhood in Los Angeles. The broader the scope, the more reductive our declarations about the world in question become (e.g., the people of North America generally have wheat and oats at the center of their diets, whereas the staple food in Asia is rice); conversely, the narrower the scope, the more specific our declarations (e.g., the median household income for downtown Los Angeles in 2021 was $69,778, with just 36.2 percent of the population holding a bachelor's degree or higher level of education). We can mentally traverse different world levels to evaluate which generalizations might be useful and, as we close into a tighter and tighter focus, decide what information holds true or needs to be modified to avoid stereotyping. For example, what characteristics of twenty-first-century North America distinguish it from other continents? How would we distinguish the United States from Canada, Mexico, Central America, and the Caribbean? What differentiates the Northeast United States from the Southeast, Midwest, Southwest, and so on? What similarities and differences exist between the states of Massachusetts, New York, and Connecticut? How is the city of Boston different from the city of Worcester? And finally, within Boston itself, how might we describe the neighborhood of downtown Boston versus the neighborhood of Jamaica Plain versus the neighborhood of Beacon Hill?

The (1977) film *Powers of Ten* provides an excellent visualization of scope.[2] It opens with a couple picnicking on a plot of grass with a camera shot one meter wide. From there, the shot zooms out vertically at a rate of one power of ten per ten seconds. After thirty seconds, the field of view is one thousand meters, and we can see that the picnic is near the downtown lakeshore in Chicago. The film continues zooming out until the entirety of Lake Michigan and the Midwest come into view, then North America, outer space, and, eventually, the view from 100 million light-years away. These zoom levels rapidly collapse back to the original shot of the couple picnicking before zooming in at the same rate down to the surface of the man's hand, his skin cells, and the subatomic level. With little effort, we could concoct a story about the different "worlds" presented at each level of the film with the spatial boundary being the frame of the shot. We can easily imagine the "microworld" of a few meters that tells the story of a couple relaxing in a park on a pleasant day that details their personalities, physical attributes, character traits, and more. In literary terms, this would be the world of a one-act play focused on the terrain of individual human relationships and experiences.

Scaling back, the film frames the world of downtown Chicago circa 1977. At this level, the opportunities for thinking through the spatial and temporal aspects of worldbuilding become more obvious, and questions of *time* arise. To begin critically considering the world of 1977 downtown Chicago, we need to answer some basic questions: What do we consider to be the border of the world of "downtown Chicago" before it transitions to something different? Do we follow the political maps of the time (i.e., determining which residents lived within the city limits), or do outlying areas have enough in common with the world of downtown Chicago that they should be included irrespective of political boundaries? The answers depend on how we articulate, at least tentatively, what does or does not constitute the world of "downtown Chicago" as it is colloquially used and commonly understood for a given worldbuilding project (e.g., population density, socioeconomic demographics, property values, environmental factors, crime rates).

We could take some arbitrary point that a reasonable person would agree is in downtown Chicago—for instance, the Willis Tower (known as the Sears Tower until 2022)—and expand outward, keeping in mind our tentative criteria. At what point do conditions begin to change on the northern side of Chicago? Evanston seems to be outside of this world simply due to the distance from the center of downtown and its designation as a suburb, but what about Rogers Park just to the south? Does it meet enough of the criteria to be considered "downtown Chicago" for our specific project? How we draw these borders depends entirely on the criteria we have specified for ourselves.

The question "what borders define downtown Chicago?" might seem superfluous because we are so used to deferring to political maps (e.g., the seventy-seven defined community areas that comprise the city of Chicago; figure 6.1), and community area 32 (i.e., the Loop) can provide a fairly efficient, no-frills answer. Yet, this produces definitional discomfort: Technically speaking, the Willis Tower and Magnificent Mile are part of community area 8 (i.e., the Near North Side). The same can be said of major Chicago landmarks like Soldier Field, the Field Museum, and the Shedd Aquarium, all of which are outside the Loop in community area 33. There is no official governmental designation for "downtown Chicago" beyond these community areas, and various websites for real estate, tourism, and crowd-sourced reviews draw different boundaries to suits their needs, often subdividing community areas into even smaller, unofficially named neighborhoods.

After even cursory consideration, some obvious uncertainties arise:

- Who drew these dividing lines in the first place?
- When and how have they changed?
- What criteria were used to define them?
- Can there ever be a "correct" assignment of dividing lines?

While well-defined borders between community areas and neighborhoods may be required for coherent governance (e.g., running local elections, collecting taxes, and providing public services), in common usage, we regularly negotiate dividing lines of different parts of a city without realizing we are doing so. Official designations can advance our understanding of the urban space alongside the western coast of Lake Michigan, but

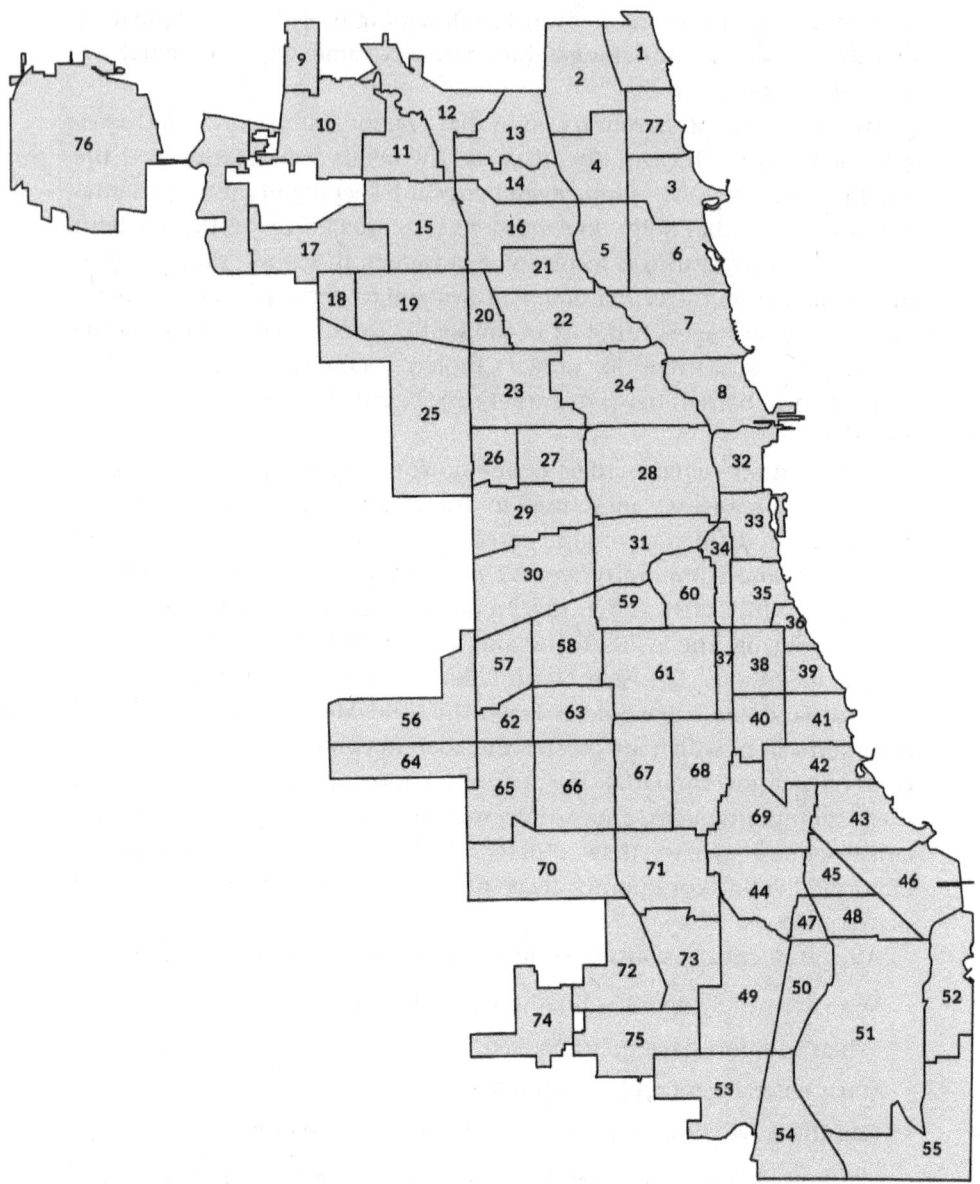

FIGURE 6.1
A map of Chicago's seventy-seven community areas; these are fixed political boundaries rather than ill-defined sociocultural boundaries. Source: American Goral, "Chicago Community Areas," map, Wikipedia, January 20, 2021, CC-BY-SA-4.0, https://en.wikipedia.org/wiki/Community_areas_in_Chicago.

constraining ourselves to those designations can become an impediment if the goal is to evaluate sociocultural, economic, or other norms that are responsive to different dynamics. We might ask, Does an individual's lived experience one block north of the Chicago River (the Near North's southern border) or one block south of Roosevelt Road (the Near South Side's northern border) differ from that of someone in the Loop? If yes, what qualities or features exemplify the difference? If not, where might we redraw our unofficial borders based on criteria we are specifically interested in?

There are ample historical examples where a few blocks of physical distance marks a significant difference in lived experience—for instance, the twenty-eight-year separation of communistic East Berlin and democratic-capitalist West Berlin by the Berlin Wall; the century-old dividing line between Republic of Ireland–controlled southern Ireland and United Kingdom–controlled Northern Ireland; the decades-long conflict in Gaza partitioning the peoples of Palestine and Israel—but disparate conditions over a short geographic space are seldom so neatly demarcated. Socioeconomic maps of major urban areas in the United States highlight that extremely wealthy neighborhoods often border poor neighborhoods even if both reside within the same politically designated area (e.g., the wealthy city of Fairfield, Connecticut, abutting the impoverished city of Bridgeport, Connecticut). Continuing with our Chicago example, the Cabrini-Green housing project, for years synonymous with inner-city poverty and crime, existed just one mile from the Gold Coast and Magnificent Mile, the city's economic hub for conspicuous consumption via high-end shopping, gourmet cuisine, and world-class entertainment. Both fell within community area 8, the Near North Side, but the life-worlds of individuals in the far west and far east portions of that designated area could not have been more dissimilar.

SEQUENCE: WORLDS IN TIME

Keep in mind that scope only tells half of the story—the other half comes from *sequence*, the world's timeline as extended back into prehistory and forward into an infinite future. At the start of this chapter, we identified the American Revolution as an eighteen-year period from 1765 and 1783 wherein thirteen English-controlled colonies coalesced into one independent nation, the United States of America. Just as we fiddled with the scope to gain different perspectives on this world, we can move forward and backward on the timeline to determine when and how specific events precipitated change. For example, if the era of the American Revolution began in

1765, what was so different about 1765 as compared to 1764? 1760? 1745? What major differences emerged in the period after 1783? 1788? 1803?

Sliding forward and backward on a timeline underscores how different forces act and inscribe themselves on physical spaces—this includes forces of nature as well as deliberate human forces (e.g., government policies, construction, technological advances, and acts of violence like war and terrorism). In most cases, change is a consequence of multiple intertwined forces acting in tandem: Properties of the natural world lead to policies that create social or political movements, and those sociopolitical movements spur human action (e.g., discovery of nutrient-rich soil → deforestation → increased agricultural activity → ecological destruction → social action → government policy → regulation of human behavior → ecological recovery).

Effective worldbuilders leverage this back-and-forth motion to evaluate the rate at which a world changes. For instance, large-scale human migrations (e.g., the late 1800s/early 1900s Italian emigration to the Americas) tend to occur over an extended period due to complex interactions between political, social, and cultural attitudes. However, dramatic Black Swan events create much more rapid change, sometimes literally overnight—the 1986 Chernobyl nuclear meltdown, the 9/11 terrorist attacks in New York City and Washington, DC, and the 2010 Haitian earthquake (see chapter 13, "Simulations").

Robert Crumb's (1993) comic strip *A Short History of America* is an excellent depiction of scope and sequence, fixing the frame on a single geographic plot of land over fifteen points in time to showcase how a natural setting can be overtaken by the forces of industrialization, modernization, and urbanization.[3] In the comic's final row are three possible futures: Ecological Disaster, Techno Fix, and the Ecotopian Solution. This demonstrates how, despite the gradual change from frame to frame, a landscape will eventually lose all traces of its original self no matter what path it takes—even the Ecotopian Solution, which features a world full of trees, bears little resemblance to the initial panel's pastoral scene. Embedded in this story is the thesis that nothing is forever, and the boundaries used to define a world in space and time are responsive to natural and human forces whether we like it or not. Ergo, worldbuilders should embrace the fuzziness of space and time as they define their worlds and establish their emergence or decline.

MACRO AND MICRO

Successful worldbuilding projects outline scope and sequence in specific terms while recognizing that the model is flexible and scalable. Widening the scope gives a broader view of the world and its surroundings through more generalizable information; tightening it provides more specific information about lived experiences. Moving backward on a timeline can show how events and conditions developed to reach a certain point, while moving forward can highlight how history will unfold beyond a certain point.

Thinking about worlds and worldbuilding in this way can at times feel cognitively overwhelming. For every level of scope to consider, it is possible to zoom in for greater granularity or further out to consider a bigger picture; each point on the timeline represents myriad constraints, opportunities, and potentialities grounded in the past and future. Add to this the notion that political borders are artificial structures (i.e., produced and policed by human societies), and a project risks languishing as an ill-defined mess of random observations rather than becoming a path to keener insights.

To keep things organized (and to protect your sanity), the next chapter details a structure- and substructure-based modeling system that can be consistently applied to both historical and speculative worldbuilding projects. As you will see, this system allows for the direct comparison of diverse worlds across space and time using categories that characterize critical political, economic, social, and cultural forces. We will explain precisely how it should unfold in a teaching and learning environment and offer a variety of worked examples that track similarities and differences between worlds. By the time we finish, you will be prepared to deconstruct everything from colonial-era Boston and ancient Egypt to the *Star Wars* galaxy and the Seven Kingdoms of Westeros.

7 STRUCTURES AND SUBSTRUCTURES

"The greatest fantasy, in my mind, is distinguished by its settings. The setting becomes almost a character. Middle Earth becomes almost a real place: The Shire, Rivendell, Minas Tirith, Mordor. Each of these is very vivid and real, and I've tried to do the same with my own Westeros, create a setting that is almost a character in its own right."

—George R. R. Martin[1]

When explaining that worldbuilding emphasizes the nature of a specific world at a given place and time, we regularly refer to its structures and substructures. We do not invoke these terms in a strict sociological sense, nor do we mean them to be read as reflecting Marx's theory of base and superstructure (though we do draw on similar concepts). Rather, we use them to describe the specific set of interrelated factors that create different social forces in a world. This invites learners to work from the broad and general down to the more targeted and complex.

This chapter will explain how our model of structures and substructures can be leveraged to interrogate historical, contemporary, fictional, and speculative worlds. We will outline four overarching structural categories—Governance, Economics, Social Relations, and Cultural Influences—to make broad statements about the features of a given society as well as describe different substructural categories to pin down granular aspects of each. Although some substructures are more or less relevant for different worldbuilding and modeling projects, we believe it valuable to consider all of them if only to expose knowledge gaps and identify areas where learners can benefit from deeper exploration.

GOVERNANCE

Governance is defined as the level of *government presence* in a citizen's daily life, from near-complete absence to total immersion. This includes the administration of regulations that affect individuals, businesses, and groups (e.g., collecting and spending taxes, delineating acceptable moral and ethical behavior, guaranteeing certain rights among citizens, intervening in the economy) as well as the creation of formalized policy (e.g., laws, executive orders) or oral histories (e.g., the word of older community members) that shape attitudes and behaviors in a given society. These activities constitute the *rule of law*—any process by which individuals are policed and adjudicated—and are associated with tools or practices used to punish transgressors. They run the gamut from arbitrary, unilateral, or uneven application of ill-defined customs to well-documented, rigorous, and transparent application of standardized procedures meant to ensure equal treatment of all citizens. While we often consider robust judicial institutions a bedrock feature of modern civilization, there is no shortage of real-world examples where governments (even contemporary democracies) fail to equally apply laws across people of different races, classes, genders, religions, sexual orientations, and immigration status.

Social services, or organizations and resources the government provides to citizens for the betterment of society (e.g., education, healthcare, transportation, housing, sanitation), are also crucial components of Governance. Some governments provide few or no social services whatsoever, while others provide high levels of support to all members of the community. As with any substructural category, the quantity and quality varies widely within a society and can be operationalized in several different ways depending on funding schemes, government agencies, private-public partnerships, and other external forces (e.g., religious institutions, technological factors, macroeconomics).

Foreign relations and government transparency are similarly important elements of Governance, and either can make or break a society's sustainability through space and time. The former accounts for a government's attitude toward and treatment of peoples and communities near and far, while the latter contends with the degree to which an average citizen within a society can understand decisions made by their government (including both predecision reasoning and postdecision consequences). A government with low transparency operates in secrecy and places strict controls on freedom of speech, the press, and assembly, whereas one with high levels of transparency empowers its citizens to engage in oversight of governmental dealings and equips them to correct for government overreach (e.g., elections) or investigate charges of corruption (e.g., independent law enforcement).

ECONOMICS

To evaluate a world's Economics, we start by categorizing its overall *economic strength*, or the total wealth across society; then, we assess its *wealth distribution*, the degree to which wealth is equally (or unequally) shared between members of society. For instance, a small nomadic community might have low economic strength but high levels of wealth distribution, where individuals and the group have minimal total wealth but the difference in economic power between the rich and poor is negligible. Conversely, a technologically advanced, highly developed country might have substantial economic strength accompanied by extreme economic stratification, where the exorbitantly rich and extremely destitute are separated by multiple levels of working-, middle-, and upper-middle-class individuals.

Agriculture and *trade* play a dominant role in determining how economic strength and wealth distribution are organized within a given world. Agriculture involves the growing of crops and raising of livestock, whereas trade refers to the buying and selling of goods and services. Much of New York State, for example, is rich in agricultural land even as New York City is a global center for trade. Most urban areas rely on rural regions to provide a steady supply of food and natural resources, while rural regions benefit from urban specialization, innovation, and taxation, which leads to improved healthcare, education, technology, and entertainment.

Widening the aperture a bit further, we can explore how substructures like unemployment rates and inflation contribute to a world's economic well-being. Generally speaking, lower unemployment rates indicate a stronger economy (i.e., more people participating in the economy as both producers and consumers), and low levels of inflation suggest economic stability (i.e., individuals making long-term investments based on reduced risk of financial upheaval). Incorporating these elements into a model affords learners the opportunity to consider how past, present, and future changes to trade, markets, spending, and agriculture can influence governmental systems like social services, the rule of law, foreign relations, or transparency.

SOCIAL RELATIONS

Social Relations describe the interactions between different demographic groups within a society as well as the levels of (in)equality among them. Common categories include *race*, *ethnicity*, and *national origin*; *socioeconomic class; gender;* and *sexual orientation*. All individuals occupy space in these groups (i.e., life-worlds; see chapter 3, "Theory to Practice") and may accrue certain advantages or disadvantages based on their membership status. This also extends to categories like age (i.e., children, adolescents, young adults, middle-aged adults, older adults) and ability (i.e., physical, cognitive, psychoemotional), each of which can have a profound impact on an individual's experience with the world.

For example, in the United States, white middle- and upper-class heterosexual men have enjoyed a great deal more privilege than non-whites, the working class or poor, women, and nonheterosexuals, which has had a demonstrable effect on who in society can land a high-paying job, receive a favorable bank loan, and be accepted into a high-quality university. Throughout the last two centuries, various social movements have sought to neutralize these privileges and guarantee equal access to all regardless of their position within society, but because privilege and the forces that create it exist in a constant state of flux, equity and fairness have required substantial ongoing vigilance even when inequities have been addressed in the moment. Therefore, Social Relations must be (1) understood as perpetually evolving and (2) treated as simultaneously individualized and systemic (within the context of a particular environment at a particular space and time).

The inverse of privilege is intersectional discrimination, where different kinds of social biases compound on a single individual to create many potential obstacles and difficulties that are not flaws of the person but a consequence of institutional classism, racism, sexism, ableism, ageism, and other discriminatory systems. Continuing from our prior example, a poor, Black, lesbian, older woman is much more likely to face discrimination than a wealthy, white, heterosexual, young man even though there is nothing fundamentally different about the two as fellow humans. This is a function of the United States' long history of empowering the latter and disempowering the former (e.g., chattel slavery, Jim Crow laws, segregation), and while it is not definitively prescriptive (i.e., the former can still succeed, and the latter can still struggle), the country's particular synthesis of Governance, Economics, and Social Relations substantially tips the scale in favor of one over the other.

Keep in mind that while it is possible to be discriminated against or gain advantage due to religious faith, political party membership, or affiliation with particular organizations (e.g., university legacy admissions), these qualities are categorically different than age, physical/cognitive ability, race, gender, sexuality, and other attributes that are inherently inflexible and unchosen. Learners should be careful not to conflate them if they are to precisely evaluate whether and how a world's intersecting systems cultivate or extinguish oppression, especially in relation to whether and how different groups may be able to act (or not) to combat any such oppression (i.e., understanding the difference[s] between choosing a way of life versus being born into a particular body with unchangeable or difficult-to-change characteristics).

CULTURAL INFLUENCES

Cultural Influences, our fourth structural category, examines a world's dominant attitudes toward *religion*, *technology*, the *military*, and different forms of *arts and culture*. Certain countries, regions, and cities are strongly influenced by one or more of these factors, but there exist others where they have little to no impact whatsoever. For instance, a (2009) Gallup poll reported that 99 percent of the population in Indonesia described religion as an important part of daily life, which stands in direct contrast to religious importance among Swedes (just 17 percent of the Swedish population consider themselves religious).[2] Silicon Valley in the South San Francisco Bay Area of California is home to several major technology, hardware, software, and internet companies; the border between North and South Korea is one of the most highly militarized in the world; and global cities like New York and Paris are known for their museums, art galleries, theaters, diversity and quality of cuisine, and more.

As a result, Cultural Influences typically act as a mirror for a local society's values. We could just as easily incorporate environmentalism (i.e., a society's attitude toward the natural world), consumerism and material culture (i.e., the presence or absence of high-end products and elite fashions), or the tolerance of drug and alcohol use. Professional sports, gambling, language, regional dialects, and other distinct local cultural practices can also fit within the scope of arts and culture, though—if sufficiently prominent—they may warrant special consideration and treatment as part of a world's (de)construction. Learners should be encouraged to explore interrelationships between various Cultural Influences and governmental, social, and economic systems as they are inextricably linked and have a manifest impact on how a society understands itself.

SYNTHESIS

Throughout the worldbuilding process, we analyze the aforementioned structures and substructures to make sense of a world's organization, the priorities of its peoples, and the nature of its past, present, and future. This

Table 7.1. A basic outline of structures and substructures

Governance	Economics	Social Relations	Cultural Influences
Government Presence	Economic Strength	Race Relations	Religious Influence
Rule of Law	Wealth Distribution	Class Relations	Military Influence
Social Services	Agriculture and Trade	Gender Relations	Technology Influence
		Sexual Orientation and Identity Relations	Arts and Culture Influence

involves pinpointing connections between each of the substructures and scaling backward into the broader, overarching structures. Importantly, we do not seek to define how a substructural category like government presence relates just to other Governance substructures but how it relates to every substructure across every structural category. We can present these structures and substructures in a table for clarity (e.g., table 7.1), though a more fitting visual metaphor would be a three-dimensional web where all structures and substructures are simultaneously interconnected and responsive to changes across the whole system (i.e., pulling on one thread causes the others to vibrate).

Consequently, the order in which structures and substructures are defined is arbitrary—anyone participating in an actual worldbuilding project will necessarily jump from category to category as they recognize relationships between them. The key is to sort observations such that causal links remain unambiguous and easily reviewable while the process unfolds. In our experience, learners often hesitate as they select a starting point, but once they have offered ideas and discussed different points of view, momentum quickly builds, and their early insights evolve into more complex debates about the nature of structural relationships (and system-wide causality).

Imagine a group of learners who choose to begin their worldbuilding efforts with the first substructural category we described—government presence, a government's role and visibility in the daily life of its citizens. Although they would surely touch on this as they brainstorm, we would encourage them to specifically define government presence as "strong," "weak," or somewhere in between as well as articulate its relationship to the other thirteen substructures:

- What does *government presence* look like in this world? What are some concrete examples of the government's presence being seen or felt? The description should include an overview of the world's laws or legal system along with an explanation of how legal decision-making unfolds, who the recognized leaders are, how leaders are appointed, and how the society's government operates (e.g., democracy, authoritarianism, totalitarianism, oligarchy, anarchy).

- How does government presence relate to the *rule of law*? How are laws or policies enforced? How does the government oversee systems used to adjudicate illegal behavior? How does the government punish transgressors (e.g., fines, incarceration)?
- How does government presence relate to the provision of *social services*? How present or absent is the government concerning the delivery of these services? How does the government assess whether the social services it provides are adequate or equitably distributed?
- What is the world's *economic strength*, and how much money does the government have at its disposal? How is the government spending that money and to what end? A world with low economic strength might have a government that cannot fulfill basic obligations to its people, while one with high economic strength may support robust government intervention in citizens' daily lives (or incentivize corruption).
- What is the world's *wealth distribution*, and what demand does it put on the government to address social questions and problems? What is the primary mechanism for wealth redistribution? How does the tax structure increase or reduce economic inequality?
- How does the government interact with *agriculture* and *trade*? Is there intense, government-led regulation of these industries, or is there a laissez-faire attitude that affords leeway for individuals and companies to shape and control the economy?
- Does the government take responsibility for addressing inequality across social categories like *race*, *class*, *gender*, and *sexual orientation*, or does it act (deliberately or not) to maintain inequalities? Does the government ensure that members of a given race, class, gender, or sexual orientation have the opportunity to hold political office? Does the government recognize same-sex marriages? What about marriages between members of different races? Each social substructure should be examined in turn as a world can have high levels of equality between some groups but not others (e.g., high equality across different races but low levels of equality between genders).
- What is the government's role pertaining to *religious influence*? Are the world's laws and legal system drawn directly from religious texts? Do

political and religious leaders or institutions operate in parallel (e.g., state-sanctioned religion), are they one and the same (e.g., theocracy), or is there a distinction between them (e.g., separation of church and state)?

- What is the government's relationship with the world's *military influence*? Are armed forces directly controlled by the government? Is the military in charge of the government (e.g., military junta)? Does the government view its role as defending its citizens from outside attacks, or is it oriented toward launching attacks on others (e.g., commandeering resources, asserting dominance, spreading ideology)?
- What is the government's relationship with the world's *technology influence*? Does the government invest in technological innovation and experimentation through grants and other funding agencies? Is the government's interest in technological progress related to improving citizens' lives, military dominance, and/or some other goal(s)?
- What is the government's relationship with the world's *arts and culture influence*? Does the government promote and support certain types of creative expression or cultural practice? Is there a desire to unite citizens around unique or specific aspects of the society? Is the law used to denigrate or ban certain types of creative expression or cultural practice?

It can be challenging to run through each substructure in this fashion (i.e., completing government presence, moving on to rule of law, and then repeating the process with social services, etc.), particularly because the process is neither mechanical nor mathematical and cannot produce objectively "true" descriptions of worlds. Thus, we recommend treating it more as a framework for identifying different aspects of a given world that facilitates the interrogation of the social forces at play. The qualitative output can then be compared with other models of the same world to determine whether and how different learners arrived at different conclusions.

Consider a literature class where students are reading Margaret Atwood's (1985) *The Handmaid's Tale*.[3] As part of the novel's analysis, the instructor asks them to break into small groups of five or six people and use these structures and substructures to model the world of the Republic of Gilead. The novel presents Gilead as a theocratic, militaristic, totalitarian state that subjugates women and controls every aspect of their lives, including and especially their bodily autonomy. Some students would undoubtedly perceive elements of Gilead's government presence, rule of law, gender relations, military influence, and religious influence as dominant within the society. All of them are central to understanding the novel's plot and themes, and finding textual evidence to support them should not require particularly deep engagement with the text.

However, once we try to account for the other nine substructures, things become a bit more nebulous. Government presence and rule of law are very strong but so are social services. Government-provided social services like education and healthcare are generally viewed as positives, but what if they are unwelcome intrusions? What if education veers into indoctrination? What if healthcare consists of fertility enhancements for unwilling patients? The substructures of Economics, Social Relations, and Cultural Influences can likewise be interpreted in multiple ways along multiple axes: If the economy generates a great deal of wealth but that wealth is constrained within a deeply patriarchal system, are the world's Economics "strong" or "weak"? Does the subjugation of women intersect with white supremacy, classism, and/or state-enforced heteronormativity? If so, does that imply "strong" or "weak" Social Relations? What function do arts and technology have in Atwood's dystopia? If they are aimed at reinforcing totalitarianism (similar to the control of symbols and imagery in George Orwell's [1949] *Nineteen Eighty-Four*[4]), should Cultural Influences be viewed as "strong" or "weak"? These second-order aspects of the novel require learners to pay more attention, especially as debatable interpretations demand textual justification. The instructor should always push their students to go beyond "How would you describe race relations in Gilead?" and toward "Where in the text do you find examples that support your claims?"

SOCIAL FORCES

We urge you to keep a few key factors in mind as you and your learners navigate this complex web of structures and substructures.

First, social forces are not naturally occurring aspects of the world but human-constructed interrelationships. Each of us is born into a reality featuring social forces that have existed for years, decades, or centuries, and it is deceptively simple to assume that our current conditions represent life as it always has been or always will be—a totalization of human experience driven by our collective binding to basic rules of biology and physics. For instance, we read the Greek tragedies of Sophocles, Euripides, and Aeschylus and find that despite being millennia old, they resonate with our modern sensibilities and struggles with the human condition. We think, "The ancient Greeks were just like us!" And in many ways, they *were* just like us. Or we are like them. After all, every civilization has sought to understand what it means to lead a meaningful life. We have found value in human-to-human relationships. We have appreciated beauty in love and grief, chaos and placidity. But if we analyze the world of the ancient Greeks using the structures and substructures of worldbuilding, we cannot help but recognize that their society was organized quite differently than ours. Tightening our focus on "the Greek world" (i.e., the Mediterranean region encompassing modern-day Greece and Turkey) reveals many significant differences in various ancient Greek societies like Athens, Sparta, and Thebes, including their governments, economies, social relations, and cultural influences. Although we find humanity in tragic Greek characters, their creators lived in worlds with very different social forces shaping their understanding in ways we (i.e., twenty-first-century readers) cannot completely comprehend. The peoples of fifth-century BCE Athens (or ancient Cairo or ancient Machu Picchu) were products of the contexts they inhabited, and that contextualization (through relationships, politics, economics, etc.) was responsible for the cultivation and maintenance of particular social forces that perpetuated particular ways of thinking and behaving among particular groups in particular places.

Second, every world's social forces exist in a continual state of change. Often, this change is so incremental that it is difficult to identify on a daily basis, and it tends to happen outside any one individual's purview. It is also a victim of short human memories, especially across vast geographic spans and generational lengths of time. The American women's suffrage movement is one obvious example: In the United States, women only secured the right to vote in 1920, hardly more than a century ago. For the majority of nineteenth-century American men, the question of women's suffrage was not an issue that needed to be addressed—it was "normal" in relation to the social forces of that time (unjust though it appears to us in hindsight). It took a decades-long campaign led by suffragettes in individual states (e.g., artistic works, debates, propaganda, and destruction of property [window smashing, arson]) before the Nineteenth Amendment to the US Constitution was ratified.

Third, not all social changes are permanent, nor are they necessarily "positive" or signs of progress. We certainly hope and expect that women will retain the right to vote, but it is possible for policies, laws, cultural trends, and attitudes to regress. Consider the Eighteenth Amendment to the US Constitution, which made the manufacture, sale, and consumption of alcohol illegal. Like the suffragettes, a committed group of activists spent years pushing for the amendment's ratification, yet it lasted a paltry thirteen years before being repealed in 1933. Prohibitionists certainly viewed the abolition of alcohol as a "positive" move that indicated progress; however, its limited lifespan demonstrates that the Eighteenth Amendment did not, by and large, change the social forces at play, and we now characterize the movement as a historic failure (i.e., though prohibition succeeded in many rural regions at the time, the corresponding amendment was never consistently enforced in urban "worlds" of the United States and ultimately collapsed under its own weight). Consequently, we should think of worlds as relativistic, context dependent, and malleable depending on the social mores of each world and its people—there is no guarantee that any particular development or trajectory will persist.

IN CLOSING

The aforementioned sections established how a given world's social forces are organized and sustained by human beings, how those social forces continually evolve, and why changes in social forces are not necessarily good nor permanent. We also described why the analysis of structures and substructures is worth including as part of any worldbuilding project: (1) it positions learners to investigate how and why different elements of a world affect its inhabitants' behavior, and 2) it gives learners an appreciation for the complex systems governing our lived reality. Moreover, it encourages them to think of history as a cumulative narrative across space and time by leveraging primary and secondary texts as snapshots from multiple contemporaneous authors with varied positioning and worldviews.

Now we can shift to even more pressing matters: Who *are* a world's people, exactly? What do demographic data tell us about them? What do they have in common, and what aspects of their identities are unique? What changes do they wish to see in the world? The next chapter will offer tentative answers and set the stage for learner-directed research on worlds and their constituent parts. Before you know it, your activity planner will be bursting with ideas and your nascent worldbuilding project will be nearing the early phases of implementation.

8 EXAMINING LIFE-WORLDS THROUGH DEMOGRAPHICS

"You've got to make your own worlds. You've got to write yourself in. Whether you were a part of the greater society or not, you've got to write yourself in."
—Octavia Butler[1]

So far, we have described worldbuilding as the analysis of a particular space at a particular time based on fuzzy spatiotemporal borders and (sub)structures that model the social forces affecting a world's people. The latter piece, specifically, draws us into the realm of demographics—the categorical conditions of those who live and breathe in a given world. As noted in chapter 3, "Theory to Practice," this is the underlying premise of a "lifeworld," the totality of a person's experience as situated in their unique environmental context. While demographics do not tell the whole story of a life-world nor act as strict determinants of a person's thinking and behavior, they absolutely factor into how one perceives the world and their place in it. These typically include race and ethnicity, gender, age, income and economic class, profession, religion, educational attainment, sexual orientation, military experience, and general state of health or able-bodiedness. All of us belong to the majority population of some demographic categories at the same time as we belong to the minority population in others, and our positioning regularly changes as definitions and/or contexts change (e.g., an individual's able-bodiedness erodes as their physiology deteriorates in late adulthood; some disabilities—like a broken arm—are temporary).

Certain demographic data may be irrelevant for some worldbuilding projects, but we err on the side of collecting and reporting as many categories for which there are reliable data. This is because, historically speaking, the experiences of marginalized peoples (e.g., women, non-whites, nonheterosexuals, disabled individuals, houseless individuals) have been treated as secondary to "normal" lived experiences. "Normal" here is defined as the "opposite" of the aforementioned demographic groups (i.e., male, white, heterosexual, able-bodied, middle or upper class), and we want to emphasize that thinking in terms of "normalcy" is equal parts lazy, disrespectful, and inaccurate. There can be robust, good-faith debates about what constitutes the average experience in a given world or how governments can and should address inequalities, but assuming that "normality" defaults to a society's most privileged demographic fails to account for the wide breadth of alternative human experiences. Opinions and judgments about "normalcy" are subjective assertions rather than facts about who actually exists or what their existence is like, and as a scholarly endeavor, worldbuilding must treat the realities of individual lived experiences as true from the perspective of those individuals (see chapter 1, "Around the World in 300 Pages"). In other words, it is not the worldbuilder's job to approve or disapprove of any particular human experience nor to claim any one demographic is "normal" but rather to ensure everyone is accounted for when developing and assessing a world's people.

The following sections detail our recommendations for demographic exploration as part of the worldbuilding process. Generally speaking, we favor a mixed methods approach that takes stock of both quantitative and qualitative information as well as introspective evaluation by the individual worldbuilder(s) themselves. This should provide a broad framework that circumvents common issues known to create consternation or confusion among participating learners. For greater effect, we encourage pausing to question your own assumptions about the world as you follow along.

NOMINAL AND QUANTITATIVE DESCRIPTIONS

Complex bureaucracies regularly need to identify and sort people into different categories quickly, efficiently, and in a uniform way, hence why we often find our unique personhoods deconstructed into a combination of quantitative data (i.e., numbers) and nominal data (i.e., labels). Consider a driver's license that features the holder's name, address, sex, height, eye and hair color, and date of birth or a tax return that includes a person's social security number, marital status, and total household income. These data are considered objectively true and cross-applicable to anyone in any place at any time. We can argue whether a man who stands five feet, six inches is "short" or "tall," but there is no debate about the quantifiable measurement from the bottom of his feet to the crown of his head—the number is what it is.

Governments, businesses, and other institutions use such data to approximate the status of individuals and groups. For example, a college admissions board will presume that students with high grade point averages are more intelligent and industrious than their peers; an athlete will be rated and traded based on their statistical performance in sporting competitions; a bank is more likely to provide loans to individuals with higher credit scores. But because this is an imperfect system (i.e., it excludes contextual information for the sake of efficiency and simplicity), the numbers may imply a narrative that we disagree with. What if a midsemester emergency resulted in unusually low grades that demolished a student's overall grade point average? What if reckless spending by one's spouse tanked the credit score associated with their shared bank account? The numbers are not a "lie" per se—the lower grade point average and credit score are technically mathematically accurate—but mitigating circumstances are not represented in the raw figures.

Labels can be similarly useful but deceiving. For instance, the US Census Bureau collects and reports data across six racial categories: White, Black or African American, American Indian or Alaska Native, Asian, Native Hawaiian or Other Pacific Islander, and Some Other Race. However, respondents are free to choose more than one race, and the Census Bureau treats the concept of race as separate from the concept of Hispanic origin, thereby confusing what is meant by "race" versus ethnicity. The challenge also extends to surveys of gender, sexuality, and economics, each of which has had to evolve beyond oversimplified binaries (e.g., man and woman, hetero- and homosexual, rich and poor) by including a wider range of options (e.g., transgender, nonbinary, agender, two-spirit, and gender nonconforming; bisexual, pansexual, polysexual, and asexual) or accounting for regional differences (e.g., an individual earning $50,000 per year might be solidly middle class in Lawrence, Kansas, while someone earning the same salary would struggle to make ends meet in Manhattan, New York).

Thus, quantitative data and nominal classification are limited in their practical application: The former omits crucial context, and the latter is a by-product of human interpretation (i.e., a series of social constructs subject to ever-changing sociocultural dynamics). Neither can be relied on to tell the *whole* story, and we must therefore adopt supplemental methods that speak to mitigating circumstances and granular situational information (i.e., what happens "in the cracks"). Happily, such tools exist in the form of narrative and qualitative description, and we can blend them with numbers and labels to provide a fuller picture of an individual's actual life-world.

NARRATIVE AND QUALITATIVE DESCRIPTIONS

Narrative and qualitative descriptions are typically more informative (though fundamentally more subjective) than nominal and quantitative data—skimming someone's driver's license or tax forms can provide a snapshot of their identity, but the documents provide no insight about the person's sense of humor, whether they enjoy the outdoors, or if they have a tendency to procrastinate. This kind of information is much more likely to be found in qualitative companion materials that allow an individual to tell a more comprehensive story than whatever is implied through raw quantitative data (e.g., a cover letter accompanying a résumé, the personal profile section of a dating app).

Of course, not all qualitative descriptions are necessarily applicable in every situation: A semester spent abroad in Tokyo, Japan, is not relevant to negotiating a desirable price on a new vehicle, nor is the savings in one's bank account relevant to getting a job counseling troubled teens. Yet, sharing a story about summers spent at your uncle's repair shop could be the deciding factor in achieving a favorable deal on a new truck, and describing your own adolescent run-in with the law could make you a compelling candidate to counsel kids in juvenile detention. Different narratives serve different purposes in different environments, and they can contextualize both broad circumstances concerning groups of people or narrow circumstances related to an individual person. As a result, we recommend combining quantitative and qualitative, nominal and narrative data to contemplate the widest possible range of life-worlds and provide as accurate and fair a representation of the human experience as possible. The more information available to a worldbuilding team, the likelier they are to identify, reflect on, and successfully speak to complex interactions between a world's structures, substructures, and social forces.

ESSENTIALISMS, STEREOTYPES, AND DRAWING WRONG CONCLUSIONS

In our introductory chapter, we described how generalizations can be used to process large volumes of information and draw conclusions that help us understand different aspects of a world. We could, for instance, proclaim "The British love their fish and chips!" and cite anecdotal evidence from a prior trip to London and/or associated demographic data (e.g., per capita fried fish consumption; the number of pubs selling fish and chips in the United Kingdom versus France, Iran, or Nigeria). Even if there are plenty of British citizens who do not eat fish or fried food and do not "love their fish and chips," the statement is *generally* true and benign enough to forgive a lack of precision.

We use the phrase "meaningful generalization" (i.e., innocuous, mostly accurate declarations that are valuable in the context of worldbuilding) to differentiate assertions like the above from stereotypes (i.e., preconceived and oversimplified conceptualizations that typify and/or defame a person or people). This is especially important when discussing large and diverse populations that have been grouped together such that some negative or poorly evidenced implications could be ascribed to everyone in the group. Any meaningful generalization we make about a population should be vague and border on the obvious—for example, if we were modeling our lived reality, it would be a meaningful generalization to say, "Practicing Christians believe in the teachings of Jesus Christ, whereas practicing Muslims believe in the teachings of Muhammad" or "Christians often identify as Catholic or Protestant, whereas Muslims often identify as Sunni or Shia." Broad statements about the character or disposition of Christians and Muslims, by contrast, would tread into the realm of stereotyping.

As much as this seems like common sense, people speak in harmful generalities all too frequently, especially as it relates to emotionally intense situations. Case in point: On October 7, 2023, the Palestinian Islamist militant group Hamas launched a surprise assault targeting Israeli civilians, injuring or killing over a thousand people in the bloodiest offensive on the Jewish community since the Holocaust. Israel immediately declared war on Hamas and began an extended siege of Gaza that devastated the territory's infrastructure and killed more than 50,000 Palestinians before the end of March 2025.

Neither author of this book is Jewish nor Muslim. We are not Israeli or Palestinian. We have no direct experience with the stresses of living in the region. Yet, we mourned the deaths of innocent Israelis killed during Hamas' terrorist attack as well as the deaths of innocent Palestinians killed during Israel's retaliation. Our misery and confusion were only heightened by a months-long mainstream and social media response during which commentators routinely propagated—and doubled down on—inflammatory accusations that followed a basic formula: "Hamas controls Palestine, and Hamas is a terrorist organization; therefore, all Palestinians (and related human rights groups/activists) condone the terroristic massacre of Jews." And on the other side, "Israel is a colonial power that has oppressed Palestinians for decades; therefore, all Israelis are interlopers, and all Jews support genocide in service of eliminating the Palestinian people."

These generalizations are entirely damaging—just one more avenue to further polarize an already-divided world. And although neither of us would pronounce ourselves expert on the topic of Israel and Palestine, we are informed enough to understand through our Jewish and Palestinian friends, relatives, neighbors, and colleagues that many people of Jewish and Palestinian ancestry are sickened by the behavior of both Hamas and the Israeli government, indicating that the sweeping judgments described above are demonstrably untrue. Nevertheless, they have persisted.

Algorithmically driven newsfeeds and short-form reporting are major contributors to this problem. It takes time, patience, and an audience interested in fact above emotional instinct to navigate the nuances of any highly charged event. The prioritization of advertising revenue via sensational headlines (versus long-form presentation and discussion) incentivizes "hot takes" over dogged journalism. Truthful, data-grounded resources do exist, but we are forced to actively search for them like needles in a metaphorical haystack.

So, how does this relate to worldbuilding as pedagogy?

When people are collapsed from diverse populations into flat monocultures through essentialism (i.e., the belief that individuals or cultures have particular characteristics essential to their being), it becomes much more difficult to think through their individual perspectives and much easier to invent snap judgments about who they are, what they believe, and why they believe it. It also fuels circular logic: "Of *course* [group of people] took [course of action]! It's in their nature!" If worldbuilding is meant to inform critical thinking and empathy, then essentialisms and stereotypes (particularly those fueled by capitalistically motivated platforms) move us further from our goal, not closer to it.

To wit, essentialisms and stereotypes lead us to draw all manner of incorrect conclusions. In extreme cases, they can be leveraged by demagogic authoritarian figures to solidify a base of support—aiming anger and grievance at scapegoats to destabilize civic, journalistic, and academic institutions that might otherwise slow or stop a hostile takeover of government. In more banal situations, they drive acceptance of essentialist truths that undermine the day-to-day choices of individuals or groups of people.

Consider the nursing profession. An essentialist would argue the reason more women become nurses than men is that women are inherently more nurturing and caring than men, and because men are more analytical, they more often choose to be physicians. A nuanced examination would question the original premise: Are women "essentially" more nurturing than men? Or does our culture socialize young girls into particular behaviors and jobs? Are young women more likely to be tracked into the profession by teachers and guidance counselors? Are career opportunities for women in healthcare more limited outside of nursing? The essentialist only needs to assert their position as if it were proven fact (whether or not it is), while the conscientious thinker has to interrogate the question and substantiate their conclusion with evidence (i.e., the former behaves like a lawyer, making a determination and working backward to justify it; the latter behaves like a scientist, conducting research before making a determination).

This is not to advocate for radical cultural relativism in circumstances involving terrorists, school shooters, white nationalists, or anyone else who commits acts of violence against innocent people. We recognize these as heinous behaviors that cannot and should not be condoned. However, we also believe there is value in probing the details of an individual's life-world and hearing the description of their worldview in their own words to better understand why they reached the conclusions (and carried out the actions) that they did. Statements like "He was a terrorist because he was [religious affiliation]" are grossly reductive and injurious; although messianic zeal *might* be a contributing factor that led someone to become a violent militant, we also need to understand how aspects of an individual's political, economic, social, and cultural situation formed them into who they were. Neither religion nor partisan politics nor socioeconomic status nor social relationships nor cultural norms are ever *the* reason, just one piece of a much larger puzzle.

We urge instructor vigilance when it comes to reviewing the generalizations learners make during the worldbuilding process so they do not mistakenly veer into essentialisms, stereotypes, and false conclusions. Remember, many traditionally aged college students (i.e., eighteen to twenty-two years old) have never been asked to think about the world in such terms before; few have had global travel experiences and/or robust multicultural/ethnic interactions; and many hold political and religious beliefs inherited from their parents or caregivers (as opposed to independently developing those beliefs for themselves). When they make mistakes—and they will—it is important to meet them where they are rather than shame them. Treat any errors as teachable moments to explore where their assumptions originated, what the implications of those assumptions might be, and how they can proactively buffer against essentialisms and stereotyping in the future.

USING DEMOGRAPHICS TO EXPLORE LIVED EXPERIENCES

Take a moment to contemplate some of the roles, positions, and/or identities you apply to yourself. Then, compile a list of those that might be applied to you by others. For reference, tables 8.1 and 8.2 feature nominal and narrative attributes that describe us (the authors).

Next, ask:

- Which of these attributes and identities best define "you"?
- Which issues, topics, ideas, skills, and values matter most to you?
- How do you make distinctions between yourself and others?
- How might others make distinctions between themselves and you?
- How have your identities changed over time? Which of them have remained constant?
- In what ways do your identities act in concert? How do they conflict?

Table 8.1. A partial list of nominal attributes that characterize the authors of this book

	Trent	Stephen
Race	White	White
Sexuality	Heterosexual	Bisexual
Gender	Male	Nonbinary
Socioeconomic Status	Middle Class	Middle Class
Age (Generation)	Generation X	Millennial
Education Level	Graduate (PhD)	Graduate (PhD)
Nationality	American	American

Table 8.2. A partial, nonexclusive list of narrative attributes that characterize the authors of this book

Trent		Stephen	
Creative Writer	Spanish Speaker	Philosopher	Illustrator
Parent	Professor	Political Activist	Learning Scientist
Advisor	Camper	Animation Enthusiast	Cosplayer
Star Wars Fan	Dog Owner	Cat Owner	Caregiver
Colleague	Collaborator	Editor	Photographer
Hiker	Game Master	Designer	Small Business Founder
Soccer Enthusiast	Director	Role-Player	Agnostic

The point of this exercise is to clarify how much of what we do on a day-to-day, moment-to-moment basis comes down to social norms, expectations, and performance. The whole of our existence does not and cannot materialize all at once nor under all conditions, which fundamentally shapes our personal attitudes and behaviors as well as our judgment of others. We depend on context to inform our understanding of the world through interaction, categorization, and culture.

Prodding at identity (and the contexts in which it applies) is necessary to demonstrate how lived experiences and life-worlds are a key feature of worldbuilding as a pedagogical approach—it helps learners connect abstract, high-level thinking about a world and its social forces to the concrete effects that social forces have on individuals' lives. The phrase *lived experiences*, in particular, refers to the "representation and understanding of an individual's human experiences, choices, and options and how those factors influence one's perception of knowledge based on one's own life,"[2] and although worldbuilding frequently involves meaningful generalization, the impact of individuals' personal beliefs, motivations, and actions can be overlooked if we fail to thread together a 40,000-foot macroscopic view with a person-on-the-ground microscopic view (i.e., missing the trees for the forest). Expert worldbuilders make it a point to examine who, exactly, benefits from certain social forces and who faces greater challenges when obstructed by them.

Put another way, we want to do our best to acknowledge *everyone* who lives in a world. The best means of doing so is to ensure that the percentage of different demographic groups within a society always adds up to 100 percent. This allows us to consider differences between groups, whether they constitute large or narrow majorities or minorities, and how different people are situated within and between them.

Imagine we are modeling the world of Rochester, New York, in or around the year 2020. A glance at contemporaneous census data tells us that the city had a population of around 209,000; gender distribution was approximately a 50–50 split between men and women; roughly 60 percent of the city's population fell between the ages of 19 and 64 years old; the city was predominantly Black (38 percent) and white (37 percent) with Latinos being a distant third (19 percent); 83 percent of citizens were high school graduates, and 29 percent of the population held a bachelor's degree or higher; and the median household income was $40,000. Taken together, this information provides a fairly comprehensive snapshot of the city at that time.

To explore the lived experiences of people in the world, we could develop a model list of 100 entries with each entry representing one citizen from the census. Based on these stats, 50 entries would be men and 50 would be women (50+50=100); 66 of the entries would be between the ages of 19 and 64, 12 would be over the age of 65, and 22 would be below the age of 18 (66+12+22=100); 38 of the entries would be Black, 37 white, 19 Latino, and the remaining 6 Asian, Native American, Pacific Islander, or another designation (38+37+19+6=100).

For the sake of simplicity, let us further narrow our set of 100 individuals to just 10 (rounding up or down). We presuppose that our chosen demographic categories are represented equally across society (e.g., one gender is not disproportionately of a specific race; one race is not overrepresented among each age bracket) and that no individual category outweighs the others. If gender is evenly split, then five entries represent men and five represent women; for age, two entries are younger than 18 years old, one entry is greater than 65 years old, and the remaining seven entries fall between 19 and 64 years old. Since there are two entries younger than 18, we will assign one to each gender and pick random ages between 0 and 18: 8 years old for male (entry 1) and 14 years old for female (entry 6). For our one entry above 65 years old, we can flip a coin—heads for male and tails for female. Assuming tails (i.e., female), we will add a random age: 79 years old (entry 7). To contend with the final seven entries, we will use a random number generator to produce seven random integers between 19 and 64. Regarding race, we will distribute our categories as four Black, four white, and two Latino. The complete dataset is depicted in table 8.3.

Table 8.3. A list of ten hypothetical Rochesterians (as characterized via the 2020 census)

Entry	Gender	Age	Race
1	Male	8	Black
2	Male	38	White
3	Male	37	Latino
4	Male	45	Black
5	Male	44	White
6	Female	14	Latino
7	Female	79	Black
8	Female	46	White
9	Female	22	Black
10	Female	29	White

We can make some educated guesses about how different individuals might see the world differently than their peers (e.g., a 79-year-old Black woman versus a 38-year-old white man; an 8-year-old Black boy versus a 46-year-old white woman). Factors like gender, age, and race would undoubtedly influence their individual life-worlds, and though limited, these hypothetical Rochesterians would offer a useful starting point to debate the potential origin and nature of each person's views on government, economics, and culture.

For all its efficiency, though, simplifying the dataset eliminates many worldviews. For starters, we know that less than 100 percent of the population identifies as either male or female; Rochester's population includes transgender, nonbinary, agender, two-spirit, and other gender identities. We also failed to account for Asian, Native American, Pacific Islander, and other Rochesterians who constitute less than 1 percent of the population (not to mention those who identify as more than one race). Age is better balanced, but relying on random numbers means that none of our entries occupy the 33-year age gap between our two oldest individuals (46 and 79 years old). We could bump one of the entries aged in their 40s into the upper 50s or lower 60s just to keep this demographic cross-section more evenly distributed, but it would still miss critical differences within generations (e.g., older versus younger millennial). Because the US Census Bureau does not maintain data with sufficient granularity to address the aforementioned issues, we would need supplemental resources to generate a more holistically representative list.

In truth, none of this is sufficient to capture the breadth of individual lived experiences, and we need to be very careful about the assumptions baked into our hypothetical population. For example, it would be irresponsible to add new columns for education or employment and randomly assign the corresponding figures to our list. Why? Because statistics indicate that only 13 percent of Black Rochesterians have college degrees compared with 42 percent of white Rochesterians. The same applies to household income: Black and Latino Rochesterians are disproportionately more likely to live in poverty (36 percent and 37 percent, respectively) compared to their white counterparts (22 percent), and *all* groups exceed the national average. Black and Latino citizens of Rochester are also more than twice as likely to be unemployed (13 percent) than white citizens (6 percent).

With only ten entries in table 8.3, we risk artificially inflating and deflating statistics to the point of creating a wholly inaccurate world model. Still, it can be a useful pursuit—building out a table like this and comparing it to actual demographic data exposes the depths of disparity in our lived-in world, leading to productive questions (e.g., "Why are Black and Latino citizens less likely to have college degrees?" or "If we as a society feel this disparity needs to be addressed, how might we increase the number of Black and Latino citizens receiving college degrees and/or lift more of those people out of poverty?"). It forces learners to confront their preconceived notions about reality and consider how societal positioning affects different individuals within different groups.

It is easy to lose perspective whenever humans are boiled down to numbers on a page rather than treated holistically (i.e., as vibrant people with complex beliefs and experiences). Ten entries in no way account for the dynamics of a world containing even a modicum of diversity; 100 entries are more comprehensive (i.e., they encompass a greater number of demographic categories and reveal a broader array of identities), but even that is impoverished compared to the list of self-assigned or externally ascribed identities we apply to one another as people socially situated in the world.

To that end, we suggest orienting learners toward the minority group(s) in each demographic they explore. If only 13 percent of Black Rochesterians have attained a college or postgraduate degree, what are *their* stories? What trajectories led them to those degrees? What barriers stood in the way of the 87 percent who did not attain a college or postgraduate degree? There are certainly well-educated, wealthy Black women in Rochester, but they are a triple minority with respect to education, wealth, and race. How might their lived experiences and worldviews differ from those of a white working-class man (a triple majority) living in a different part of town? Individuals represented in the narrowest wedges of our demographic pie charts are every bit as real and valid as those who occupy the wider, more common slices.

Constructing a table to reflect the demographics of a world's population should be undertaken with caution, but it introduces teachable moments regarding how and why we think about that world's structures and substructures (see chapter 7, "Structures and Substructures"). For instance, if we were to model the Western Front during World War I rather than Rochester, New York, in 2020, the gender split would not be 50–50 between men and women; likewise, the median age on a university campus would be much younger than in a retirement community. These situations bring to light interesting life-world dynamics, and they encourage learners to interrogate power relationships between minority and majority groups (e.g., the lived experience of a woman on the Western Front, of a nontraditionally aged university student, of a nursing home administrator surrounded by a majority of people three or four times their age). Despite the challenges, it is a crucial component of any worldbuilding project, and it should be included as part of your instructional toolkit.

SOMEONE ELSE'S SHOES

To paraphrase other portions of this book, we define empathy as "wearing someone else's shoes" for the purpose of seeing the world from an alternative perspective. Although empathy shares some characteristics with sympathy, sympathy suggests an emotional investment that typically involves feelings of sadness, pity, or guilt for another person based on their situation or circumstance. The difference is meaningful insofar as our goal is to examine individual worldviews without necessarily obliging ourselves to coddle or change another person's mind—the former is evaluative, and the latter is action oriented.

Practicing empathy—that is, stepping out of ourselves and (at least briefly) suspending our personal opinions, judgments, and beliefs—is vital to understanding the world as it actually exists. For instance, a white student from financially well-off suburbs might be inclined to believe that the world more or less operates as a meritocracy and that people, as individuals, make their own luck through the maintenance of a strong work ethic, a well-calibrated moral compass, and adherence to the rules and laws of society. Many twenty-something university students subscribe to this interlocking system of beliefs and presume that so long as they make all the "right" choices, they will achieve success in their careers and personal lives. Consequently, when approaching questions such as what can be done to support houseless individuals living in inner cities, they are inclined to suggest that the root problem lies in a lack of personal responsibility; that people in difficult living situations must work harder to extract themselves via school, not breaking the law, and saving money. These are values that they have been raised (by professional-class parents and a doting media ecosystem) to accept as a kind of essentialist truth (i.e., the just-world fallacy; people get what they deserve).

Through the empathetic act of worldbuilding, we can help them suspend their preexisting belief systems, substitute different sets of conditions, and develop a greater understanding of fellow humans. Worldbuilding may be the first time they are asked to imagine themselves as someone of a different racial or ethnic background. It may be the first time they have considered what it would be like to live in an urban, economically depressed area. It may be the first time they have questioned how their existence would be affected by local acts of violence and illicit drug use. It may be the first time they are asked to work through what it means to be the child of a single absentee parent—no one ensuring that they attend school, stay out of trouble, wear clean clothes, eat nutritious food, or get sufficient sleep. It may be the first time they confront the underlying assumptions of a self-serving, self-aggrandizing "personal responsibility" worldview and reflect on the impact of complex political, economic, and sociocultural dynamics.

We want learners to question what it means to have few role models who hold down good, professional jobs with adequate salaries, and we want them to wonder about the implications of few adults in their world having high school or college degrees. How might someone whose parents received undergraduate or graduate degrees benefit from their parents' institutional knowledge? How would they navigate applying to (and paying for) college differently than someone whose parents did not attend? How many people in their day-to-day lives would they encounter who have such knowledge and experience? What value comes from an insider's perspective—not just financial but social, political, and cultural value?

Even though "hard work" and "making your own luck" might apply in some circumstances, we operate in a big, unforgiving system, and learners should understand that personal efforts alone can seldom overcome circumstances. If our role models regularly engage in illegal activity, then that becomes our baseline; likewise, if our role models regularly facilitate one another's success in business or education, we gain intangible benefits that are not available to all people. Staying in school and working hard in entry-level service jobs cannot save us if we lack the resources and know-how to escape precarity; we depend on clearly cognizable examples from others to take advantage of relevant tools and systems.

Never lose sight of the fact that the instructor's job in these kinds of demographic discussions is to guide learner metacognition (i.e., thinking about thinking) and expose how and why competing worldviews may be incomplete. This is categorically different than proselytizing or converting students to partisan political positions—we instead want them to think through problems from different angles and appreciate that their own worldviews are, in fact, subjective. They should be encouraged to ask, Upon what information or data are different worldviews based? Do others in the room find one rationale more compelling than another? Does anyone (student or instructor) have direct life experience that contradicts anything being said? What alternate ways of understanding complex systems and their interactions have not been raised by anyone in the room but can be found in external literature?

As echoed throughout this chapter, the heart of life-world analysis is distinguishing between highly biased gut feelings and dispassionate deconstruction, particularly as it pertains to demographic grouping. Standing in someone else's shoes is not a free pass to assume that all perspectives are equally "correct" but rather an opportunity to explore different perspectives as equally legitimate *to those who hold them*, hence why we emphasize the strategies described above: to establish a framework for how to think such that whatever conclusions your learners draw—in the classroom and beyond—they will gravitate toward substantive and informed argumentation grounded in the situated nature of lived experience and appreciation for others' life-worlds.

9 CLASS PREPARATIONS

"It is good to have an end to journey towards; but it is the journey that matters, in the end."

—Ursula K. Le Guin[1]

Incorporating worldbuilding into a unit, course, or program requires careful preparation for things to run as smoothly and successfully as possible. In designing personal worldbuilding courses and helping colleagues develop theirs, we have found that even the best-laid plans can wither upon contact with learners. For one thing, different group compositions yield different, unpredictable results: Some groups catch on to certain concepts very quickly and are eager to accelerate the process, while others stew over one portion of the project as emergent questions lead them in unanticipated directions. For another, worldbuilding tends to be slippery, messy, and idiosyncratic for the instructor, requiring constant tinkering to adjust for whatever comes your way. Yet, despite all the risks and unknowns, *it is entirely worth the effort*.

Many instructors want to be seen as the authority on a given topic, which makes some sense—nothing demonstrates expertise quite as well as being able to answer questions from left field and adjust for on-the-fly, in-the-moment curveballs. Where some of us struggle is in admitting the limits of our knowledge, concerned that learners will see any admission of not knowing facts or figures as a weakness and cause for lack of confidence. It might be a psychological hangover from being grilled while defending theses and dissertations—impostor syndrome abounds—but there is value in acknowledging gaps in our understanding and, crucially, being able to bridge those gaps. Colearning and communicating across life-worlds is much more important than memorizing esoteric bits of content; to invoke a Vygotskian turn of phrase from chapter 2, "Road to Contemporary Learning Theory," our students depend on us to be their guide on the side rather than a sage on the stage.

DEVELOPING YOUR PROJECT OVERVIEW

Whether you plan to employ worldbuilding for a single assignment or a semester-long project, the best results will come from proceeding through a series of stages. Below, we discuss the foundational stages that should be completed before your project begins in earnest: articulating the project's purpose and length, selecting primary and secondary sources, and introducing the worldbuilding project to students. The project itself consists of a few additional stages, including world modeling, writing the world's metanarrative, and populating a catalog with people, places, things, events, and groups. Where you go from there—either discussing and analyzing the project as a group or moving on to simulations or role-play scenarios—is up to you.

Note that refinements and revisions throughout each stage are usually necessary and time commitments can vary, but you *should not* skip any steps or else you will miss out on important checkpoints and sow a combination of confusion and disappointment. Particularly expansive worldbuilding projects can continue beyond the listed stages (e.g., simulations, role-play scenarios), but those endeavors will be discussed in future chapters.

With that, it's time to prepare. Let's get planning!

STAGE ONE: PROJECT PURPOSE AND LENGTH

Before putting pen to paper or fingers to keyboard, ask yourself, "What do I hope to gain from adding worldbuilding to my curriculum?" The best designs and experiences come from well-articulated learning objectives, and it will be much easier to craft instructional activities and assessments if you have your goals set in advance (see chapter 3, "Theory to Practice"). Some possibilities:

- You want small groups of learners to construct their own understanding of the social forces at play in a given place at a specific time—this will contextualize broader course content and help them appreciate the level of complexity concerning real-world social problems and the interconnectedness of different strands in the fabric of society.
- You want learners to model the same world at different points in time so they can track political, economic, social, and/or cultural changes (speculating as to the cause[s] of these changes based on historical, literary, scientific, or other evidence).
- You want learners to engage in deductive reasoning about how the conditions of specific worlds came into being, or you want to encourage

speculative thinking about how worlds may change over time (including how we can generate positive changes in lived reality).
- You want learners to occupy different subject positions or viewpoints and reflect on how different individuals' experiences or life-worlds shape their beliefs and attitudes (including introspection about learners' personal feelings and opinions about the problems they face and changes they would like to make in the world).

In many cases, worldbuilding will encompass one or more of the above, or you may have different objectives than those listed here. Regardless, it is vital to have a clear idea of what you want to accomplish so you can carve out sufficient time in the course or program schedule. There is often a snowball effect where students take a little while to acclimate to the process, but once they understand the project, they do not want it to end.

The next section will explain how to translate your objective(s) into a manageable timeline for both the instructor and learners.

STAGE TWO: SCHEDULING

In a typical classroom environment, worldbuilding projects last anywhere from a few weeks to one or two months or the entire semester. Your time should be budgeted based on your desire to engage in one or more interrelated worldbuilding activities (i.e., world modeling, simulation, and role-play).
- Even the most basic world modeling project will take at least two to three weeks depending on how much time is spent scaffolding the project, how much time is allocated for learners to research different aspects of the world, and how much collaborative writing learners are asked to engage in (e.g., cowriting summaries about different aspects of the given world, including its political, economic, social, and cultural structures). This should be sufficient for all participants to "go meta" on the complexities of accurately representing a world and connecting its diverse (and seemingly unrelated) parts.
- The process of developing a representative wiki catalog (i.e., People, Places, and Things) will take at least two weeks. This will ensure that learners have time to develop a fully representative set of entries.
- Each simulation, whether moving the world forward or backward on a timeline, will take at least one to two weeks depending on how much change occurs (e.g., a few years versus several decades). For example,

modeling Singapore between 2010 and 2020 might require one week since it represents relatively minimal change over a short period of time, whereas modeling the country between 1920 and 2020 might require two or more weeks owing to the comparably dramatic breadth of change occurring over a century.

- For role-play scenarios, expect each round to take one to two weeks. You should assume learners will need a few class periods to properly situate their characters in the world and several more to position those characters in project-relevant social situations.

Both simulations and role-play are repeatable, meaning you can perpetuate them for varied spatial and temporal conditions or introduce new scenarios/complex systems that alter how the world works. Doing so improves the likelihood that learners will grapple with different lived experiences and life-worlds as well as transfer their learning outside the classroom context. Because the process is cumulative—that is, learners will understand what is being asked of them without the need for substantial direction each time they repeat the process—the instructor can adjust the calendar as needed throughout the semester. If portions of the project are taking longer than expected, simulations and role-play can be trimmed to make additional space for world modeling; conversely, if learners complete their world modeling faster than expected, simulation or role-play experiences can be added. The instructor can also divide learners into multiple simulation groups, where one examines fifty years before the present, a second examines the present, and a third examines fifty years after the present; alternatively, the instructor could engage learners in two sequential role-play scenarios, the first involving characters with particular ideological or socioeconomic positioning and the second involving characters with the opposite ideological or socioeconomic positioning.

PRIMARY AND SECONDARY SOURCES

Worldbuilding instructors need to strike a balance between how much information they provide and how much they require learners to find for themselves. Both have potential benefits and drawbacks: On one end of the spectrum lies something akin to *Reacting to the Past* (*RTTP*), a game-based educational program wherein a manual describes the "world" in its totality (i.e., major social forces, personalities, maps, locations, and a summary of the central problem to be resolved), and learners are tasked with replicating (through role-play) a specific moment in space and time (with limited space for imaginative deviation). On the other end, an instructor may forgo any existing scaffold and provide no resources so that learners must model or construct the "world" via open-ended, inquiry-driven research (maximizing creativity but losing definition). Our worldbuilding methodology falls between these two poles.

Although *RTTP* has an avid following and has successfully introduced role-play into history classrooms, there is a reason we have not adopted this approach. First, the manual presents *RTTP* scenarios in definitive, didactic terms without many opportunities for students to research the content for themselves—they are asked to simulate real-world events using scripted content rather than engage in discovery learning (as defined by Dewey; see chapter 2, "Road to Contemporary Learning Theory"). Second, *RTTP* is an overtly competitive game complete with a victory condition for one or more sides. Having specific victory conditions requires quantification of "correct" choices based on known outcomes, which diminishes learner agency and fails to contextualize how and why complex systems interact; reality is not so neatly zero-sum, and attenuating playfulness constrains how learners engage with the content. While we do not contest *RTTP*'s appeal among a subset of educators, we believe our approach affords greater opportunities for coauthorship rooted in a more theoretically sound set of constructivist learning principles. Additionally, the playful nature of worldbuilding—emphasizing learner choice and innovation over rigid game mechanics and win-loss conditions—provides greater flexibility and customizability than *RTTP*'s comparatively strict, single-purpose role-playing scenarios.

On the flip side, we do not believe that instructors should forgo any kind of template, primarily because a lack of structure makes it easy for learners to get lost in the weeds. We instead tend to (1) assign a range of secondary sources that describe the conditions of a world in broad terms, (2) supplement our secondary sources with relevant primary sources (often excerpted), and (3) allow the worldbuilding process to reveal gaps in learner knowledge that can become the basis for independent research. For example, Trent tasked one of his classes at the Rochester Institute of Technology with creating a model of 1920s Rochester, New York. As the instructor, he provided a map of the city from that era (when the university was located downtown), which allowed learners to explore the region before New York State bisected the campus to construct a new freeway (an act that prompted the Institute's move to its current location—the suburb of Henrietta—in 1968). He likewise invited a colleague specializing in local history to provide a guest lecture paired with readings from Steven L. Piott's (2011) book *Daily Life in the Progressive Era*,[2] relevant chapters from Dane Gordon's

(1982/2007) *Rochester Institute of Technology: Industrial Development and Educational Innovation in an American City, 1829–2006*,[3] and a handful of scholarly articles concerning women's suffrage and prohibition. Taken together, these materials afforded learners adequate context to outline basic elements of the world's governmental, economic, social, and cultural (sub)structures. They also laid the groundwork for a class session at the university library where a research librarian was able to answer questions related to learners' individual interests.

Some students researched tensions between labor and management, while others looked into organized crime and prohibition. Some became interested in the Progressive movement, and some sought to better understand race relations and demographics within the city. What they discovered through their research and collaborative writing is that the world of 1920s Rochester was both similar and different to the world of 2020s Rochester. They were surprised to find a crossover between the women's suffrage movement and the labor movement; that local philanthropist George Eastman's many contributions to the city—including the Eastman School of Music and the Rochester Philharmonic Orchestra as well as parks, green spaces, employee benefits, and profit-sharing—were an attempt to defuse class tensions; and that social disputes often centered on different immigrant groups from Europe (as opposed to the present situation in which a large economic gap divides Black and white Rochesterians in the city versus the suburbs; a post-World War II influx of Black citizens occurred between 1945 and 1960, increasing the Black population by 300 percent). Other learners became interested in the social religion of Spiritualism; the Fox sisters, famous mediums who held public seances; the pseudoscientific health movement that accompanied Spiritualism; or stories of World War I veterans and victims of the 1918 influenza pandemic.

Most desirably, learners were eager to exchange their independent discoveries with peers and begin drafting a shared narrative. The final product was a bit uneven (i.e., sections about women's rights and bootlegging were lengthier than those describing the labor movement), but the project was undoubtedly a success (keeping in mind that the goal was *not* to construct a fully comprehensive model of the world—it was to highlight similarities and differences between 1920s and 2020s Rochester). And, through it all, the instructor remained positioned between the two aforementioned poles of the intervention spectrum, acting as a guide on the side who strategically introduced secondary sources before letting learners loose to interrogate more specialized primary sources. Responsibility was intentionally distributed across the entire Community of Practice (see chapter 4, "Collaboration and Community") so that the instructor (i.e., the relative expert) could focus on coordinating the actions of different learners/groups, ensuring that learners/groups stayed on topic, and providing insights or recommendations based on emergent fact patterns.

UNLEARN WHAT YOU HAVE LEARNED

When learners are asked to model a historical place in the real world, they do so based on a combination of their (usually unfounded) assumptions about the given place and time as it has been presented in films, television shows, and other forms of media. The obvious problem is that not all sources of media accurately depict times and places, especially when those sources are meant for entertainment—rather than academic—purposes.

One particularly pernicious example comes from the popular Extra Credits YouTube series (2011) video entitled "Tangential Learning: How Games Can Teach Us While We Play."[4] The video's creators mean well—they describe how players can learn about a variety of topics by playing games—but they fail to account for the fact that games (like films, television shows, and historical fiction) have no obligation to truthfulness. Unlike academia, where there is an entire ecosystem designed to monitor for accurate depictions of people, places, things, and events from other times and places (e.g., peer review, editorial oversight), game development optimizes for engagement and profitability over facts, often playing fast and loose with history to create maximally interesting and/or fun user experiences.

Many popular video game franchises take this quasi-historical route with their storytelling: *Fallout 3* has players scavenge the ruins of a postapocalyptic Washington, DC, and *Fallout 4* moves them further north to postapocalyptic Boston; *Grand Theft Auto* features locales that strongly resemble New York City, Los Angeles, and Miami; and a number of *Assassin's Creed* games incorporate historically significant cities and cultures as compelling backdrops for gameplay (e.g., Florence and Venice during the Renaissance, the Northeast United States during the Revolutionary War, Paris during the French Revolution, London during the Second Industrial Revolution, ancient Egypt, ancient Greece). Students commonly enter the classroom having spent dozens of hours in these simulated environments, but without refined media literacy skills, they are prone to uncritically accept incomplete or inaccurate facsimiles as if they are genuinely representative of real places and times.

In a (2021) study of reconstructed colonial Boston for *Assassin's Creed III*, Aurélien Catros and Maxime Leblanc noted that the city was "faithful enough to convey a feeling of verisimilitude," but they "were able to discover numerous differences in the urban fabric" of setting and concluded the game world to be an "imperfect historic reconstruction"—something they referred to as "a useful lie" that prioritized gameplay and the expert rendering of a few notable landmarks over strict historical accuracy.[5] They further argued that because these reconstructions were presented as if they were real, players would struggle to parse fact from fantasy and walk away believing they learned a great deal despite knowing quite little.[6] Whereas previous generations of college students may have had no preconceptions about the layout of colonial Boston or eighteenth-century Paris, today's may be arriving with incorrect preconceptions about these places and times owing to their interaction with the simulacra embedded in popular media.

Of course, a student's knowledge of entertainment media can fuel their desire to gain a deeper, more well-rounded understanding of a particular world at a particular historical moment, and it can even become a point of discussion as part of comparative analysis (i.e., what, why, and how a creator chose to highlight or accentuate, downplay or outright omit)—essentially the argument underpinning anchored instruction. However, it is incumbent upon the instructor to convey that entertainment media is incomplete and/or modified to suit a specific creator's goals. Directly comparing video games and film with lived reality is the best way to empower learners as critical media consumers who can reflect on their own authorial choices and decide which world structures are most worthy of attention (versus those that have been misrepresented in media and should be unlearned).

WIKIPEDIA AS A SOURCE OF INFORMATION

Left to their own devices, learners are apt to use Wikipedia as a preferred if not sole source of information about the world. Their inclination is somewhat understandable—not only is it usually a top search engine result, but it does (for the most part) an excellent job of summarizing the main features of a given society. In fact, Wikipedia provides countless models of how to describe a world even if it lacks specifics about economic conditions or demographics in very narrow windows of space and time (see chapter 10, "Wikipedia as a Model for Worldbuilding"). For instance, entries concerning "Rochester, New York" and "History of Rochester, New York" allocate several paragraphs to events that transpired in the decade of the 1920s, but they do not devote much space to the specific year 1920. Because learners often experience temporal confusion (e.g., mentioning Silver Stadium in a narrative about 1920 Rochester even though the baseball field was not built until the late 1920s), it is good practice to review any relevant Wikipedia pages before launching into your worldbuilding project. This will allow you to strategically select primary and secondary sources that complement and/or challenge whatever information students are bound to find for themselves.

In general, students' familiarity with Wikipedia is more boon than bane as the worldbuilding process relies on the website's basic article template as a model for organizing researched information. Additionally, the site's entries typically offer dozens of primary and secondary sources as citations or hyperlinks throughout different sections of each page. Wiki entries thus serve as a familiar model (for article structure, page linking, and citation) and provide information breadcrumbs for students to follow as part of their self-guided research and discovery.

Introducing a variety of media can also pay dividends with respect to inducing a sense of immersion in the world. Biographies, films, and historical fiction provide more subjective positioning of an individual's experience, which may or may not align with an academic article or textbook chapter. Rather than having learners judge sources based on which is most historically accurate, the instructor can turn conversation to points of tension that emerge between different modes of creation and world modeling. A fiction writer or a film director may take certain liberties with the historical record if it suits their creative purposes, but the depiction of lived experiences through the eyes of a specific character can make a world come alive in ways that drier historical accounts sometimes cannot.

Overall, your assigned resources should provide ample information for students to create a representative model of the world that covers broad aspects of governance, the economy, demographics, social relations, and unique or prominent facets of the culture. Because they will be inclined to view reading material assigned by the instructor as objectively "correct," the use of multiple sources representing different perspectives across a variety of modalities will help establish how differences in depiction can lead to a more comprehensive, multivalenced picture of daily life.

STAGE THREE: INTRODUCING THE PROJECT

Educators are trained to spend the first few class periods outlining learning objectives for the term, which is essential for learners to understand complex, multistep projects like worldbuilding as fluid, collaborative efforts that require a great deal of communication between themselves and their peers. We try to be as clear as possible that the process can be messy, but if they trust in and follow the instructions, they will be rewarded with a deeper appreciation of the material and a more memorable learning experience. This is *not* a magical corrective for engagement—some students prefer passive learning environments, struggle with social anxiety, and/or detest any kind of group work, occasionally leading them to drop the class upon hearing what is expected of them; others are uncomfortable with the prospect of open-ended assignments and ungraded evaluation procedures. The majority, though, are intrigued by the promise of an interactive experience and will set aside any harbored suspicions.

It can help to underscore that the flexible, ill-defined nature of the process is intentional. Learners who are used to rigid class structures will sometimes perceive adjustable scheduling and customizable assignments as indicative of reduced academic rigor rather than adaptable, responsive instructional design. Preemptively addressing these concerns goes a long way toward heightening confidence in the instructor and project as a whole, which comes in handy if or when you need to make midsemester changes to the plan.

You should also stress that learners will not be copying and pasting information from other sources but summarizing and synthesizing multiple sources in their own words. Their summaries will be revised, expanded, condensed, combined, and/or challenged by other students. They and their coauthors will constructively critique language use and whether core ideas are suitably conveyed to the audience. In sum, they will attend to linguistic nuance (e.g., why certain words mean different things in different circumstances and/or come with different connotations) and come to understand that worldbuilding does not establish a singular, objective, static capital-T "Truth" but rather portrays worlds—including our own—as complex webs of ever-evolving, individualized realities.

PREPARATIONS COMPLETE

Circling back to where we began this chapter, worldbuilding scarcely goes 100 percent according to the instructor's plan. Some educators see this as a fatal flaw, but as long-time implementers, we see it as a benefit: Not only are all learning environments prone to unpredictability, but the vast majority of students find the unpredictability (and consequent opportunities for creativity) to be motivating and exciting. If you are not reaching your target objectives, you can simply modify your approach; if you are hit with in-the-moment inspiration, you can go completely off script. The mix of personalities, processes, and areas of study ensures that every project offers something new and unique, and this dynamism is what has compelled our return to the practice time and time again. Every cohort represents a chance to try something new. Every world allows us to reinvent ourselves. Every story yields a different conclusion.

Should you pursue worldbuilding with your own learners, we expect that your experience will be just as richly gratifying.

10 WIKIPEDIA AS A MODEL FOR WORLDBUILDING

"Wikipedia is the best thing ever. Anyone in the world can write anything they want about any subject, so you know you are getting the best possible information."
—Michael Scott, *The Office*[1]

Learners have near-universal familiarity with Wikipedia—the world's largest online encyclopedia—but they are much less likely to have thought about how Wikipedia frames the collaborative writing process and templatizes collaborative knowledge building. In fact, they may never have considered who writes a given article nor what norms help maximize readability across the website.

To address this disconnect, we offer this chapter to introduce the basics of wiki organization and guide wiki integration into your worldbuilding projects. We will begin with an overview of wiki structure before delving into best practices for article layout, strategies for content curation, and affordances of wikis for group-oriented writing. By the conclusion, wikis should seem like a natural extension of the worldbuilding process and neatly fit into your broader curricular design, especially through a social constructivist lens.

GETTING STARTED

While there are many variations on individual Wikipedia pages, there is typically consistency between parallel categories (e.g., locations like nations, regions, cities, and neighborhoods). All Wikipedia entries require an article title followed by a lead section that precedes the full body of content. It is very common for an infobox to be featured in the top right-hand corner of the page to showcase a representative image and any relevant facts about the entry. Locations, specifically, tend to feature facts about a city's founding, geographic size, current population, elevation, and similar data, which can be categorized as an expression of both quantitative and nonnarrative data; a page's body of content, by contrast, usually features qualitative and narrative data.

Commonly recurring sections of location pages include (most often in the order delineated below) the following:

- **History:** A brief recounting of major historical events from the past through the present
- **Geography:** A description of the location's main geographic features (e.g., rivers, lakes, mountains) as well as descriptions of the regional climate, amount and type of precipitation, and other weather-related information
- **Government:** An explanation of the system by which the society is governed, including different governmental structures, explanations of political systems, rules relating to voting, systems of succession, political parties, political borders or boundaries, and anything having to do with how decisions are made within the society
- **Economy:** A summary of the location's wealth, including major sources of income or revenue, natural resources, trade relations, major employers, average household income, economic trends over time, and other matters relating to production, distribution, and trade
- **Demographics:** Statistical data about the population (often expressed in data tables accompanied by a narrative description) that highlight percentages of the population across many categories (e.g., race, religion, household income, education level, crime)
- **Culture and Society:** A broad category that is often subdivided but includes a description of local art, music, film, food, sports, and clothing as well as museums, parks, recreation activities, and anything else deemed a prominent or unique aspect of the society

Other common sections include infrastructure, art and culture, education, transportation, parks and recreation, healthcare, and media. These may be integrated with the aforementioned sections rather than treated as distinct, and their order may diverge across entries. Irrespective of minor differences, most location entries include all of these topics at varying levels of detail.

When employing worldbuilding pedagogy, we recommend tasking learners to review a handful of Wikipedia pages so they can practice interrogating "big ideas" related to their own project(s):

- The content—that is, the type and range of information that can be gleaned from an entry (and/or what information has been omitted)

- The structure—how information is organized and divided into different categories and subcategories and/or links to other relevant entries
- The writing style—whether and how the page adopts Wikipedia's endorsed neutral point of view, described as "fairly, proportionately, and, as far as possible, without editorial bias, incorporating all significant views that have been published by reliable sources on a topic" (considered a "fundamental principle" of Wikipedia specifically and other Wikimedia projects generally)
- Embedded hyperlinks—any words or phrases that link to other pages, where those links lead, and their relation to the original entry
- Accompanying media—which images, tables, maps, audio or video files, and other types of media are embedded in the page as well as how they contribute to or otherwise shape the reader's understanding of the topic

Wikipedia also features a robust Manual of Style that provides both advice and warnings concerning a Neutral Point of View (NPOV). For example: Words to Watch, including those that may introduce bias or use language that lacks precision; suggestions for proper Categorization, including sections on Overcategorization and how to avoid problems when it comes to the ethical Categorization of People; and best practices for a sensible Layout and instructions on appropriate Linking. It may be worth discussing assigned Wikipedia pages in class to allow learners to reflect on different aspects of collaborative knowledge building and how different pages do (or do not) adhere to the stated guidelines.

Consider encouraging your learners to think through questions of breadth and depth (i.e., how Wikipedia writers speak in both general and specific terms) regarding a geographic area. If the authors of this book were to choose Rochester, New York, as the subject of a world modeling project, we would ask our students to begin by examining the city's Wikipedia entry with a focus on how the article's contributors describe a familiar location. Then, we would ask that they "zoom out" to Monroe County and analyze its page before seeking articles about the larger Finger Lakes region and Western New York (a process that could continue across multiple additional layers, such as New York State, the Northeastern United States, the United States, and North America as a whole). Upon completing this task, we would request that our students recenter their attention on Rochester to repeat the process in reverse, zooming inward to examine different areas of the city (e.g., Downtown Rochester, Browncroft, South Wedge, and others) or substantial suburbs (e.g., Greece, Irondequoit, and Henrietta).

This activity functions on two levels: (1) to deliver content (i.e., describing the most salient features of Rochester and its surrounding areas) and (2) to provide a metacommentary about Wikipedia authorship, NPOV tone, and what/how much information belongs in each section. It is also an effective means of identifying different types of information and how they are conveyed—for instance, specific moments where the authors make meaningful generalizations; how the authors couch some of their descriptions with qualifiers such as "most," "many," or "few"; and how data, charts, graphs, images, and so forth are deployed to support statements in the narrative.

Additionally, it opens the door to frank discussion about Wikipedia as a source of information, including the site's claim to being a "free encyclopedia that anyone can edit." In reality, a core group of Wikipedians (the title given to Wikipedia editors) are predominantly middle-aged white men located in the Anglosphere, meaning the site is curated less from an objectively "neutral point of view" and much more by a highly specific subsegment of the global population. This has led to a number of controversies about contentious historical figures and events, but speaking openly about this issue provides yet another avenue to understand knowledge as socially formulated and continuously supplemented, rethought, revised, reworded, and reconsidered by new generations of human interpreters.

A deep dive into the workings of Wikipedia could make for an informative and impactful class in its own right, but for most projects, a simple discussion of the site's affordances and limitations is sufficient to ground student thinking. We call this "going meta" on worldbuilding, a valuable component of critical thinking and a core feature of anchored instruction (see chapter 3, "Theory to Practice").

ORGANIZING ENTRIES

Even a small worldbuilding project can give rise to several dozen entries of many types, while larger and longer projects can produce several hundred. For example, a typical worldbuilding catalog assignment might ask a class of thirty-two students to create a sampling of 5 entries per person (totaling 160 entries). Because learners work at different paces and have very particular areas of interest, the instructor needs a clearly articulated plan to prevent entries from becoming messy or duplicative (e.g., multiple entries for the same topic, missing content, too many of one type [people] and not enough of another [things]). Consequently, it is in the instructor's (and learners') best interest to develop a forward-looking blueprint before kicking off entry creation to prevent major headaches further down the road.

The instructor should have a general idea of how many catalog entries will bring the worldbuilding project to critical mass. For short worldbuilding projects with a very tight scope (e.g., the "world" of the Love Canal environmental disaster), the catalog may have just a few dozen entries covering key people, places, things, events, and groups. For much larger projects (e.g., the "world" of the Vietnam War), the number may run into the hundreds.

We suggest that entries be no fewer than three hundred words and no more than a few thousand words. Entries with fewer than three hundred words often feel incomplete or irrelevant, while those exceeding two or three thousand words tend to lose their sense of purpose, veer into tangents, and become redundant with other entries. Additionally, these limits allow learners to complete their initial drafts in a single sitting while making evaluation (and providing feedback) a much easier task for the instructor.

Take a moment to contemplate which topics you would like learners to focus on and the number of entries you expect them to compose—for instance, each learner must create three entries that describe a person, place, and thing, or everyone must create five entries featuring at least two people, one place, and one thing (in a category of their choice). Asking learners to collaborate on their entries can be quite effective so long as the total number of entries remains the same (e.g., if you plan for each learner to write five entries by themselves, you can offer the option for them to collaborate with two peers on a total of fifteen entries). Regardless of which strategy you choose, be sure that every learner has the opportunity to work across different categories and not, say, write five entries solely focused on locations.

The rest of this chapter will highlight best practices for managing the catalog portion of the worldbuilding project. It should come as no surprise that entry construction seldom works out as intended: Some learners complete fewer entries than required, while some complete extras; some learners interpret the instructions in unforeseen (and incorrect) ways, while others do precisely as directed. Like so much of worldbuilding, collaboratively sifting and reorganizing information is the primary goal, and it is perfectly acceptable to end the process with something less than an immaculate result—we care much more about learners refining their research and writing skills than their ability to regurgitate rote information.

WIKI MANAGEMENT

For much of the last two centuries, university students have been expected to attend lectures, jot down notes, and demonstrate mastery of content and skills through independently written essays, multiple-choice tests, and final examinations (e.g., comprehensive questioning and/or term papers). Aside from out-of-class study groups, authorship was an exclusively individual endeavor, and in-class discussion was strictly forbidden at exam time.

The act of worldbuilding could not be more different—it is a collaborative process that assumes knowledge must be coconstructed for learners to connect disparate ideas into a broader, deeper, and richer understanding. With free digital tools at our disposal, different threads of knowledge can be bound together via hyperlinks between wiki entries, multimedia objects, and interactive stories that allow users to traverse information in a personalized and nonlinear way. These road signs guide users along a suggested route while affording them a chance to explore topics that interest them or are centrally relevant to their long-term learning goals.

Hyperlinks: Internal, External, Sources, and Citations

It is not uncommon for internet users to fall down a Wikipedia rabbit hole by searching for something like the history of voting rights in Argentina and—just a few dozen clicks later—engrossing themselves in an article about Lydia Litvyak, the most successful Russian woman fighter pilot in World War II. This is possible because Wikipedia hosts nearly sixty million entries across every imaginable subject, all of which are interconnected with other articles through a complex network of hyperlinks. Worldbuilding projects are far smaller in scope and scale (i.e., between a few dozen and one hundred articles), but learners can create similar webs of information to organize and make accessible their research into a given domain of interest.

If our learners were to do this for colonial Boston during the American Revolution, an entry for Samuel Adams might mention (and link to) fellow revolutionaries John Adams and John Hancock (People); Faneuil Hall and the Boston Custom House (Places); the *Boston Gazette* and tea (Things); the Stamp Act of 1765 and the Boston Massacre (Events); and the Sons of Liberty, Revolutionaries, and Loyalists (Groups). Each article can and should lead to as many others as possible, though hyperlinks should be used only in the first instance (to prevent the text from becoming a stream of redundant interactables).

Additionally, learners can add outbound links to external sites for subjects that go beyond the scope of the given worldbuilding project. If our sample American Revolution project focused on changing social forces and the deteriorating relationship between the Thirteen Colonies and Great Britain rather than details of the conflict itself, it might be useful to create an Event article entitled "Battles and Turning Points in the Revolutionary War" that provided a chronological list of links to Wikipedia entries for the Boston Massacre, the Battle of Lexington and Concord, Washington's crossing of the Delaware River, and other military engagements. Alternatively, our learners could embed citations to resources such as the Library of Congress, USHistory.org, or the National Park Service. Different style options can help to differentiate internal and external links, so those directed within the worldbuilding project might appear blue, while links to external sources appear green.

Most Wikipedia articles feature a References section that lists support resources. This is one way the instructor can ensure students are drawing from different course texts and not plagiarizing Wikipedia or other online encyclopedias. Requiring links to primary sources also provides insight into learners' interpretation of primary and secondary texts, inferences about the subject matter (rightly or wrongly), and misinterpretations, oversimplifications, or overgeneralizations.

Branching and Nesting

As the project progresses, some articles may grow to be several thousand words, while others remain much shorter (i.e., fewer than one hundred words; "stubs"). We suggest keeping them as focused and concise as possible (within a range of three hundred to three thousand words) to optimize efficiency for both learners and the instructor. If an article becomes too long and unwieldy, its authors can branch it into one or more different, shorter articles; conversely, if there is difficulty extending an article beyond a few hundred words, you may consider combining (or nesting) related stub articles into one longer article.

Articles often become overly wordy when the authors lack focus and begin inserting ancillary information or duplicate content from other entries. Rather than veering into a tangent or restating preexisting content, Branch links should be used to connect articles. Wikipedia recommends three primary techniques to accomplish this: *main article, further information,* and *see also.* Main article is used when the topic of another article has been quickly summarized for context (directing the user to a separate full entry about the topic at hand). Further information is used when the topic of a particular section continues beyond the scope of the immediate article. See also is used to draw attention to articles that are related to—but somewhat distinct from—the current article.

For example, if we were to write a People article for Samuel Adams that aims to discuss his political activities, we might provide a one- or two-sentence summary concerning the Sons of Liberty along with a link to the main article. From the main Sons of Liberty article, we could include two links for further information, one for the Loyal Nine (a group that preceded the Sons of Liberty), and one for the Improved Order of Red Men (an 1834 group whose members claimed to be descendants of the Sons of Liberty). Finally, we might add a see also link to an article about the Daughters of Liberty, a contemporaneous but unmistakably different group. The distinctions between the three categorizations can be narrow, so it is not terribly important whether an author chooses further information or see also so long as they recognize that the information is better relayed elsewhere.

Nesting is the opposite process, grouping related topics that do not warrant separate and distinct articles. We might, for instance, author one article for Beer, one for Vegetables, and one for New England cuisine, and although we initially thought there would be sufficient information to justify three different entries, each is only between one hundred and two hundred words. We could choose to nest these three in a new article titled "Food and Drink of Colonial Boston" with subsections for each of our original topics. This is also useful if we want to add stray thoughts but do not have enough new content for a standalone article. Instead, we can identify a related article, integrate the additional information, and retitle the page as necessary.

Images and Media

Many Wikipedia articles contain one or more multimedia objects related to the article's content, including photographs, illustrations, or paintings of People, Places, and Things as well as pie charts, histograms, maps, videos, and more. Although Wikipedia, specifically, limits users to freely licensed images (i.e., in the public domain), worldbuilding projects often qualify for educational "fair use" wherein learners can feature copyrighted media so long as they include a citation to the original source. It obviously falls beyond the scope of this book to navigate the labyrinthian minefield of intellectual property law, but we have successfully incorporated such materials into our worldbuilding projects for over a decade without any removal requests (stipulating that all worldbuilders should proceed with appropriate caution and respect for others' intellectual properties).

Contributor Pages
Because worldbuilding projects involve dozens of articles with multiple authors and resources, it can be challenging to determine who created or developed each entry. One way to simplify assessment is to have learners curate an authorship page that summarizes their individual contributions. For example, one learner might make a series of edits to the Social Relations section of the world's metanarrative and substantiate their work via hyperlinks to five articles they solo-authored, two articles they coauthored, and two peer articles they revised for consistency. The instructor can track these values in a spreadsheet and evaluate them with a project rubric, directly comparing the number, type, and quality of articles that different learners volunteered or were assigned to write (see chapter 5, "Assessment"). Not only does this clearly define the workload for each learner, but it facilitates accountability across the larger group.

III WORLD MODELING

11 CONSTRUCTING THE WORLD NARRATIVE

"There is a theory which states that if ever anyone discovers exactly what the Universe is for and why it is here, it will instantly disappear and be replaced by something even more bizarre and inexplicable. There is another theory which states that this has already happened."

—Douglas Adams[1]

Once learners have finished outlining a world's scope and sequence and delved into a range of primary and secondary sources, they can articulate its structural and substructural categories as part of a cohesive world model. This model serves as the foundation for their coauthored metanarrative, a macro-level story describing the world's social forces as if frozen in time.

This chapter will explore how metanarrative construction connects early stages of the worldbuilding process with later ones, including wiki creation, simulation, role-play, and reflection. Such bridging will help your learners more closely associate their own life-worlds with the social forces they interrogate as well as make the real world's metanarrative (as defined by different individuals and groups from different times and places) more comprehensible.

Now, let us board the passenger car to improved empathy and critical thinking with a few brief stops at data collection, analysis, and summarization along the way.

CHARTING COMPLEXITY

Depending on a world's complexity, modeling can be a delicate task that requires thoughtful engagement with both quantitative and qualitative data. Quantitative data, as noted in chapter 8, "Examining Life-Worlds Through Demographics," come in many forms, most notably demographic information concerning the population. Still, other numbers can help us make sense of a world's organization, including miles or kilometers;

elevation; date founded or date destroyed; gross domestic product (GDP); the Gini ratio, which measures income inequality; and the Human Development Index, which indicates average lifespan, education level, and per capita income. Qualitative information similarly comes from all manner of places, such as texts, audio materials, and visual content embedded in primary, secondary, and tertiary sources. Neither is inherently better than the other, and we believe the two must be integrated to create a coherent depiction of the world. In fact, cross-applying them can clarify important details—for instance, narrativizing quantitative information by putting it in its proper context, or quantifying qualitative information by condensing data extracted from interviews, discussions, and focus groups into numbers, charts, and graphs.

Modern urban areas normally provide more and better data, whereas worlds far removed in space and/or time tend to be data limited. Census data from the first half of the twentieth century or earlier may be inaccurate or incomplete, only capturing whatever information *seemed* true to a particular census taker. Or, the census questions themselves may have included biases, voluntary or involuntary omissions of certain kinds of data, and impoverished context. Until quite recently, sexual orientation was very poorly tracked even though there is ample evidence that nonheterosexual people have always existed. Just because the question was not asked does not mean that the total nonheterosexual percentage of the population was lower in the past nor that the number has grown exponentially since 2010. We can also point to the quantification of undocumented immigrants who—because they are undocumented—are understandably reluctant to volunteer information to government officials. Various statistical models enable us to make educated guesses about how many undocumented individuals live in a particular region, but there is no way to definitively test our estimates.

For policymakers, these information gaps fall somewhere between troublesome and intractable—yet they provide an excellent framework for exercising learners' research and critical thinking abilities. Without omniscient insight, they must identify what information they possess, assess its reliability, and decide if it should be included in the model; then, they need to determine (1) what question(s) they seek answers to and (2) how any newly emergent variables should be addressed. They cannot know a priori whether a given solution will stick, so they have to ensure the model remains contingent, flexible, and open to change. It is the instructor's job to guide curation of quantitative and qualitative resources in service of that goal.

QUANTITATIVE APPROACHES TO MODELING WORLDS

On a (2014) episode of *The Colbert Report*, astrophysicist Neil deGrasse Tyson argued, "When different experiments give you the same result, it is no longer subject to your opinion. That's the good thing about science: It's true whether or not you believe in it."[2] This is a great slogan for chemistry and physics. It is not, regrettably, well suited for questions of sociology, culture, and politics.

To contend with such fuzzy-bordered subjects throughout the world modeling process, we suggest the (2018) *Collaborative Worldbuilding for Writers and Gamers* system described in chapter 7, "Structures and Substructures."[3] This system asks learners to assign each of the world's structures and substructures a numeric value from 1 to 5, where lower values indicate the absence or scarcity of some factor in the society, and higher values indicate a factor's importance or prevalence in that society. Selecting a low value for the Rule of Law governance substructure would mean that the society has a weak or absent formal justice system; a low value in the Wealth Distribution economic substructure would mean that little effort is placed on equalizing wealth, thus creating significant wealth disparities. Conversely, a high value in the Gender Relations social substructure would suggest substantial gender equality across the society, and a high value in the Religious Influence cultural substructure would imply that matters of faith are a high priority. Learners can also decide whether a value is stable or trending: A stable value is not experiencing change, a rising value is becoming stronger or more prevalent, and a falling value is becoming less common or scarcer. If a value is changing, learners should be able to explain the rate of change—either the society's attitudes are slowly shifting (e.g., gradual acceptance of a minority group into the majority zeitgeist) or a major event has precipitated rapid distortion (e.g., natural disaster).

This approach is most effective when the group is modeling worlds that are very polarized and/or different from their own. For instance, Octavia Butler's (1993) *The Parable of the Sower* may result in some quibbling about exact values and rates of change, but learners generally agree that the Rule of Law substructure is a 1 and the Wealth Distribution substructure is a 1 or 2.[4] Outside of extremes, though, it is rare for two people to model a world in the same way, which galvanizes discussion about divergent interpretations of various structures and substructures as well as appropriate values to define them. That is where the instructor can intervene to request textual support: "Your model assigns a 3 to Race Relations. What evidence from the text informed your choice? If this is a 3, what would a value of 2 look like?

What about a value of 4 or 5? What concrete details about the world would you need to model it differently?"

The point of this exercise is not to arrive at an objectively "correct" model but to provide an on-ramp for learners to deliberate complex sets of intertwined social forces grounded in the text. We want them to build off of one another's ideas and comments, challenge alternative interpretations, and add nuance or make new connections concerning a society's structures and substructures. Even though the bulk of worldbuilding projects explore fictional worlds portrayed in different types of media—text, television, films, comics, games—it is a two-inch putt to connect the construction of those models to constructing a model of the real, lived-in world.

However, a funny thing happens when we ask students to model reality: High and low values are almost universally abandoned in favor of middling 3s. Even when pushing on hot-button topics of race, gender, and sexual orientation or the relationship between religion, politics, and economics, learners shy away from moving to the poles on the 1-to-5 scale. This is, notably, an anecdotal observation from our experiences in the classroom rather than a rigorously studied phenomenon, but over many years in many different classrooms and disciplines at different universities, there is a distinct willingness to use the numeric system for fictional or historically far-removed worlds such as the Aztec or Roman empires that does not exist for the contemporary United States, Europe, or other regions. Suffice it to say that supplemental, nonquantitative methods may be our best bet to improve the quality of learner-generated models and close the gap between their perception of fictional versus nonfictional complex systems.

QUALITATIVE APPROACHES TO MODELING WORLDS

Like the aforementioned quantitative approach to world modeling, the qualitative approach begins with concrete observations. Learners are assigned a particular substructure—say, technology influence—and the instructor engages in Socratic questioning: "How prevalent is technology in this society? What evidence can you provide to support your analysis? In what ways has its prevalence changed over time? How does technology interact with other substructures?" If the process seems too ill-defined, it can help to open with a Likert scale poll that asks learners to rate the degree to which they agree or disagree with specific statements about the world (e.g., "On a scale from strongly disagree to strongly agree, how would you rate the statement 'There is a clear and transparent Rule of Law applied equally to everyone in the society?'"). Precisely wording these questions and statements is vital because even minor alterations can yield dramatically different respondent feedback, and while we are not aiming for learners to arrive at an agreed-upon, objectively "correct" answer, the instructional framework we present can dramatically influence their definition of various structures and substructures.

Consider the evaluation of policing in New York City: By introducing Rule of Law in terms of the city's robust police presence and federal laws dictating due process, the instructor may immediately bias learners *toward* policing. Contrarily, introducing Rule of Law in terms of institutional racism and classism (i.e., non-white and poor citizens being incarcerated at higher rates than white and middle-to-upper-class citizens) may immediately bias learners *against* it. To the greatest extent possible, we should encourage them to draw their own conclusions based on the available evidence rather than our editorializing, especially as the purpose of worldbuilding is to foster critical thinking and empathy over singularly "right" ways of understanding reality.

There is no reason that learners cannot use a blend of quantitative and qualitative methods to define each of the fourteen substructural categories. What matters is that they tie their ideas and observations to those categories and determine how they are interdependently related. Initial observations will usually evolve as more connections are made, and we want them to understand that it is both good and productive for them to change their minds. Sometimes this means rewording or restating observations in clearer terms; other times, it might require deletion and rewrites. Both are not only acceptable but desirable—we want them to become better coauthors, editors, and problem solvers as they wrestle with the interconnectivity of complex systems.

In practice, we organize learners into small groups and advocate that they share information with and ask questions of one another. There is always a bit of pressure to develop as realistic a model as possible, but the messy, recursive process through which they arrive at a final product is inarguably more important than whatever they create. These discussions expose weak points and false assumptions that can be interrogated by others with different life experiences, which forces learners to work through cognitive dissonance and the discomfort of being "wrong." Of course, while tension and discomfort can create powerful learning moments, the instructor should stay deeply involved to defuse any acrimony or recrimination. We want to cultivate an environment where learners can speak their minds openly and honestly, but the debate should be bounded by mutual respect, good-faith positioning, and reverence for evidence above and beyond individual egos.

DRAFTING THE WORLD METANARRATIVE

After discussing the structure and style of Wikipedia pages, learners can draft an initial world metanarrative, otherwise known as its overarching story. Be as clear as possible that everyone's writing will be reviewed and revised by the entire group—worldbuilding projects are long-term endeavors shaped by many hands, and each hand adds a unique layer of perspective, language, and descriptive information to convey depth and nuance. It is a collaborative process that depends on a wide cross-section of contributors coming together to form a whole greater than its constituent parts (see chapter 5, "Collaboration and Community").

To begin, choose a document-sharing platform and create new blank documents for the world's major structural and substructural categories (starting with the metanarrative lead and following with history, geography, government, economy, demographics, and culture and society). Although you may be tempted to include other top-level categories—infrastructure, healthcare, or transportation—hold off on introducing them until your learners have addressed the topics listed above.

Their metanarrative lead should be a high-level summary that briefly characterizes the details described further down on a wiki page. Its composition demands that learners carefully consider which information is essential for a reader to understand the world, and it emphasizes the point of the present, or the current moment in which the world is set. However, both of these qualities can introduce errors into the drafting process: (1) the inclusion of too many details (such that the metanarrative lead becomes bloated and unhelpful) and (2) the addition of substantially more content about the world's prehistory than the point of the present. It may help to compare the lead with a movie or video game trailer that compresses multiple hours' worth of content into a thirty- or sixty-second overview—strategic truncation to introduce an idea or subject from a 40,000-foot view.

For example, the metanarrative lead for a location tends to follow the same three- to five-paragraph structure found on Wikipedia location pages.

- The first word of the metanarrative lead is the article title, and the first sentence provides a factual statement describing what the entry is—a nation, province, city, neighborhood, and so on. The rest of the first paragraph identifies the location's global positioning, describes its geography, accounts for its population, and presents other relevant information including whether it is a capital, whether it is well-known for a specific reason (e.g., Philadelphia and cheesesteaks), and whether it is known by any other name or nickname (e.g., New York City as the "Big Apple").

- The second paragraph provides a short historical perspective describing the location before human settlement and/or at its founding. Subsequent sentences cover only the most important historical events associated with the location and, with few details, connect the past with the point of the present.
- The third paragraph describes the point of the present with emphasis on qualities that make the location unique or notable. This can include information about the location's economy, some of its demographic data, its specialized industries or organizations, its general reputation, and more.

Many entries continue with fourth and fifth paragraphs that describe aspects of the location's political power, specific challenges or societal problems, and recent high-profile events or changes in condition. The number of paragraphs matters less than the overall length, which should be limited to 1,000 words or fewer—keeping it under 750 words is best for concision and readability. If learners struggle to meet this threshold, remind them that anything they trim from the lead can be moved into one of the article's main categories.

It can be instructive to show students the Wikipedia entry on Rome or some other ancient city with a long and consequential history. Even though Rome and Roman culture have had an enormous influence on Western culture over a few dozen centuries, the city's Wikipedia article has a metanarrative lead of just three paragraphs and fewer than 700 words. The middle paragraph covers twenty-eight centuries in only 275 words, and the first and third paragraphs describe Rome in the twenty-first century, not the Rome of ancient times. The complete entry contains more than 16,000 words and fifteen separate categories, but this wealth of information does not equate to a longer metanarrative lead. You can also compare the succinct metanarrative lead of Los Angeles (three paragraphs, about 400 words) to the longer-winded metanarrative lead for New York City (eight paragraphs, over 1,000 words) and discuss the merits and drawbacks of longer versus shorter summaries.

We suggest drafting your initial metanarrative lead as a whole-class activity so learners can emulate the process while completing the remaining sections in small groups. Remind them of the lead's three-part structure—location and geographical information first, brief history second, and unique aspects third—before asking them to suggest single sentences of general but factual information about the given world. If you like, create a column for each of the three categories and have the learners state which column should contain their statements (rather than deciding for them). Be sure to write their answers on a whiteboard or in a shared document so they are visible to all participants. Regardless of how they are displayed, learners should verbalize their statements in their own words without instructor editorialization so their peers can respond and/or critique. Even if a statement is factually incorrect or uses problematic language, it is vital to give the rest of the class a moment to challenge the idea, articulate it differently, or build from it. It is indeed the instructor's job to guide the students through the brainstorming session, but the discussion should focus on learner-to-learner conversation.

Once the brainstorming subsides, review the list of learner-generated statements. If anything questionable remains, provide constructive feedback via probing questions to see whether the group can or will posit improved framing or vocabulary. As a last resort, explain where you feel the statement falls short and provide a few alternatives. The vast majority of this exercise should entail learners coconstructing knowledge while the instructor guides verification and wordsmithing, never engaging as a didact with a singularly "correct" answer.

Next, organize the learners' statements into a logical sequence according to the standard structure (i.e., first paragraph general information, second paragraph history, third paragraph characteristics) to determine which belong in paragraphs one or two and whether it is necessary to have three, four, or more paragraphs that characterize unique aspects of the location. The final step is to convert these bulleted statements into a coherent narrative. Consider the Wikipedia article for Rio de Janeiro:

- Nickname is Rio
- State capital
- Third most populous state, second most populous city after Sao Paulo
- Name means River of January

These statements could be converted into a narrative such as "Rio de Janeiro, often referred to as Rio, is the capital of a state by the same name. 'Rio de Janeiro' means River of January. It is Brazil's third most populous state and the second most populous city in Brazil after São Paulo."

It may be faster and more efficient to split your learners into groups of four or five so that each group completes one paragraph of the full metanarrative lead. Alternatively, you can split them into small groups that each write their own versions of the full metanarrative lead, and then compare and contrast how different groups chose to communicate the same set of facts—these separate narratives can be combined into a single narrative, allowing learners to select from the clearest and most succinct sentences.

Once the class is satisfied with their metanarrative lead, have them break into groups of no more than five people to develop the entry's main sections: history, geography, government, economy, demographics, and culture and society. Learners can either choose their partners or be randomly assigned; the same is true for the sections, which can be chosen by the groups on a first come, first served basis or via random assignment. There are benefits and drawbacks to both methods: Learners who choose their own groups may work more efficiently if they already know one another's strengths and weaknesses, but this can also introduce behavior management problems (i.e., learners moving off task), lopsided knowledge and proficiency (i.e., friends having similar interests/strengths), or uneven work distribution throughout the project. Dividing learners into random groups is more likely to yield diversified knowledge and skills, but it can also lead certain students to dominate the conversation while others are left out (depending on the group's social dynamics). Similar issues abound for topic selection, where learners may have greater motivation to research a subject they have chosen, but if two or more groups want to work on the same subject, it can lead to resentment and frustration that manifest as lackluster final products (though this can be mitigated by mentioning that there will be many different sections and groupings throughout the project, so nobody should become attached to any one section or grouping). Just know that no single approach is definitively better than the others, and which is optimal will depend on your personal preference as the instructor, the class size, and the group's internal relationships—the setup will be different for particular localities based on their particular needs.

Drafting article sections unfolds much in the same way as drafting the metanarrative lead: Learners create a bulleted list of what they know about their chosen or assigned section category, repeat the process of organizing the bullet points in a logical order, and then cite sources to support their statements. If they are ever unsure about what to write next, they can consult Wikipedia to see what kinds of information those pages usually contain. As a side benefit, reviewing exemplar pages can highlight the need for additional research or supporting evidence as well as demonstrate the many ways in which Wikipedia authors differentially include, exclude, and/or convey information. Completing this work in class affords the free flow of conversation and exchange of ideas, both of which reinforce the notion that knowledge is neither static nor obtained but dynamic and constructed.

The instructor should dedicate themselves to moving between groups, reviewing what has been accomplished, and making suggestions. Learners, by contrast, should commit their brainstorming and bullet points to online documents that the instructor can access as needed. Keep in mind that observation can be deceiving: Very quiet groups may be extremely productive with respect to generating ideas, and highly talkative groups may fail to capture their ideas in writing. You should open each document in a different browser tab and jump from one to the next to track progress as it is being made, ensuring that learner contributions are relevant and appropriate for their section(s) and identifying any obvious gaps that must be addressed. This will give you a chance to assess language use and point out unintended biases, editorializing, or failures to account for both majority and minority perspectives on contentious matters. If your learners need additional structure, set a target word count to keep their eyes on the prize.

When the class session draws to a close, learners should have a bulleted list of statements and drafted summaries for each of their sections. Some groups may have met or exceeded the desired word count, while others might have fallen short. In either case, ask the students to review what they have written and revise as necessary *or* keep writing outside of class until they reach the minimum word count for the section. Also inform them that they will be working on a different section next time, including new writing partners and new learning objectives. As with the first round of groupings, you may opt to allow student self-selection or exercise instructor judgment in assigning groups.

Once class convenes again, have your learners join their new groupmates and review bullet points authored during the previous session. They should be encouraged to revise, reword, and rewrite anything they find to be lacking or problematic. Since the original writers will be in the same room, they can directly ask those writers for clarification about what they meant by certain statements and/or ask the instructor for their opinion. The goal is to begin converting bullet points into sentences and paragraphs and then chunking paragraphs into subsections as necessary. Throughout this process, students will almost always add more new information or alter bullet points to add qualifications, present a wider range of opinions or views, and otherwise round out what has been written. This tends to be slower than brainstorming and generating bullet points, especially when learners are conscientious about editorializing and attempting to maintain a neutral point of view. Again, the instructor can watch the writing happen in real time, insert themselves when necessary, and be on hand to answer questions or encourage productivity.

There exists a full suite of online project management tools and team worksites that allow students to carry on synchronous or asynchronous discussions outside of class (e.g., Discord, Slack, Microsoft Teams). Encourage students to use the commenting features of word processing software to ask questions and leave notes or remarks to keep the conversation going even when they are not face-to-face or working at the same time. Depending on the amount of progress being made, students can either continue to work with the same teammates as they convert bullet points into sections and paragraphs, or the instructor can once again scramble groups as students finish each section.

At this stage, the entire class will have worked on the metanarrative lead, and each student will have contributed to about half of the sections of the metanarrative. The group should review all sections for content and tone, ensuring that no problematic statements, simplistic generalizations, or editorializing remain. The overall organization of the information can also be assessed with specific attention being paid to the division and titling of subsections and whether some information belongs in separate entries. This audit may highlight more specific or niche topics that can be added under the main sections; for example, a specific type of cuisine, cultural practice, or industry that is particularly relevant for the entry.

By now, you should have a collaboratively written statement that describes the world in the project's present moment, including a brief history of where this world came from, the types of people who have lived and currently live in it, and its prominent features as related to its governance, economy, and local culture. This is a high-level view that synthesizes many different aspects of the world to create a broad, value-neutral explanation incorporating both majority and minority perspectives on a variety of topics. Finally, you will be prepared to transition from the general (a metanarrative that captures the "big picture") to the specific (the People, Places, and Things situated within the world's web of social forces).

12 CATALOGING PEOPLE, PLACES, AND THINGS

"To grow interested in any piece of information, we need somewhere to 'put' it, which means some way of connecting it to an issue we already know how to care about."

—Alain de Botton[1]

If organizing a world's structures and composing its metanarrative lead are the metaphorical counterparts to laying a house's foundation and adding its sheetrock, plumbing, and electrical, then creating a world catalog is akin to the interior design process. We can, of course, infer something about the building and its inhabitants based purely on its curbside facade, but entering the front door and wandering around each room is what provides an intimate sense of the house's character and organization. Hence, People, Places, Things, Events, and Groups are the worldbuilding equivalents of handpicked color palettes, furnishings, wallpaper, molding, and drapery—the bits and bobs that make a generic dwelling feel like a customized home.

- People are the human beings who live in or are directly affected by a given world. The combined list of People should approximate the world's demographics and be evenly distributed across categories such as socioeconomic status, gender, sexuality, class, race, religion, age, and (dis)ability.
- Places indicate a world's naturally occurring and/or human-created locations of varying size, layout, and dimension. For example, Lakeview is a Place within the city of Chicago, the baseball stadium Wrigley Field is a Place within Lakeview, and the Nisei Lounge—a Northside bar—is yet a smaller Place near Wrigley Field.
- Things represent a particular world's material culture(s). Although a Thing can be just about any item or artifact, the best entries tend to define a particular place and time as well as express some deep meaning, connection, and/or value within the given world. Pizza, for instance, is

found in many Places, but deep-dish pizza has unique properties that represent the culinary preferences of Chicagoans, specifically.

- Events denote significant historical moments that necessitate explanation beyond the broader metanarrative. Consider the difference between a generic house fire and the Great Chicago Fire of 1871—the former can be characterized as localized and ordinary, but the latter was a uniquely influential moment with an outsized effect on the city's long-term development.
- Groups describe formal and informal institutions or organizations to which People belong. These include political parties, membership clubs, religious communities, and governmental or nongovernmental associations. Like Things, the best entries are deeply connected to the given world and help define that world's socioculture (e.g., "criminal gang" is a general term, but Al Capone's Chicago Outfit is a specific crime syndicate that dramatically influenced the politics of 1920s Chicago).

These categories are meant to cover a broad swath of material, but you may find that the details of your worldbuilding project demand the creation of additional entry types not listed here.

HOW MANY ENTRIES?

As a rule of thumb, we suggest including at least five entries per category to avoid dilution through overspecification. However, the number of entries developed for a worldbuilding project will depend on both the total number of learners and the level of detail desired for each entry. Thirty-five learners each creating one Person, one Place, and one Thing will net over one hundred (low to moderately detailed) entries. Alternatively, if each learner focuses their attention on a single Person, Place, or Thing, the group will net thirty-five (moderately to highly detailed) entries. There are merits and challenges associated with either approach; the key is striking a balance between *breadth* and *depth*.

Favoring breadth emphasizes diversity and/or concentration within a volume of entries—each entry is relatively short (anywhere from a handful of sentences to a few short paragraphs), but you end up with a wide spectrum of content to draw on for thought experiments, simulations, and role-play sessions. For example, tasking thirty-five learners with the creation of five People apiece will yield a whopping 175 entries for a single geographic region. It is improbable, especially with limited time and resources, that learners will be able to write full biographies about so many individuals, but a large cast of characters can provide a more comprehensive picture of a particular world in a particular space and time (i.e., more summaries mean more opportunities for life-world comparisons).

Favoring depth, on the other hand, emphasizes granularity and/or significance—the group will have fewer total entries to compare and contrast, but each entry will yield several hundred (or over one thousand) words of detail about the world. Such strategic targeting ensures that only the most important or influential People, Places, and Things receive attention, and though the world catalog will be a bit thinner, the entries are likelier to be instructionally valuable and meaningfully threaded through the broader project.

Whether you pursue breadth or depth, it will be crucial to articulate your baseline requirements and assessment measures to prevent learners from slacking on their writing, a frequent problem if/when they believe they are providing common sense information or are merely copying and pasting text from an encyclopedia. This can be mitigated by acknowledging that the project is less about conducting original research to unearth hitherto unknown facts than synthesizing a selection of resources into a narrative that directly maps to the project's learning objectives (see chapter 3, "Theory to Practice"). Put another way, each entry's value comes from its relationships to and with other entries, not each entry being a brilliant, standalone composition.

ENTRIES FOR PEOPLE

The act of worldbuilding takes as given that human society is a consequence of human decision-making, including the formation of governmental institutions, economic structures, social relations, and cultural norms (see chapter 7, "Structures and Substructures"). This bears some similarity to other animal populations (see chapter 4, "Community and Collaboration"), but from the earliest moments of recorded history up to the present, we have been in unique control of our shared fate through a blend of ingenuity, social collaboration, and problem-solving. Most distinctly, we possess a combination of personal and community knowledge that transcends time and allows us to embrace or reject the cultures and customs we were born into, thereby shaping the environmental context to suit our moment-to-moment (individual and societal) goals.

Thus, we catalog a world's People not to account for every possible opinion or attitude but rather to consider the interactions between different life-worlds and how particular structures function (or fail to function) according to particular human wants and needs. Prominent factors include gender, race, socioeconomic status, sexual identity, religion and strength of religious convictions, age, familial status, education level, and (dis)ability (see chapter 8, "Examining Life-Worlds Through Demographics"), but it can be helpful to consider a person's specific personality traits (e.g., extroversion or introversion), the degree to which they are open to alternative points of view, and whether they tend to have an optimistic or pessimistic outlook. It is the interface between identity and societal circumstance that grounds an individual's worldview, attitudes, and motivations, and by exploring this interface, we can interpret why different people make different decisions (even if those decisions substantially diverge from what we ourselves might do in a similar situation).

We recommend dividing People entries across two categories: historical figures, or individuals who actually existed, and historically accurate characters, or individuals who never existed but nevertheless reflect a high level of historical accuracy. In many cases, it is beneficial to curate a mix of both historical figures and composite characters to highlight differences in lived experience. For example, it would make sense for learners studying the US Civil War to model major historical figures such as President Abraham Lincoln and opposing army generals Ulysses S. Grant and Robert E. Lee. They could then model lesser-known soldiers based on the historical record and/or use demographic data to generate fictional but plausible character records for soldiers who could have served on either side of the war.

Why create entries for people who never existed? In addition to affording learners an opportunity to practice empathy and critical thinking, it gives the instructor a chance to formatively evaluate core content mastery.

Imagine asking learners to author People entries for two fictional soldiers, an upper-class Protestant white man with English heritage from Vermont and a working-class Irish Catholic immigrant man from Maryland. They would need to explain how and why these men joined the Union Army, how they felt about the politics of the day, and how their respective home states and socioeconomic classes might have contributed to their understanding of the conflict. This would provide creative leeway to underscore how someone from Vermont—a strongly abolitionist state—would view the conflict differently than someone from Maryland—a border state with more substantial ties to the Confederacy. Interrogating these men's individualized wartime experiences would stress how personal identity, social standing, and religion accounted for deviations in lived reality, thereby reinforcing how interactions between one's life-world and environmental context affects the maturation of their perspective and behavior (which could then be transferred to contemporary political, economic, social, and/or cultural conditions).

Catalog entries for People are structured in the same way as a meta-narrative lead, including a summary of the person's background and a list of their notable accomplishments. Following the introduction can be any number of subsections, such as:

- **Early Years:** Describes the person's family life from birth through adolescence. This normally features information about parents and siblings, the location and nature of their home, early education, and other facts that contribute to a reader's understanding of the subject's past.
- **Education:** Outlines formal education beyond elementary or high school, especially if the person graduated from a prestigious institution (though it may be appropriate to note any vocational or practical training).
- **Profession:** Explains the person's career history, usually listing positions and significant achievements in chronological order by year.
- **Works:** Highlights specific, named work products that may or may not relate to the person's profession. This commonly includes books, articles, formulas, processes, and/or artwork listed in chronological order by production year or when the work gained in popularity or made a notable impact.
- **Awards and Accolades:** Recounts major awards or acknowledgments bestowed on the person, including the award name, organization, year of conferral, and whether the award was accompanied by any material benefits.
- **Personal Life:** Chronicles aspects of the person's background apart from their profession and public profile. This includes romantic relationships, marriages, friendships, children, and topics like political activism, health problems, and hobbies.
- **Late Life and Death:** Relates the person's activities in their later years as well as the date and cause of their death.
- **Legacy:** Characterizes the person's enduring impact on the world. Although their legacy may begin before or at the time of death, it is also possible that they were not widely recognized until many years later.

Two additional subsections you may want to consider are a person's personality profile and socioeconomic standing. These attributes can clarify why multiple individuals who share certain tendencies respond differently upon finding themselves in similar situations (i.e., why some people are less or more motivated or able to act under certain conditions).

Constructing the former requires humanistic and holistic thinking that accounts for a person's entire life-world. An inventor may revolutionize an industry through a mix of drive, stubbornness, and force of will, all of which are traits that Western culture tends to valorize. However, these qualities tell us nothing about whether that inventor was kind to their employees, contributed to their family's well-being, or engaged in any philanthropic causes. Were they assertive or soft-spoken? Did they have grand ambitions of fame and fortune, or were they working to right a perceived wrong? Our respect might increase if they succeeded without engaging in morally dubious behavior, acknowledged others who contributed to their rise, and supported friends and family through thick and thin, but our respect may diminish if they used lies and deceit to forge their way, took undue credit for the work of others, or believed their ambitions trumped the needs of family and friends. Crucially, this is not an invitation for students to pass judgment about an individual's "goodness" or "badness"—it is a tool for nuanced interpretation beyond a reductive "hero" and "villain" framing of history.

Detailing socioeconomic standing requires equally humanistic and holistic analysis. The term "socioeconomic standing" can be shorthand for one's wealth and class, but it can also describe a person's education, occupation, and family lineage. To invoke an obvious example, a young man from one of Russia's noble families would have more influence in society than a middle-aged peasant woman. Why and how they choose to conduct themselves is entirely interconnected with their station in life; where our Russian nobleman might face considerable pressure to improve his family's reputation, our middle-aged peasant woman would face little scrutiny beyond serving her family and community. This explodes the false notion that everyone begins at the same starting line—our respective advantages and disadvantages are a consequence of random geographic, familial, and financial factors imposed upon us at birth. Accordingly, becoming the CEO of a Fortune 500 company would be far more impressive for someone who rose out of desperate circumstances than someone who inherited that role from a parent.

A traditionalist might argue that this kind of "political correctness" threatens to smear high-achieving individuals and erode any sense of cultural pride in individual triumphs, but we firmly believe that teaching critical interrogation is a force for good, demythologizing human accomplishment and leading us to carefully reflect on how we (collectively) form expectations and adjudicate outcomes. It also allows for meditation on factors that are difficult to quantify, like whether experiencing a lucky break or being in the right place at the right time made a difference in someone's trajectory. Ideally, learners should be scaffolded toward contextualizing individual lived experiences to understand why and how different lives unfold differently. Did a particular person fit well within the social status quo and make the most of the opportunities available to them, or were they a contrarian who raised objections that wider society did not recognize (or, worse, expressed hostility toward)? Do we respect the sacrifices a person made to change the world around them? How willing would we ourselves be to sacrifice time, energy, money, credibility, and/or relationships without foresight of the long-term consequences?

Such profiling has the added benefit of structuring thought experiments within alternate timelines and/or counterfactual histories. What might have happened if a person made different decisions? What if fate had presented different conditions or opportunities for action? The historical record tells us what decisions people *did* make and what the consequences of their choices were (i.e., matters of fact that can be memorized, regurgitated, and forgotten); more interesting (and instructionally meaningful) is the act of probing scenarios to speculate on multiple branching applications of richly authentic, highly situated knowledge (see chapter 13, "Simulations").

ENTRIES FOR PLACES

Catalog entries for Places can be created for everything from gigantic geographic areas to minutiae on a map.

The "top level" for most worldbuilding projects consists of boundaries drawn to define the given world—for instance, if your project were focused on the world of Chicago, it would not be necessary to create entries for the state of Illinois, the Midwest, the United States, or North America. However, depending on your needs, it may be advantageous to create entries for neighborhoods or other spaces *within* the scope of the world (e.g., Hyde Park, the South Side, River North) to underscore variation and compare different parts of the city.

The "zoom in" and "zoom out" nature of physical space allows for nested information (i.e., where one location encompasses or contains several others). Returning to Chicago, Hyde Park could be one Place location, and the University of Chicago could be a second Place located within Hyde

Park. Swift Hall would be a third entry that specifies a location on the University of Chicago campus, and the coffee shop Grounds of Being would be a fourth entry that further specifies the basement of Swift Hall (on the University of Chicago campus in the Hyde Park neighborhood of the city of Chicago). Because every building, business, and intersection could generate dozens of potential entries, we need to unpack which Places are most relevant to the project and why.

The best entries fulfill multiple overlapping goals:

- Most obviously, they **identify the exact location** where important events unfolded. It is common knowledge that John F. Kennedy, the thirty-fourth president of the United States, was assassinated in Dallas, Texas, in November 1963. Even more precisely, the assassination happened when Lee Harvey Oswald fired from the sixth floor of the Texas School Book Depository on the north side of Dealey Plaza, adjacent to the infamous grassy knoll. Depending on the desired level of detail, this could be a single Place entry for Dealey Plaza containing two nested locations, or it could be broken into three separate entries (i.e., Dealey Plaza, the book depository building, and the grassy knoll).

- High-quality Place entries **create spatial relationships** between locations. For the era of the Crusades, we might spotlight distances between Rome, Byzantium, and regions that would become the so-called Crusader states of Jerusalem, Edessa, Antioch, and Tripoli. We could contrast the overland journey with the route over the Mediterranean Sea to better understand the European monarchs' challenges with long supply lines and the fortification of lands they settled. We could also analyze how geographic differences contributed to the clash of cultures between the Europeans of France and the Holy Roman Empire, Byzantium, and the Islamic kingdoms.

- Place entries should **provide insights into unique aspects** of the local culture(s). The US capital Washington, DC, is known for vital governmental locations—the White House, Capitol Hill, and the Pentagon, to name a few—as well as historic monuments, museums, and world-class universities. A traveler to Mecca, Saudi Arabia, might be engrossed by the abundant holy imagery. Camp Humphreys, an enormous army garrison near Pyeongtaek, South Korea, can be identified by its uniformed inhabitants and their military exercises. Milan, Italy, is known as a fashion center with many designer clothing stores, and the area surrounding the Shanghai Stock Exchange in Shanghai, China, is predictably packed with banks and other financial institutions.

Even with some (loose) constraints, the range of options—from a city to a neighborhood to a baseball stadium to a concession stand to a mouse hole in the back-left wall of that concession stand—is virtually infinite. Learners should thus only create entries for locations that have special significance to the area or provide insight into a particular lived experience. To simplify and clarify the process, ask them to organize their work around each of the four major structural categories (Governance, Economics, Social Relations, and Cultural Influences) at multiple, varying levels.

For example, a class seeking to model present-day Chicago might assign one group to identify a high-level governmental Place, a mid-level economic Place, a specific social Place, and an individual cultural Place. After some preliminary research, the group chooses Daley Plaza, the city's civic center and home to many governmental buildings; the Miracle Mile, a hub for shopping and retail; the former site of the Cabrini-Green Homes, a notorious public housing project known for problems with drugs and crime and predominantly populated by Black citizens from the 1960s into the 2000s; and the Chicago Theatre on State Street, a widely known and respected cultural landmark. They could then be advised to connect their entries to those developed by other groups, each of which should have targeted different Chicago Places at different levels.

It can be quite helpful to mark Place entries on a physical world map as a means of accentuating spatial relationships and determining whether certain types of Places cluster together or spread out. Digital tools, too, are great for indicating specific Places via shapes, colors, and levels of opacity—consider encouraging learners to hyperlink mapped locations to their web-based wiki entries. Although using maps to visualize datasets and trace patterns through time goes well beyond the scope of this book, we endorse the adaptation and incorporation of such practices by those with the time and resources to do so.

ENTRIES FOR THINGS

Think of Things as material objects that can be separated and organized into logical groupings. You are likely surrounded by all manner of them as you read this passage—books, furniture, electronics, tools, food, articles of clothing, and dozens of others. Yet, despite (or because of) their ubiquity, learners often struggle with this entry type and may need assistance parsing the stuff that matters from the stuff that does not.

On the desk in Trent's home office are, at the moment of writing, two pens, a marker, a digital tablet, a mobile phone, a glass of water, a balled-up sweatshirt, a planning calendar, and a box of tissues. They could be described using categorical entries for similar objects (e.g., pens) or, if warranted, individual entries for discrete objects (e.g., Uni-Ball Signo 207, TRU RED 0.7 mm). Then again, they could be assigned to broader categories that include many kinds of objects (e.g., all writing implements; the pencils, markers, and highlighters in the coffee mug pushed to the corner of the desk). How these Things should be organized depends on what they say about the world (i.e., "Are any of these desk objects meaningfully different than those owned by other middle-aged working professionals? If not, why are we describing them?").

Looking dispassionately at what occupies the desk surface, there are a few Things that most middle-aged professionals probably *do not* have. One is an old saffron tin full of polyhedral dice with a deck of cards sitting on top of it. Neither the tin, the dice, nor the cards are especially noteworthy in and of themselves, but in the context of Trent's workspace, they speak to a few personal quirks: The saffron tin comes from one of his many visits to Spain, and he regularly uses the dice and cards to randomize different aspects of assignments for his classes. Owing to their relative uniqueness, these items would do a lot of heavy lifting for any onlooker who wanted to get a sense of Trent's personality and interests as a scholar and an educator.

Thing entries should generally fit this mold. Sure, a vodka martini is a Thing, but it is not uncommon or noteworthy among drinks, so it would tell us little about the world in which it is embedded. A caipirinha—a cocktail made with cachaça, sugar, and lime—is the national cocktail of Brazil and provides intriguing contextual information about the region. Agua de Valencia, an even more niche drink made from the juice of Valencian oranges, cava, vodka, gin, ice, and sugar, is a local favorite in Valencia, Spain. To decide whether an object (or category of objects) should be included, ask yourself if it is definitional or anomalous in some way: Medieval Europe was awash in swords, but there is only one Excalibur, the mythic sword of King Arthur; there are many types of religious texts, but there is only one set of the Dead Sea Scrolls; there are countless paintings, but there is only one Mona Lisa.

An alternate entry point is the intersection of Things with People, Groups, Events, and other Things. If, for instance, the worldbuilding project incorporates one or more Tibetan monasteries and/or monks, it would be sensible to create entries for elements of the material culture that represent Tibetan Buddhism—robes, a standing bell, a prayer wheel, and/or some other object(s). Descriptions of each object could be included in a single catalog entry for Buddhist holy ritual items, or they could be authored as individual entries for an added layer of detail.

No matter the object or its relation to People, Groups, and Events, focus on traits that make it *exceptional*. Relatively common or well-known items should be excluded unless they have a special relationship to the given world at a specific point in time (e.g., oil is abundant enough that it need not to be highlighted in most worlds, but it could warrant an entry if the world is being modeled to examine the environmental damage caused by an oil spill). Likewise, you should avoid rare, bizarre, or odd items that are only notable for being rare, bizarre, or odd. Prepare to do some trimming if learners miss the mark, and ensure that they provide a rationale for every entry they develop. At worst, you may need to facilitate some editing, and at best, they may impress you—what seems like a too-obvious or too-obscure Thing can occasionally reveal extremely clever lateral thinking.

GROUPS, EVENTS, AND OTHER TYPES OF ENTRIES

Depending on your instructional objectives, you may opt to create two additional wiki categories for Groups and Events.

Groups are political parties, organizational affiliations, professional memberships, and/or other designations that a group of People has adopted or had ascribed to them. Like with the other entry types, we could spend a lifetime imagining ways to sort Groups and establish separate or nested entries for each. Therefore, learners should be directed to justify whether and how their entries have relevance to the project topic and highlight differences between People in the world's society. For instance, during the Spanish Civil War, the overarching conflict was defined by the Nationalists on the political right and the Republicans on the political left, but the Republicans were subdivided into dozens of smaller Groups that included socialists, communists, anarchists, unionists, and Basque and Catalan nationalists (all of which could be further subdivided by their discrete ideological flavors). The names of each Republican subdivision are not as important to modeling the Spanish Civil War as their sheer number and the fact that their infighting weakened collective resistance to the fascist Nationalists, reinforcing the notion that the level of detail should parallel the given world's metanarrative scope.

Event entries should likewise track only the *most* noteworthy historical happenings within a world's spatial and temporal borders. For example, the world of the United States' New Deal era would likely be bookended by two major Events: (1) the stock market crash of 1929 and (2) the outbreak of World War II. Each topic could be worthy of its own worldbuilding project, but if we are primarily concerned with the New Deal, an entry about the stock market crash would explain what precipitated the Great Depression, and an entry about the war would explain what ended it. The project timeline could then be filled with any number of smaller-scale Events, such as the creation of the Tennessee Valley Authority in 1933 and the Social Security Act of 1935. This clarifies pre- and postworld conditions, thereby enabling discussion about the size and speed of Governmental, Economic, Social, and/or Cultural change.

Nearly all entries should fit within the five base categories—People, Places, Things, Groups, and Events—though there may be occasions to create additional buckets that synthesize or characterize unusual outliers. Is Punxsutawney Phil, the famous groundhog who predicts the coming of spring, a Person or a Thing? Is the Large Hadron Collider, Earth's largest and most powerful particle accelerator, a Place, a Thing, or both? Answers usually land somewhere between "it depends" and "it doesn't matter," and either attitude may be warranted depending on the world in question. For our New Deal example, we could split each piece of legislation into an independent Event entry, but doing so would only account for the moment a law passed, not how it evolved over time. It would thus be appropriate to create a sixth entry type called Legislation to group information around a specific idea or topic that would otherwise be subsumed into another category.

Some learners will delight in finding such straddle cases, and they should be encouraged to critically interrogate their classification system(s). The best outcome would be for them to uncover qualitative challenges with meaningful generalization and reconcile those challenges with the chaos and complexity of cataloging a world that lacks defined edges.

YOU'VE GOT A WORLD... NOW WHAT?

By the time learners close out catalog construction, they will have generated dozens (if not hundreds) of People, Places, Things, Groups, and Events to the tune of thousands of words. These articles will be messy and underdeveloped in some regards but overdeveloped in others, so the urge to tinker will be strong, and learners will likely ask to add or edit "just one more entry" (which may become another, and another, and another). We plan for this—even applaud it—so long as proposed changes are relatively minor and unlikely to send shockwaves through the entire project. Sometimes, though, a hard stop is preferable if you want to debrief about the group's work as it exists in a specific moment (rather than as it might have existed under ideal conditions).

If your project is self-contained and meant to conclude after metanarrative lead and wiki development, congratulations—you are now finished! Jump ahead to chapter 15, "Wrap-Up and Critical Reflection." If, however, your wiki is intended to bridge and support further learner interaction, press on through the next two chapters for recommendations concerning simulation and role-play.

13 SIMULATIONS

> "Mental simulation is not as good as actually doing something, but it's the next best thing. And, to circle back to the world of sticky ideas, what we're suggesting is that the right kind of story is, effectively, a simulation."
>
> —Chip and Dan Heath[1]

Simulations have long been employed for educational and job training purposes, particularly in domains that involve dangerous, expensive, or technical tasks—healthcare, the military, aviation, construction, and more. In a broad sense, they imitate realistic situations so that learners can experiment with novel strategies and analyze the consequences of their choices. Police, firefighters, and emergency medical technicians regularly simulate conditions to test their decision-making skills and reaction times; several long-running video game franchises simulate complex governing, economic, social, and/or cultural systems (e.g., *SimCity*, where players manage different aspects of growing a city over dozens or hundreds of years; *Civilization* and *Age of Empires*, where players guide a society's evolution over centuries or millennia); and virtual reality applications simulate a variety of professions, including rollercoaster development, surgery, farming, race car driving, and cooking.

Of course, the degree to which simulations bend or break the rules of physics has implications for transferability, and trade-offs must be made if we want learners to detect the similarities and differences between a simulation and its real-world equivalent. A home computer with a specialized controller can simulate some elements of being a fighter pilot, but professional simulators duplicate the cockpit, provide a 360-degree field of vision, and subject the trainee to g-forces akin to those experienced when flying at top speed. Vehicle simulations similarly allow the user to customize their car and race around a track from the comfort of a desk chair, but that is a far cry from a professional simulator that incorporates acceleration, top speed, maneuverability, and other qualities of real-world driving.

So, do all high-quality, effective simulations depend on pricey, specialized equipment? Not exactly. For conceptual experiences in particular, it is much more important for a simulation to afford realistic experimentation with cause and effect—"Will choosing X or Y yield the desired outcome?"—than to be grounded in any specific technology. How does raising or lowering taxes affect a city's inhabitants? How does choosing violence or diplomacy resolve a dispute with a neighboring civilization? These questions are rooted in malleable, socially constructed systems, and their answers entirely depend on how we as individuals classify, interpret, and react to the *human* perspectives that undergird their function, not any universally applicable physical properties of the universe. Consequently, we should think of simulations not just as technical marvels for training nurses and engineers how to save lives and build spacecraft, respectively, but as tools that allow us to "think like" someone of a different perspective and take a longer view of potential downstream events.

THE SIMS

Following from above, we recommend concept-oriented simulations as a way for learners to set a world in motion and model the trajectories of its systems over time. This provides a snapshot of the world's spatial and temporal boundaries that can be run forward or backward on the timeline to explore what changed and why.

The reason this approach is so exciting is because there are seldom any definitively "correct" answers. How might the Pacific theater of World War II have concluded if the United States did *not* develop the atomic bomb? What if President Truman had chosen *not* to drop two of them on Japan? Experts have weighed in to offer their best guesses (as supported by evidence), but in truth, we cannot know because we cannot run the counterfactual—all that exists is the historical record, which indicates that Japan was unlikely to surrender regardless of the odds and that a great number of Allied soldiers' lives would have been lost while retaking island after island in the Pacific. We contend that the underlying questions matter more than any hypothetical rejoinders; it is the act of engaging and assessing learners' critical thinking abilities via what-ifs that allows us to determine (1) the process by which they draw conclusions and (2) what can be done to shape their critical thinking skills into the future.

In simulations, changes can happen quickly (e.g., living through a natural disaster) or span decades (e.g., achieving social justice reforms). While there are many different ways to run instructionally useful simulations, this chapter will consider three different approaches:

- Examining social, cultural, and environmental changes by moving forward or backward on a timeline based on actual historical events;
- Considering the potential ramifications of speculative Black Swan events or other unforeseen occurrences with far-reaching impacts; and
- Studying specific "wicked problems" that plague modern society, tracking the causes and effects of such problems as well as any attempted solutions.

SIMULATIONS FOR WORLDBUILDING

For worldbuilding projects, simulations are intended to be macro events that see the world change in one or more fundamental ways, rapidly or gradually, over a period of years or longer. That is, they focus on the temporal aspects of change and how worlds develop or regress through time. Sometimes the simulated change can be social, such as the implementation of a policy to redistribute wealth or an act of aggression that results in two nations going to war; other times, change can be the result of natural phenomena, such as earthquakes, volcanic eruptions, or meteorite impacts. Sometimes, it is a combination of both (e.g., raging wildfires, nuclear meltdowns, rising sea levels). Regardless of cause, learners are told that the world they built is undergoing transformation, which positions them to reflect on how the world model could or should respond to new conditions and how those conditions will ripple throughout a society's structures and substructures.

SOCIAL AND ENVIRONMENTAL CHANGES ON A TIMELINE

The further we become removed from a historical event, the more likely we are to "flatten" time, compressing long periods into easier-to-manage chunks that belie how they were actually experienced. For example, growing up in the 1970s and 1980s, American history was framed with Columbus's discovery of the continent, the landing of the Pilgrims at Plymouth Colony, and a jump in time to the establishment of the Thirteen Colonies as they existed at the start of the Revolutionary era; then, we leaped ahead to the Civil War and then to World War I. This narrative arc—from 1492 to 1607 to the 1770s to the 1860s to the 1910s—compressed entire generations into a narrow band of information that streamlined our modern conception of the United States and its national identity (often in factually incorrect and/or obtuse ways; e.g., the fiction that Columbus was the first to discover America, the mythologizing of America's Founding Fathers, the underlying rationale for the US Senate and Electoral College, the core cause of the American Civil War, the reason[s] Reconstruction failed, the tendency to gloss over the Gilded Age). Effective simulations slow down the process and expand (rather than flatten) context so we can better understand specific agents of change and their respective roles in shaping reality.

The Women's Suffrage Movement
One worrying facet of the early twenty-first century is the frequency with which learners underappreciate the long-term commitment of activists seeking social change. Major victories for equality appear retrospectively self-evident, while objections seem like dusty relics of a bygone era, but this outlook diminishes the accomplishments of individuals and groups who fought for decades to achieve their desired outcomes. Much more often than not, the codification of equal rights is an exceedingly long and frustrating battle where relatively few contributors live long enough to witness the fruits of their labor.

Take women's suffrage. The American suffrage movement culminated with the 1920 passage and adoption of a constitutional amendment that prohibited states from denying the right to vote based on a citizen's sex. From the time of the country's founding (1776) to the movement's greatest expansion (Upstate New York during the 1840s) to the ratification of the Nineteenth Amendment (1920), there were nearly 150 years of struggle—five or six generations—before the goal was realized. Contrast that with the amount of time women in the United States have enjoyed this right (i.e., about a century, or less than half of the nation's history). At no point was success guaranteed, and the road to it was pockmarked with disagreements, feuds, setbacks, and incremental gains.

Traditional history courses typically characterize important social movements like this in chronological order, focusing on the life and works of influential figures (e.g., Margaret Fuller, Lucretia Mott, Elizabeth Cady Stanton, Susan B. Anthony), stressing the arguments in favor of and against the central organizing principle, and gradually progressing through different phases of the movement (in the case of women's suffrage, emphasizing how women's rights became intertwined with the cause of abolitionism up to and through the Civil War). Reading materials and discussion tend to focus on a specific subgroup's role in society and highlight different experiences based on class, race, religion, and other demographic factors.

Historical worldbuilding projects, on the other hand, shift attention to a particular world model (or a few coexisting models—e.g., the American Northeast, Southeast, and Midwest) and describe extant Governmental, Economic, Social, and Cultural forces of the time. This reformulates questions like "When did the women's suffrage movement start?" and "Who led the movement?" as "Where, why, and how did the women's suffrage movement expand?" and "What people, events, and circumstances contributed to the movement's eventual success?" Were there specific conditions that made Seneca Lake, New York, a natural hub of suffragette activity? Were certain personalities primed to act in response to the world's structures and substructures? Why and how did race map to different conceptions of voting rights, both in favor of and against the inclusion of Black Americans? Inquiring about broad, interconnected relationships more effectively positions learners to explore the outcome-determinative nature of human-environment interactions while lowering the likelihood that they will view the past as a series of decontextualized points on a number line.

Equipped with one or more world models, we can migrate forward or backward through time to examine whether and how circumstances evolved. What, if anything, changed over this period and why? Where were gains the most dramatic? Where was there little or no progress? Tracking movements spatially and temporally allows us to adapt our conceptualization of the world based on transitional data and see how change occurred differently for different people in different places. Moreover, it introduces opportunities for learners to study how changes in one area affect changes in another. Rather than collapsing into isolated strands, these complex systems become overlapping pieces of a larger puzzle where local structures and substructures multiply the effects of individual or group attitudes and beliefs across society.

The Exxon Valdez Oil Spill

On March 24, 1989, the supertanker Exxon Valdez ran aground just west of Alaska's Prince William Sound and went on to cause one of the worst ecological disasters in world history. Nearly eleven million gallons of crude oil streamed into the water, devastating wildlife habitats and turning the local economy upside down. Unlike the suffrage movement—which unfolded over the course of centuries—this catastrophe transformed a remote corner of the planet literally overnight.

We could initiate a worldbuilding project centered on the Exxon Valdez by asking learners to reconstruct the world of the Kenai Peninsula and Alaska's oil industry as it existed in February or early March 1989, accounting for each of the structures and substructures that defined the area's governance, economics, social relations, and cultural influences. Equipped with a picture of predisaster Alaskan society, the group could advance time in intervals of hours, days, and/or weeks to showcase short-, medium-, and long-term ramifications—first the immediate environmental consequences, then the impact on local human activities, and finally effects on the broader economy and regulatory apparatus. Next, they could analyze the collective human response across multiple timelines and perspectives: politicians at the local, regional, and national levels; oil industry employees, including technicians, communications professionals, and executive management; individuals working in Alaskan tourism; activists; and Indigenous tribes.

Stepping forward again, the group could consider changes that extended beyond the early weeks and months of the disaster when it remained a fixed part of the news cycle:

- What steps were taken to counteract the ecological consequences?
- How long did the response last and why?
- What were the long-term effects on the economy and community?
- What new federal regulations were created postdisaster, and to what degree were they successful?
- What effects did those regulations have on the oil industry?

Learners could further ask whether the answers differ at different points in time, exemplifying how attitudes and viewpoints vary depending on our temporal removal from a traumatic event. For instance,

- What did the region look like in 1994, five years postdisaster?
- What about 1999 and 2009, ten and twenty years postdisaster?
- If we were to build a new model of the Kenai Peninsula and Alaska's oil industry set in the present, how would it compare to the world of 1989?
- How many of the world's changes can be directly attributed to the Exxon Valdez oil spill?

There are no "correct" responses here. Learners must reflect on cause and effect, the efficacy of specific enacted solutions, the difference between managing an ecological disaster versus a public relations one, the impact on lives and communities that do not make the headlines, and outcomes that persist after the media circus has moved to the next crisis. Ideally, they will also connect their individual areas of expertise to the given world—chemical engineering, social work, healthcare, and so on—and engage in collaborative interpretation based on one another's disciplinary lenses.

BLACK SWAN EVENTS

Nassim Nicholas Taleb's (2007) *The Black Swan: The Impact of the Highly Improbable* describes a Black Swan event as being composed of three components: First, [the event] is an outlier, as it lies outside the realm of regular expectations because nothing in the past can convincingly point to its possibility. Second, it carries an extreme "impact." Third, despite its outlier status, human nature makes us concoct explanations for its occurrence after the fact, making it explainable and predictable.[2]

Some common examples include the outbreak of World War I, the 2000 dot-com bubble burst, the 9/11 terrorist attacks on the World Trade Center, the 2008 Great Recession, and the COVID-19 pandemic. In each case, the specific event (1) was unexpected for a majority of observers, (2) inflicted enormous global harm, and (3) seemed in hindsight as though its potentiality should have been glaringly obvious long before it occurred.

Perhaps unsurprisingly, this theory comes from the world of finance, where the primary goal is neither to predict nor prevent the unpredictable but to safeguard financial assets through diversification of investments. The concept of unexpected yet paradigm-shifting events can be usefully applied to many disciplines: economics, yes, but also political science, public policy, and other social sciences, or as thought experiments in the humanities and natural sciences. Whereas our prior examples—the women's suffrage movement and the Exxon Valdez oil spill—ask what happened and how did people respond, Black Swan events work in a more speculative mode, asking what *if* and how *might* people respond?

Analyzing Black Swan events involves a thorough review of actual historical occurrences before speculation about the future (or, potentially, the past). As with the previous section, there are no definitively "correct" answers, but learners should be expected to provide a rationale grounded in precedent. For example, nuclear weaponry has proliferated in the decades since World War II, yet as of this writing, the only such bombs used in warfare have been those dropped on Hiroshima and Nagasaki. Even if a nuclear attack is within the realm of the all too possible, a learner claiming a state would fire nuclear weapons must account for why the simulated situation is so different from other international crises that did *not* result in such an action.

Black Swan events can be violent and political in nature (e.g., the sudden outbreak of war, a carefully orchestrated terrorist attack), but they need not involve military conflict nor politics, per se. The Wall Street stock market crash of 1929 is generally regarded as the worst in the history of the United

States; other major crashes occurred in 1987, the early 2000s, in 2008, and once more during the COVID-19 pandemic. Although we could reasonably debate whether four major crashes in the span of thirty years fits the Black Swan criteria of "unpredictable," we are more interested in whether and how the then-present worlds of these events can be compared across time. For instance, we could examine the regulations proposed and adopted prior to each crash and then contrast long-term outcomes of postcrash legislative "fixes" to evaluate how different aspects of society reacted to the downturns and subsequent recoveries.

We often concentrate on high-level consequences of Black Swan events (e.g., how different branches of government react to sudden, unpredictable change), but it can be valuable to narrow the aperture and study smaller subgroups or individuals—say, drilling down to different socioeconomic classes and/or affected families to understand how a market crash impacts blue-collar laborers, white-collar professionals, and the very wealthy in similar or different ways. Are rural families forced to change their lifestyles more or less than urban ones? How likely are individuals to struggle if they live on the coasts versus inland regions? And, as always, *why* and *to what extent* do differences between different people exist? What do those differences tell us about the society as a whole?

WICKED PROBLEMS

The phrase "wicked problem" refers to any sociocultural issue that (1) involves opaque or confounding information, (2) requires compromise between clients and decision-makers with conflicting values and/or motivations, and (3) has confusing or unknowable ramifications for the broader system. The adjective "wicked" is meant to invoke a sense of mischievousness or evil reflective of how a problem's proposed curative measures often lead to as much collateral damage as the problem itself.[3] Common examples include poverty, crime, the outlawing of certain drugs, socioeconomic and educational inequality, the global proliferation of nuclear weapons, pandemic diseases and their containment, and climate change.

What these varied issues have in common is their persistence across political, economic, and sociocultural systems—history is littered with attempts to alleviate or resolve them, and though there are occasional success stories, the vast majority end in stalemate or outright failure. Fortunately for our purposes, this is precisely what makes them superb fodder for deconstructing complex systems. Given that different societies define problems in different ways and that cultural conditions may vary so greatly that a moderate success in one location might be a spectacular disaster in another, wicked problems position us to review what has and has not worked as well as prospectively contemplate what we might try next.

Consider the long-tailed wicked problem of climate change. Before getting to any potential solution(s), we should establish that "climate change" encompasses many different climate-related issues—weather phenomena like storms and droughts as well as power generation, electricity transmission, human migration, and other non-climate-specific challenges (e.g., housing, engineering, healthcare). Each subcategory comes with locational differences that lead to substantially different consequences for highly industrialized nations like the United States versus developing nations like Ethiopia, Haiti, or Pakistan. The underlying causes, the effects on various populations, the governmental responses, and so on share some similarities but are, overall, quite diverse. Thus, any solution(s) we conceive of cannot and will not be one-size-fits-all.

To properly model causes and responses, we must establish spatial and temporal boundaries that define the world's scope—a 40,000-foot macroscopic view, a hyperlocal microscopic view, or some combination of the two. For this example, we will focus on Pakistan's Balochistan and Sindh districts (impoverished rural areas that are more difficult for relief teams to reach) during the 2020s (a period of record-breaking climate-change-driven flooding and landslides). We can develop a metanarrative lead that describes the worlds of Balochistan and Sindh in terms of their structures and substructures to get a better sense of how they operate on a daily basis; then, we can layer in climate data to consider how this wicked problem intersects with Governance, Economics, Social Relations, and Cultural Influences. Questions might include:

- **Governance**: To what degree is the Pakistani government interested in the problem of climate change, and what proof—in terms of legislative action or lack thereof—addresses this problem? What relationships exist between climate change and local, regional, and/or national politics? What social services aim to alleviate the consequences of climate disaster?
- **Economics**: How much overall wealth exists in the worlds of Balochistan and Sindh? What are the mechanisms for wealth distribution, and how evenly is wealth distributed across society? What are some of the main drivers of agriculture and trade, and how do those drivers relate to the causes and effects of climate change?

- **Social Relations:** When we compare the smaller Balochistan and Sindh populations with the broader Pakistani population, do we see any anomalies where climate disaster disproportionately affects individuals based on their race, gender, sexual orientation, or other characteristics?
- **Cultural Influences:** What relationships exist, if any, between climate change and the Pakistani military, the country's dominant religion (Sunni Islam), citizens' relative access to technology, or regional artistic and cultural endeavors?

Through this process, we gain a clearer understanding of the social forces at play in different areas of Pakistan, thereby staging a more nuanced conversation about climate change and its far-reaching consequences. This sets us up to study the history of climate change and determine whether current conditions have persisted for a long time or certain events—war, famine, economic downturns, migration—have triggered newly emergent challenges. The process can be repeated as desired to examine which facets of governance, economics, social relations, and/or cultural influences have changed over time and created conditions that increase or decrease climate-related harm.

All of the above serve as a foundation for critically examining potential solutions and their relative probability of success or failure given on-the-ground conditions. What efforts have already been made to alleviate climate suffering in Balochistan and Sindh? Which approaches have been successful and which have not? Why? Are there other regions in other nation-states with similar conditions? If so, what have they tried? Would those approaches be more or less likely to work in Balochistan and Sindh?

Our aim is to grapple with the genuine wickedness of the problem. Learners will frequently offer pat solutions without considering why, if the answer is so obvious, it has not already been implemented. For instance, the Pakistani government can just allocate additional resources toward building climate-resilient infrastructure in rural regions, right? It is never that simple—resources are finite, and the money has to come from somewhere. What other programs or initiatives would need to be eliminated for parliament to fund safeguards against climate disaster? How would the population react to paying higher taxes for potential solutions? What degree of confidence do we have that the proposed plans would have the desired impact? Given that Pakistan's per capita carbon footprint is so small relative to larger, wealthier countries, why does it bear these costs in the first place?

We presume that most educators seek to inspire their learners to create positive change in the world, but the aforementioned questions emphasize how incomplete preparation or oversimplification can precipitate naive optimism and jaded cynicism. Young people should be able to recognize sexism, racism, classism, ableism, and corruption, and we should want them to confront those issues on behalf of themselves and others. Yet, to do so, they must also appreciate why wicked problems exist, why resolving them is so difficult, and why we cannot give up when the going gets tough. Hence the benefit of simulation through worldbuilding—to illustrate how, for better or worse, tugging on one thread makes the whole web vibrate and how we, as individuals and a society, can gradually affect the "big picture" without descending into incredulity and hopelessness.

SIMULATIONS IN THE CLASSROOM

The chapter opened with a description of how simulations introduce users to situations that, in most cases, replicate cause and effect processes as they exist in lived reality. Although these tools strive to be realistic, we can and should critically examine any values baked into a given scenario and decide for ourselves whether the outcomes resemble what happens in practice or if the designers allowed certain biases—conscious or unconscious, intentional or unintentional—to affect how their simulations unfold.

We caution instructors to look out for and minimize such biases in their own simulations, where predetermined outcomes can lead learners to singularly "correct" conclusions. As with video games, this will motivate them to learn less about cause and effect and more about how the simulation (or instructor) *wants* them to engage. Such textbook learning hinders creative thinking, and while not all open-ended answers are equally well reasoned, argued, or articulated, it is much more important to focus attention on reasoning, sound argumentation, and articulating one's case using data and facts over gut instinct and emotionally driven decision-making.

To ease the process, consider randomizing elements of what you ask learners to reflect on and do. While running a class about public policy and Black Swan events, you could randomize both the nature of a changing situation and the speed and scale of the problem. Exams and papers could be grounded in scenarios where different learners address different issues—a third of the group assigned to think through a massive economic downturn, another third assigned to analyze consequences of a terrorist attack, and the final third assigned to evaluate a climate catastrophe. Within those thirds, there could be further randomization where effects are immediate and immense or long term and subtle. Only a handful of learners would answer the same question, but all learners would be assessed on criteria dealing with their ability to articulate a chain of plausible causes and effects as well as their aptitude for supporting claims with quantitative and qualitative data.

Alternatively, you could switch from traditional exams and papers to group presentations where learners share their scenarios and outcomes with peers. While the presenters articulate their collaboratively developed ideas and corresponding rationales, learners in the audience could be tasked with evaluating the presenters' claims, asking questions, and providing constructive criticism. This would allow you, the instructor, to assess both presentation quality and active participation among learners in the audience, noting when someone asks a particularly deft question or exposes gaps in reasoning. You could likewise note any lack of participation resulting from ill preparation or engagement with the content.

In sum, simulation-based activities are particularly useful for facilitating depersonalized, systems-based thinking grounded in historical events and/or events that continue to unfold around us. They compel learners to consider what a president or a scientist might do and how those individuals might react to changing circumstances. They further underscore the fact that procedures and contingency plans already exist for all kinds of unexpected challenges as well as the reality that the leaders we depend on in times of crisis often follow predetermined guidelines rooted in historical precedent.

To probe and inhabit even more intimate perspectives (e.g., asking not what *a* politician would do but what *a specific* politician would do), we suggest a subset of up close and personal simulations called role-plays. The next chapter will introduce relevant definitions, best practices, and our thoughts on the risks and benefits of this approach, having learners adopt—and enact—someone else's life-world.

14 ROLE-PLAY

"All the world's a stage,
And all the men and women merely players."

—Jaques, *As You Like It*[1]

What does it mean to role-play?

José Zagal and Sebastian Deterding's (2018) *Role-Playing Game Studies: A Transmedia Approach* spent no fewer than thirty-two pages addressing this question, but even they could not come to a wholly satisfying answer—not for lack of effort, mind you, but because there was no expert consensus as to what does and does not constitute a role-playing game.[2] In addition to evaluating a catalog of different activities that could, in part or in whole, be considered role-playing games (or at least incorporated multiple elements that people commonly associate with role-playing), the duo identified a broad set of commonly recurring qualities that characterize role-playing (generally). Their conclusion was that role-play loosely consists of "play activities and objects revolving around the rule-structured creation and enactment of characters in a fictional world. Players create, enact, and govern the action of character, defining and pursuing their own goals, with great choice in what actions they can attempt."[3]

Fictional worlds like those assessed by Zagal and Deterding need not contain speculative element. Plenty of role-playing scenarios posit plausible situations where players assume the role of historical figures (e.g., *Reacting to the Past*'s [2010] *Patriots, Loyalists, and Revolution in New York City, 1775–1776*, where learners reenact the lives of various Patriots, Loyalists, and Moderates, all of whom lived through the events of the scenario[4]) who are historically accurate (e.g., *Mission US*'s [2010] *For Crown or Colony?*; learners adopt the persona of a fictional fourteen-year-old apprentice [Nat Wheeler] living in Boston in the days before the Revolutionary War[5]) or purely imaginary (e.g., the [2021] commercial role-playing game *Flames of*

Freedom, in which players create custom characters in a fictionalized version of colonial America that features magic, monsters, and the occult[6]). Crucially, the characters are embedded in times, spaces, and events for which we possess a great deal of historical knowledge, creating opportunities for players to control and make decisions on behalf of characters in some version of the "real" world (though the nature of possible decisions and solutions is rooted in the individual worlds described in each game; i.e., there are varying degrees of complexity and realism). That is, we do not need to invent conditions or contexts out of whole cloth—we can draw on actual history.

In so doing, there is an obligation to treat the subject matter with the respect it deserves, particularly in the case of controversial and nuanced topics. Although adding speculative elements to an otherwise historically accurate worldbuilding project does *not* necessarily imply that the project is unserious or disrespectful, care must be taken to avoid distorting history and circumstance to the point of absurdity (e.g., denigrating individuals or populations, perpetuating stereotypes, excusing demonstrably harmful behavior; see the section "A Cautionary Tale").

For example, the 1920 Rochester worldbuilding project described in chapter 9, "Class Preparations," involved learners adding advanced steampunk technology to an otherwise realistic model of the city. Class conversations centered on the types of technologies that different societies tend to develop and how those technologies reshape the societies that produced them. A few ideas fell on the whimsical side (e.g., a network of East Coast dirigible air traffic, a single-pilot submarine used to bootleg liquor from Canada across Lake Ontario), but most were rooted in genuine concerns of the day, including steam-powered prosthetics for soldiers who had lost limbs in World War I and mechanical exoskeletons that allowed construction workers to more easily build skyscrapers (thereby inspiring the Empire State Building's construction a decade later). Learner-generated characters ran the gamut from scientists, inventors, and engineers to mafiosos, speakeasy owners, and captains of industry. Some fought gender discrimination, while some faced anti-immigrant sentiments; some struggled to enforce laws they did not believe in, and others evaded police to smuggle dangerous materials into the city. Despite a handful of fantastical quirks, the project created space for learners to research and interact with a real moment in space and time—making decisions, taking risks, and witnessing the consequences of their choices. The actual plights and perils of 1920s Rochester remained front and center throughout, and learners gained an appreciation for what Rochesterians lived through a century prior (albeit with fewer dirigibles and exoskeletal suits).

Twenty students.
Twenty characters.
Twenty unique experiences.
And history at the heart of their learning.

A CAUTIONARY TALE

Role-play can be powerfully instructive. It has the potential to deliver us in mind and spirit to others' life-worlds, introduce us to foreign cultures and arts, and encourage reflection on our positioning within complex systems. However, as with their obligation to respect the subject matter, instructors must ensure that these experiences do not result in the reinforcement of reductive assumptions, minimization of historical traumas, or inadvertent harm.

To be blunt, not all content is suitable for role-playing. Scenarios that involve the Atlantic slave trade, the horrors of the Holocaust, or similarly harrowing themes should be off-limits; they can easily traumatize participating learners, not least of all those whose ancestors lived through such events. We are not saying that game-based learning is never effective in this arena—some games can be powerful tools for tackling difficult concepts (e.g., Brenda Romero's [2008] *The New World* and award-winning [2009] *Train* contend with the Middle Passage and Holocaust, respectively[7,8])—but risks are heightened whenever players are directed to assume individual identities. For instance, a role-play scenario centered on chattel slavery would position learners as assailants and victims, thereby creating an uncomfortable power dynamic, weaponizing trauma for the sake of gameplay, and failing as an instructional simulation (especially given the distance from classroom reenactment and real-world application, begging the question "What *is* the real-world application of this activity?"). As history professor Hasan Kwame Jeffries highlighted in a (2019) interview with Cult of Pedagogy's Jennifer Gonzalez, "You can't really simulate what it would feel like to be dehumanized on an auction block and separated from your parents. What you would need to do to actually re-create these scenarios would put you in jail."[9]

On role-swapping race or ethnicity, specifically, he argued, "Essentially you would be telling these other children, okay, you're going to be the Black people for today, right? That doesn't really help, because they can just walk in it, and then they walk out of it. And then how do they carry that into the playground? It's like, okay, I had my Black experience, and that is about being sold. In other words, even pretending that we're going to do something that is race-neutral around a subject that is not race-neutral doesn't really help the scenario either."[10]

Nevertheless, even in this emotionally charged example, Jeffries acknowledged the potential value of abstracted, depersonalized playful reflection: "You don't say, hey, what would you do if you were this person? You say, what did this person do? And what were some of their options?"[11] This halfway approach encourages learners to inhabit the headspace of another person (i.e., their life-world) without assuming responsibility for anyone's actions—the learner and subject remain distinct and at a distance, while the learner embodies the subject only inasmuch as is necessary to deconstruct the subject's behavioral rationalization (no emulation required).

But there remains a separate challenge concerning the tendency of learners to revert to essentialisms and stereotypes (see chapter 8, "Examining Life-Worlds Through Demographics"). They may, for example, assume that a young Black man living in an economically depressed city is involved in the drug trade or a gang, or they may assume that an Indigenous woman has some inherent mystical connection with the natural world. There are reasons these stereotypes persist (e.g., the relationship between institutional racism and poverty, some cultures' long-recognized and celebrated approaches to human-earth interaction), and instructors should aspire to dispel the notion that any one trait or quality of a group is biologically engrained (i.e., essentialism) or so prevalent that alternatives seem improbable (i.e., stereotyping).

Generally speaking, we can avoid these problems by applying Benjamin Franklin's (1735) adage that "an ounce of prevention is worth a pound of cure."[12] Essentialism and stereotyping should be thoroughly discussed during the worldbuilding portion of the project to tune learners' perceptions of how context shapes individuals' attitudes, beliefs, and actions. Equally important is the instructor's revisiting of these concepts before any role-play scenario begins, including the explicit direction that learners must provide evidence-based reasons for their portrayal of any given character. Leave exaggerated accents and assumptions about race or ethnicity outside of the classroom—instead, emphasize how environmental pressure and complex systems (not genes) lead to the development of traits and skills.

Keep in mind that precautions are not foolproof, and learners are apt to make mistakes (more through inexperience than malice). The only instructionally responsible thing we can do is remind learners that very little in life is cut and dry, and both positive and negative stereotypes oversimplify how and why people make the choices they do. A student who cares passionately about climate change might view the CEO of a company whose products increase carbon pollution as irredeemably evil, but moral judgments like "goodness" or "badness" are not the same as the thoughtful interrogation of incentive structures that drive behavior (i.e., is the CEO categorically "evil," or do the incentives to grow their company, expand job offerings, and compete in a crowded business environment outweigh the prioritization of climate sensitivity?). Thus, during a role-play scenario, the CEO may refuse to change, but we can insist that our learner portray the character as fearful of failure or conflicted about their choices over and above a cackling, one-dimensional villain who enjoys polluting.

This is where well-designed role-playing scenarios can become some of the most potently transformative learning experiences a student will ever have. Continuing with our hypothetical environmentalist from above, they may revel in righteous indignation at the harm being caused by a massive corporation, but their inability to see the problem from the opposition's perspective implies a lack of vision toward generating meaningful real-world change. Worldbuilding and role-play lead us to get inside the head of someone with different values and test our preconceived judgments against a competing point of view. If, for instance, the CEO's motivations are rooted in profitability, protesting that person's moral turpitude is unlikely to change their behavior; however, jeopardizing the company's profits—through a media campaign to decrease product sales or lobbying for legislation that would make polluting more expensive than a climate-friendly business model—is far likelier to make a difference. In short, this kind of scenario provokes learners to empathize and critically think their way through an issue to arrive at more plausible, practical, and actionable solutions, honing the skills needed to wrestle with the challenges they face in their lived reality.

Lest we belabor the subject too much, we close this section by repeating that forethought and peer consultation (i.e., discussing your plans with colleagues) are the keys to guaranteeing that your learners will have a successful role-playing experience. The following bullet points come from Ingrid Drake's (2008) list of best practices for role-play and should be used as an instructional preparation checklist:

- Before facilitation, clearly identify the learning objectives.
- Avoid simulations that can trigger emotional traumas.
- Allow students to opt out.

- If applicable, notify parents in advance (especially with younger students).
- Do *NOT* group students according to characteristics that represent real-life oppression (e.g., race, gender, socioeconomic status).
- Strive for a diverse facilitation team.
- Schedule ample time for debriefing, including journal writing for students who are uncomfortable discussing their experiences aloud.
- During debriefing, avoid telling students what happened—instead, ask open-ended questions (e.g., "What happened in today's simulation?" or "What were your takeaways from today's session?").
- Remind students to disengage from the role-play at the activity's conclusion.
- Connect to real-life experiences and ways to apply what has been learned (i.e., facilitate transfer).[13]

Working through this list and sharing your role-play scenario(s) with a diverse group of fellow instructors will help you identify oversights and possible unintended ramifications. Often, reframing the way you think about your setup and implementation is sufficient to nail down an optimally productive, positive, and reflective process that will keep your learners from falling into essentialisms, stereotypes, and half-baked conclusions.

ROLE-PLAYING PERSPECTIVES

For the purposes of worldbuilding-based role-play, we borrow terminology from the field of fiction writing to describe narrative distance and point of view. At the most removed is third-person distant, which asks participants to adopt an omniscient, god-like perspective that considers multiple characters' life-worlds and describes how their thoughts and/or feelings might influence their choices. By contrast, third-person limited—also called close third person—has participants consider the perspective of just one character and decide what kinds of decisions that character would make when presented with a specific situation (or set of situations). Both approaches involve participants using third-person pronouns (e.g., he, she, they) when describing character thoughts, feelings, and actions to maintain distance between the participants and the character(s).

First-person scenarios are those in which participants adopt the identity of individual characters and portray those characters' thoughts, feelings, and actions using personal pronouns (e.g., I, me, my). Rather than asking about hypothetical situations, participant-controlled characters are typically embedded in a specific context (i.e., environmental setting and set of conditions) where their choices have consequences and generate new situations that unspool into additional choice-making. If the player characters have quantified skills and abilities (e.g., Strength, Intelligence, Perception, Dexterity, Insight), dice rolls can add an aleatory element to determining whether player actions succeed or fail (see the section "Successes and Failures"). For example, a player character who wishes to bluff their way past a pair of guards and access a closed-door meeting might need to roll a specific die value that exceeds some manipulation or persuasion statistic. The act of speaking like a character (i.e., the colloquial meaning of "role-play") can be incorporated in several ways depending on the intended amount of distance between a participant and their character.

Below are three potential implementation strategies that can be modified by the instructor and/or community of learners to fit the need:

- **Third-Person Distant:** Task learners with creating a random encounter; as individuals or groups, learners generate two or more wiki entries per category (i.e., "People," "Place," "Thing") and provide a rationale for how these entries might come into contact with a character and/or how different characters might feel about it.
- **Third-Person Limited:** Task learners with engaging in "role-play lite"; learners assume the headspace of one "People" entry and explain how that character would contend with a given situation, problem, obstacle, or opportunity (i.e., how the character understands the situation and what their most and/or least likely courses of action might be).
- **First-Person Live Action:** Task learners with engaging in "live role-play"; each learner assumes the role of one "People" entry and acts in character, answering questions and making snap decisions based on different scenarios presented by the instructor. This can include two or more students interacting in their roles (e.g., responding to one other in a given scenario), short scenes where one or more players work toward achieving some objective (supplied by the instructor or emergent from player interactions), or both.

A fourth possibility could include offering learners the opportunity to choose a preferred perspective distance and engage in different tasks based on which perspective they select (e.g., allowing learners to opt out of spontaneous playacting if they suffer from social anxiety during public performance). As a general rule, the shorter the distance between the participant and the character, the more the participant will *feel* the effects of the character's actions, successes, and failures. This can be remarkably useful in cases where the activity is intended to build empathy for others; conversely, it is potentially detrimental in cases where the activity is likely to surface historical trauma.

THE WORLDS OF *EL CID*

To further demonstrate how role-play can manifest in a teaching and learning environment, we offer the following worked example. Read the project description and trace its application to each of the three role-playing perspectives in their respective sections below.

Imagine a group of thirty learners that spent weeks modeling the world of eleventh-century medieval Spain based on the epic poem *El Cid*, in which the Muslim kingdoms of Al-Andalus waned in power, the northern Christian kingdoms grew in strength, and the Reconquista (to push Muslims out of the Iberian Peninsula) gained momentum. They modeled the specific worlds of León-Castile and Aragon-Navarre (i.e., Christian kingdoms) as well as the worlds of Zaragoza and the Almoravid Empire (i.e., Muslim kingdoms). They learned about the values of Christian, Muslim, and Jewish cultures; the differing levels of religious tolerance in each culture and kingdom; and how some Christian kingdoms had better relations with Muslim kingdoms than other Christian kingdoms (especially as pertained to economic structures). They also learned about the social hierarchies and class divisions of these cultures, and they researched how race, gender, and sexuality were understood by the people of this era. The project's "present" is set in 1080 CE, just before El Cid's exile (which occurred for political reasons and on trumped-up charges).

The thirty learners created two People wiki entries apiece, totaling sixty characters. They were provided criteria for generating historically accurate figures that would include a diverse range of Christians, Muslims, and Jews; men and women; young, middle-aged, and older people; the poor, peasantry, middle class, clergy, and nobility; and so on. Additionally, they were given leeway to develop character personalities, skills, attributes, values, and attitudes on religion, government, and other factors. Their wiki incorporated several locations (e.g., regions within each kingdom, specific points on the map [palaces, throne rooms, holy places, agricultural sites, battlefields, etc.]), and the role-play scenarios centered on teaching proficiency with perspective-based interpretation under variable conditions.

Third-Person Distant

A university instructor states that the course midterm will require students to write short essays from the perspectives of two different characters evaluating a major current event in their world. On the day of the exam, each student receives the names of two characters randomly drawn from the catalog (with care being taken to ensure that one student did not get two very similar perspectives). After a brief grace period, the students are assigned (by last name or student choice) to describe what their characters would think about one of the following scenarios:

- Last names beginning with A–G: Rodrigo Diaz, one of the king's most successful champions, has been exiled on charges of treason. His military prowess has been key for the Christian kingdom of Leon and Castille, and he will be a great loss for the military. However, treason is a serious charge that usually results in death rather than banishment.
- Last names beginning with H–P: Heightened tensions between Leon-Castille and Zaragoza lead the two kingdoms to sever economic ties—perhaps for a short time, perhaps forever. Leon-Castille benefited from spices and other goods sourced from Muslim merchants, and Zaragoza used those funds to pay for military upkeep.
- Last names beginning with Q–Z: The kingdom of Leon-Castille has increased taxation on Zaragoza to keep them from raiding Muslim lands. A few vocal members of the sultan's court in Zaragoza are demanding that he refuse to pay and instead launch an armed conflict with the Christians (though their armies are rumored to be evenly matched).

In the first part of the essay, the students must provide a short explanation of the relations between the two kingdoms and how that history contributed to the current scenario. The second portion should feature an explanation of how different segments of society would plausibly react to the situation. Finally, in the third part of the essay, students need to make a case for how their two random characters would respond based on their respective positions in society. It is unlikely, for instance, that a peasant would know about the intrigues of royal courts, whereas an aristocrat would be privy to rumors and confidential information; a young soldier may look forward to conflict as a way to raise their social standing, while a mother might fear for the lives of her husband and sons; a zealot could celebrate a bloody religious conflict, but a profit-minded merchant would prefer peace to maintain the flow of trade.

Students ought to balance the more objective aspects of these societies with their more subjective opinions about how different people would react to the changing conditions. Because each student has two different characters and a different scenario, no two essays will be identical, and there are no "right" or "wrong" answers. The instructor must assess how well the student can articulate the state of the world in the given moment, think through the broad social implications, and ground their response via two different viewpoints. This is no different than other types of exams where students choose from multiple prompts; the responses are adjudicated according to their internal logic and the quality of supporting arguments and/or evidence. However, this approach encourages (if not requires) students to more carefully consider the context and respond with greater creativity than in a typical five-paragraph essay.

Beyond essay writing, a third-person distant perspective can be employed if some (or all) characters are on a trajectory toward an unpleasant fate. This is more or less how the US Holocaust Memorial Museum in Washington, DC, organizes its exhibits: At the start of the museum narrative, visitors are invited to take an identification booklet that recounts the life of someone who directly experienced the terrors of the Holocaust. Each page chronicles their relationship with content embedded in surrounding museum resources, and the final page reveals whether that person survived or perished. Macabre though it may sound, this contextualizes an abstract figure by grounding it in a singular life-world: Out of eleven million people murdered during the Holocaust, this is just *one* person, and this is *their* story. Much of the museum's emotional weight derives from that fact, and despite differences in age, sex, profession, economic class, and other attributes, there is a chilling consistency between the victims—the vast majority had no means of escape. In the present, where so much emphasis is placed on personal responsibility, a third-person limited perspective can highlight how innocent people become swept up in world-changing events with little or no agency, hence why we recommend this approach for the study of other traumatic events, such as the military deployment at the beaches of Normandy during D-Day, the 2004 Indian Ocean earthquake and tsunami, Hurricane Katrina, the COVID-19 pandemic, and the wars in Ukraine and Gaza.

Third-Person Limited
In a third-person limited role-play, each student assumes the identity of an individual character. While those engaged in third-person distant activities must think about the (potentially opposing) viewpoints of two different people at a single hypothetical moment in time, third-person limited role-play can put time in motion by having characters make multiple decisions based on an unfolding series of events (informed, if not dictated, by

the character's previous choices). Such scenarios can take multiple forms, including:

- Multiple students assume the role of the same character facing a given problem or choice. Then, students compare opinions and rationales for what decisions they believe the character would make.
- Students work in small groups, with each student adopting the role of a different character. They control only their respective character and may be privy to information that other students/characters do not know.
- Similar to a third-person distant exercise, students are divided into pairs, and each person takes a different perspective. The dyad discusses how their respective characters would think and act in a given situation.

What differentiates third-person limited from a first-person perspective is that the role-player remains one step removed from their character—that is, they participate as over-the-shoulder witnesses to the action and use third-person pronouns (i.e., he, she, they) rather than first-person pronouns (i.e., I, me, my). This additional distance makes complicated or emotionally charged scenarios more manageable by allowing for reflection on a character's thoughts and motivations without forcing students/players to assume those beliefs for themselves. For instance, third-person distant would be preferable to first-person if a student were asked to interrogate the mindset of a plantation owner in early nineteenth-century America, considering how the Kansas–Nebraska Act would impact the westward expansion of slavery.

It should go without saying that students can understand the immorality of slavery without being asked to condone or sympathize with an enslaver's views; however, because the issue of slavery was the root cause of the Civil War, they should be able to conceive of how a plantation owner viewed the world (i.e., someone who considered the enslaved not as human but as property and thus outside a system of morality). A third-person role-play scenario could stretch from the Kansas–Nebraska Act of 1854 to the 1857 *Dred Scott v. Sandford* decision and then to the 1860 election of Abraham Lincoln, where students could be directed to reflect on how a particular person (or set of people) would have felt and acted during each point in that chain of events (though it would be important to emphasize that historical hindsight must be set aside; e.g., a plantation owner in 1851 could not have known that the South would start—and lose—a Civil War just ten years later).

The same can be said for individuals who have previously supported and promoted (and/or still do) fascist or totalitarian regimes. When polled as to whether they would have supported Hitler, Mussolini, or Stalin during the 1930s, respondents in the present claim near-universal denial. Yet, there were clearly millions of supporters at that time, and there is clearly support for their contemporary equivalents. Understanding how so many people could endorse (or at least passively allow) tragic crimes against humanity is a painful lesson to both teach and learn, but it is wholly necessary to deter future threats (and is much more effective than assuming the moral superiority of "we know better"). Third-person limited activities are perfectly structured to facilitate this type of thinking, encouraging learners to shelve their personal worldviews and see—through the eyes of another—how someone (or an entire population) can end up on the wrong side of history. Such exercises are particularly effective when followed with questions that connect the past, present, and future (e.g., "What do we see in today's news that, fifty years from now, may be viewed as confounding and unconscionable?" or "What widely held positions in the present may age well or poorly given what we know about the past?").

First-Person Live-Action

More than other types of role-play, first-person live-action thrusts students into alternative perspectives. These activities work best when students are directed to create historically accurate characters from scratch, building affinity for their creations as they choose background experiences, personalities, skills, motivations, and other qualities. In addition to being entertaining and engaging, the process makes it easier for them to assume the mindset of someone from the relevant space and time (e.g., a medieval peasant) than imagining what a specific historical figure (e.g., Charlemagne) must have thought or believed—the latter requires a substantial amount of research about the figure's personality, disposition, politics, and personal life, making it much more challenging and less rewarding for the learner.

Regardless of which kind of character a student chooses, their role-play will rely on the use of first-person pronouns (e.g., I, me, my) and an embodiment of their character within the given world. This is accomplished through a mix of quantitative and qualitative descriptors similar to those detailed in chapter 12, "Cataloging People, Places, and Things." In general, we ask students to provide something we refer to as "driver's license and tax information," or the kinds of data commonly recorded on official forms (e.g., birth name, sex, height, weight, race, class, hair and eye color). These aspects of a student's character can be chosen by the student, assigned by the instructor, or randomly generated—different projects are regularly built around different strategies, but in all cases, the characters should resemble the demographics of the world being modeled. It is perfectly acceptable for students to work with sexes, races, religions, and socioeconomic classes different from their own, though we do suggest that when they are role-playing characters of a different sex, race, gender, economic class, and so on, the instructor should be on guard to ensure no one trips backward into stereotypical representation.

Perhaps surprisingly, a character's age is often the most consequential choice a student will make during the creation process. This simple figure represents much more than just an abstract number—it implies a series of life-world-shaping experiences and dictates which events fall within the world's *living memory*. A character who turned eighty years old in 2020 would have been born in 1940, and though they might be seen as just another person in the current moment, their knowledge extends eight decades into the past. It is the foundation of their being as well as a historical record of the communities in which they lived.

Suppose that the bulk of our fictional eighty-year-old's life was spent in Newark, New Jersey. From that fact alone, we can infer the following:

- Their parents lived through the events of World War II, and their grandparents lived through the events of World War I.
- They would have few (if any) memories of World War II, save perhaps a hazy recollection of V-E Day and V-J Day or the dropping of atomic bombs on Japan.
- They were in their mid-twenties during the 1960s, a decade of significant social upheaval; they would have been attending university, starting a family, or meeting other young adulthood milestones. They would have been twenty-three years old when President John F. Kennedy was assassinated. In 1969, the year of the first moon landing, they would have been twenty-nine years old; that same year, they would have been two hours (by car) from the famous Woodstock festival.
- They would have been fifty-three years old when the internet became widely available to the public. They would have been sixty-one years old during the 9/11 terrorist attacks (in addition to having seen the devastation firsthand).
- They would have been sixty-eight years old when Barack Obama was sworn in as the first Black president of the United States.

These are just a few of the seismic events marked in this character's memory, and their worldview would reflect how they had internalized each moment. If they were committed to the Civil Rights Movement during the

1960s, the inauguration of the first Black president would conceivably carry a great deal of emotional weight after decades of work pursuing equal treatment of minorities. That effect compounds when you consider how their experiences would contrast with people of other ages and from other places—their memory of 9/11 would be substantially different from someone born in 1993 Seattle (i.e., just eight years old and living across the country).

Age is also the limiting factor in a character's goals and achievements. A teenager is unlikely to have as broad a worldview as a well-traveled, middle-aged person. Those who earn advanced degrees tend to be in their thirties, and it often takes additional decades of experience, opportunity, and trial and error before an expert makes a scientific or artistic breakthrough. Charles Darwin and Albert Einstein developed their theories only after completing relevant training and preparation, and both scholars depended on the work of earlier researchers and lesser-known contemporaries to find success. No paradigm-shifting idea is ever born in isolation.

A character's personality is likewise intertwined with their life-world, and their interactions with the world (as well as their responses to significant events) inevitably affect their attitudes and behaviors. We generally ask students to provide a few adjectives that capture their character's most prominent attributes (e.g., developing a short list of words or phrases describing personality traits) and intentionally limit them from selecting more than three. This may seem reductive, but there are two major benefits: (1) it reduces the likelihood that students will get carried away with overspecifying (i.e., burning precious time), and (2) it forces students to focus on quality over quantity (e.g., reflecting on interactions between the character's traits, the environment, and their goals/motivations versus navigating how to role-play a maze of [potentially conflicting] traits). If we were to build out a character model of Martin Luther King Jr., we might say his defining adjectives were "determined," "persuasive," and "righteous." How do we decide whether they are central to our understanding the person? We can test our assumptions by asking thoughtful questions about how they have responded to the world around them: Would Martin Luther King Jr. have risen to national attention and cemented his place in Civil Rights history if he had not been determined to see through opposition? If he was not persuasive enough to convince people of his views? If he was not righteous in his belief that minorities deserved equal rights? If we were to erase any one of those qualities, he might not be remembered by history in quite the same way.

When synthesizing "driver's license and tax information," demographics, age, and personality traits into a comprehensive character biography, the finished product should run from the character's birth up through the world's present. If your worldbuilding project aims to be historically accurate, take care that students do not confuse the directionality of cause and effect or causation and correlation. For instance, when Martin Luther King Jr. delivered his "I Have a Dream" speech in 1963, he did so without knowing that the Civil Rights Act would be signed in 1964. According to a (1969) newspaper article citing his wife Coretta Scott King, MLK Jr. harbored the belief that he, like President Kennedy, would be assassinated, though he obviously could not have known his death would come in 1968.[14] To us, historical events can seem as though they were part of an inevitable trajectory, but MLK Jr. did not possess powers of precognition and could not act on information he did not have. His decisions and beliefs were formed as in-the-moment responses to a complex, chaotic reality paired with an unknowable future. Thus, any representation (i.e., character) should reflect what he reasonably could have known at a *specific* time and place, not the full set of events/experiences that transpired during his life, across all times and places, and after his death.

This principle applies to role-play scenarios as well: They should remain open-ended rather than pointed toward a single, predetermined outcome. If, for example, students are participating in a foreign policy exercise where they assume the roles of prominent world leaders during the early 1930s, they should not act as though Hitler's rise to power and declaration of war on Europe are a forgone conclusion. To do so would be to suggest that future events are already decided, stripping individuals of in-the-moment agency to influence the present and days ahead. These kinds of activities are more effective when students leave their knowledge of outcomes to the side and focus solely on information the characters had in that particular moment.

The precise form of a given first-person role-play is inherently adjustable and can resemble any of the aforementioned third-person examples—the only substantial difference is that students must elaborate on their characters' choices and motivations from the first-person perspective. Not every activity needs to include live-action, but live-action can be threaded in and out as desired: Students can write diary entries or letters to the editor on the day after a significant historical moment; conduct one-on-one interviews in peer dyads, incorporating their characters' personalities and values as they respond to questions; and work in small groups to discuss how a particular character should think and act, role-playing that character (collectively) as part of a whole-class interaction. Just be aware that while some students thrive with unorthodox assignments and on-the-fly thinking, performance in front of any audience (big or small) can lead to social anxiety. Always double-check before transitioning into live-action role-play so that anyone who harbors doubts can select a less nerve-racking option (e.g., assuming a third-person perspective or completing the role-play as part of an online, asynchronous experience). It is also good practice to check in as live-action activities unfold (e.g., every character action, every twenty minutes, every session) to reaffirm participant consent and student comfort with how the narrative is developing (i.e., reducing potential harm).

CONSEQUENCES FOR ACTIONS

Like other types of simulation, role-play activities blossom over time as students witness and interpret the consequences of their characters' choices. The effect is cumulative when the scenario is split into two or three phases where each decision branches into a new environmental context and presents new options for exploration, interrogation, and/or reflection. Common in interactive narrative games, such "decision trees" clarify that there are multiple paths to achieve a particular outcome or that there are multiple paths to completely divergent outcomes; which approach is the best fit for a given project is entirely up to the instructor.

To illustrate, what if John Wilkes Booth had failed to assassinate Abraham Lincoln in April 1865? How might have Reconstruction proceeded if Lincoln remained president through his entire second term? Naturally, we cannot run the counterfactual to produce a definitive answer to either question—but we *can* encourage students to exercise creativity and critical thinking to propose alternative timelines. Applying a combination of research and discussion skills, they could introduce an evidence-supported range of outcomes from most to least likely; explain how the failed assassination attempt would have influenced Lincoln's actions; or develop multiple plausible pathways and debate differences of opinion with their peers. The process places the proverbial ball in the students' court by galvanizing the refinement of their reasoning and argumentation abilities.

This works best with close instructional oversight and "teachable moment" interjection. Lacking supervision, students gravitate toward implausible or silly options that provoke their peers to respond in kind, perpetuating a cycle of unseriousness and farce. Students can and should enjoy themselves during these open-ended exercises, but the instructor needs to firmly focus the group on planned learning objectives so that the scenario reinforces pertinent concepts rather than comedic tangents (a figurative sandbox on rails).

Role-Play

SUCCESSES AND FAILURES

All types of role-play scenarios can incorporate randomized elements to interject chance into student decision-making. Using an abstract example, a character may be presented with option A, option B, or option C. First, the player must decide which option to pursue, and then the instructor must resolve whether the action was a success. That means option A, option B, and option C can lead to six potential outcomes: option A success or failure, option B success or failure, or option C success or failure. Irrespective of the result, the instructor's follow-up should be "What do you do next?"

Note that unpredictable does *not* mean arbitrary. Branching pathways should account for both the relative difficulty of the action and the relative skill or ability of the person attempting the action. In many tabletop role-playing games, this is achieved by asking players to roll a number of dice that determine whether their attacks hit their enemies or resolve nontrivial, out-of-combat challenges (e.g., persuading a skeptical listener or solving a tricky scientific problem). The same strategy applies in classroom role-play scenarios, which can shorthand the process by estimating chances of success as a flat percentage (e.g., "This character has an 80 percent to succeed at this action") and determining success or failure via cards or dice. Below are two ways to implement this:

- **Cards**: Organize a stack of twenty index cards with the same layout/backing. Write "Success" on ten cards and "Failure" on the other ten cards. If the given action has an 80 percent chance of success, combine two "Failure" cards and eight "Success" cards into a deck, shuffle them, and have the student draw one card from the deck. These decks can be assembled and shuffled very quickly so long as your percentages are grounded in multiples of ten (e.g., a 50–50 chance deck consists of five "Failure" and five "Success" cards).

- **Dice**: Have the student roll two ten-sided dice (also known as percentile dice; available at any gaming store). They can choose the order in which the dice will be read: the first is the "tens" column, and the second is "ones." If the action has an 80 percent chance of success, any roll of 80 or below (i.e., "8" plus "0") would meet the standard, and any roll above 80 (e.g., "8" plus "1") would be a failure. This allows for greater granularity than a card-based system using multiples of ten (e.g., a 7 percent chance of success for a longshot challenge ["0" plus "7"]; a 99 percent chance of success ["9" plus "9"]).

The instructor should be clear about probabilities of success or failure and the gravity of potential consequences *before* a student makes their choice. Cards should not be redrawn nor dice rerolled—we want students to conduct in-the-moment risk-benefit analyses without the reassurance of a mulligan safety net (e.g., going for a longshot if there are no consequences for failure; choosing the safest option if the consequences for failure are grim). The instructor should follow the card draw or roll by asking what the student would have done if the situation had turned out differently (i.e., engaging the success/failure counterfactual).

Depending on your level of familiarity, introducing popular, entertainment-oriented tabletop role-playing games into the classroom can also be exceptionally effective. *Dungeons & Dragons* (*D&D*)—the world's most popular tabletop role-playing game—is a well-known option, but there exist myriad game systems (both more and less complex than *D&D*) that dovetail nicely with the structure and goals of various worldbuilding projects. Two particularly useful game systems are *Powered by the Apocalypse* (*PbtA*) and *Year Zero Engine* (*YZE*), each of which is published under an Open Gaming License that allows for user adaptation and revision. These systems simplify gameplay by prioritizing narrative and live-action role-play above statistics and mathematics (i.e., limiting the complexity of challenge checks to rolling six-sided [d6] dice—the type included with most tabletop board games).

Integrating *D&D*, *PbtA*, *YZE*, or other systems with a worldbuilding-based role-play scenario adds complexity but comes with several benefits. In *PbtA* and *YZE*, players are provided with a limited number of points to distribute across their characters' abilities and skills. As a result, different characters are more or less likely to overcome a given challenge owing to their particular point distributions (e.g., a player who assigns their character's points to mental and social skills is less apt to succeed at physical challenges like breaking down a door or pulling an injured companion to safety; however, they are more apt to discover a new invention or convince another character to participate in a controversial plan). Just as in real life, this encourages players to resolve their problems by leveraging their strengths (rather than testing their weaknesses), thereby simulating how different people view and react to the same challenge or context in dynamic, interesting ways. Paraphrasing the Greek philosopher Heraclitus, no student ever steps in the same role-play twice, for it is not the same role-play, and they are not the same student.[15]

USING ROLE-PLAY TO VIRTUALLY EXPERIENCE WORLDS

In closing, we reiterate that role-play can transcend mere entertainment to enrich your teaching and learning environment. Immersive storytelling, lively character development, and collaborative problem-solving collectively allow learners to experience and deconstruct vibrant worlds both like and unlike their own. Stepping into the shoes of diverse characters bestows invaluable insight into the human condition, the intricacies of the world's interconnected structures, and the forces that shape our respective lifeworlds. Done conscientiously, this can foster higher-order thinking skills, promote social interaction, and nurture empathy that can be transferred out of the classroom and into day-to-day life.

It is the camaraderie and accomplishment running through role-play that cultivates strong, lasting bonds between learners and course content. Many of those who participate ultimately forge lifelong friendships and new Communities of Practice based on their shared experiences. Such prosocial activities are part and parcel of constructivist education, and having observed this many times over, we can attest to its power to influence personal growth and development. It is our sincerest hope that upon trying these methods, you will reach the same conclusion.

15 WRAP-UP AND CRITICAL REFLECTION

"Read not to contradict and confute; nor to believe and take for granted; nor to find talk and discourse; but to weigh and consider."
—Sir Francis Bacon[1]

The conclusion of a worldbuilding project frequently leaves participants and the instructor feeling as though something is incomplete or that more could have—or should have—been done.

Truthfully, any worldbuilding-based lesson, unit, or course could continue ad infinitum. There are always more People, Places, and Things to catalog, ideas for role-play sessions, and points on the timeline to explore. It is not uncommon for learners to view the denouement as a somber occasion, equally regretting that they did not attend to everything they wanted and dreading a return to more conventional coursework. We ultimately view such sentiments as compliments, and they give us faith that the experience will stick with participants for years to come. To increase the probability that your own project(s) will yield this kind of lasting meaning, we offer some exercises to soften the landing.

You may remember that chapter 5, "Assessment," recommended self-assessment and one-on-one conferencing as useful means of facilitating learner reflection about their learning (or lack thereof) throughout the project. Self-assessment usually takes the form of a brief, introspective essay (no more than a few thousand words) where students compose a narrative explaining which parts of the project were most and least affecting. One-on-conferencing, on the other hand, is an oral exercise wherein learners dialogue with the instructor to clarify what they have written and expand on their ideas.

Below, we introduce three additional approaches you may want to consider: large-group debriefing, self-accounting, and peer evaluation. Although all can be employed in isolation, you will likely choose to combine two or more for maximum effect, especially if your learning objectives are geared toward social collaboration and self-actualization.

LARGE-GROUP DEBRIEFING

We suggest carving out at least one session for a large-group debriefing—an open, free-form discussion covering the full breadth of the project. Rewinding the clock reminds learners that they began with a nearly blank slate and few, if any, preconceived notions about the final product. It also draws attention to the delta between what they knew at the beginning versus the end of the process, sharpening their understanding of how they have changed over time. Keep in mind that if the group has been worldbuilding for weeks or months, your early sessions will feel like a distant memory by the time you reach the finish line. Thus, asking them to articulate what they accomplished during each stage of the project can go a long way toward mitigating any sense that it remains unfinished.

Resist the urge to tightly constrain the conversation, focusing instead on open-ended brainstorming and unstructured feedback about planning strategies, aspects of the process that could use refinement, and tasks that were emotionally engaging, enjoyable, surprising, and so on (or not). Doing this in an open forum with all participating learners is crucial for them to hear and learn from their peers' responses. Some will undoubtedly describe the time they spent probing the world's structures and substructures, while others will highlight catalog entry creation. Others still will contend that simulation and role-play were the best parts. Allowing them to voice these opinions publicly will reinforce the notion that every step along the way was worthwhile—you cannot create a diverse catalog of articles unless you understand the world's fundamental social forces, and you cannot run a role-play session without a diverse catalog of People, Places, and Things. Learner-directed arguments and counterarguments tend to prompt more thoughtful meditation on the experience as a whole, and it may change the perspectives of those who began the project with a healthy dose of skepticism. Ideally, this will prime everyone to furnish highly granular, personalized commentary in their self-assessments and/or one-on-one conferences, providing fodder for you to determine precisely how and why they learned—exactly the kind of qualitative, contextual (and invaluable) data absent from traditional evaluative measures.

SELF-ACCOUNTING

As both a bookkeeping and instructional measure, it can be helpful for learners to provide a record of the work they performed over the project's duration, otherwise known as self-accounting. This often takes the form of a curated list that learners annotate in cooperation with their peers. Some of the requested information on a typical self-accounting sheet includes:

- How many assignments did you complete? How many were completed by the deadline?
- To which specific parts of the metanarrative did you contribute? Approximately how many words did you write?
- List and provide links for each of your wiki articles.
- Explain other work you did on behalf of the project (artwork, design, organization, revision, etc.).

This subset of self-assessment prevents learners from claiming more credit or a higher grade than their work supports. After all, they may have genuinely enjoyed the project and learned a great deal from enthusiastically participating in group discussions, but failing to follow up with a written product would have left their peers at a significant disadvantage. Should a student who only wrote four wiki entries receive the same grade as someone who wrote ten or twelve? What about a learner who debates the finer points of how the world functions but leaves writing the metanarrative to others?

Self-accounting should be cross-checked against the instructor's records, calendar, and other available information. Such triangulation helps establish whether any due date or word count revisionism has crept in, buffering against honest mistakes and white lies while bolstering the credibility of your assessment measures. Because there is so much to digest, though, we recommend pairing this approach with another popular ungrading method capable of providing qualitative insight into the coauthorship process: peer evaluation.

PEER EVALUATION

Instructors cannot be everywhere at once, nor do they have the benefit of directly witnessing out-of-class discussions and collaborations. It is easy to assume that a well-organized project comes with an equitable workload distribution, but appearances can be deceiving—we never *really* know who is completing which task at what time and under what circumstances. Sometimes, the most talkative group member contributes little when the instructor is out of eyeshot, and other times the learner who rarely speaks in the thick of large-group discussions is responsible for the lion's share of writing. Hence, peer evaluations allow us to confirm or challenge our perception of a project's overall progression.

Peer evaluation is not the same as peer grading; it is a qualitative mechanism for extrapolating group dynamics. It can, of course, be taken into consideration when tallying final grades, but it should emphasize whether and how class expectations were met rather than attempt to quantify some specific aspect of performance. Relevant forms commonly ask learners to record their groupmate's names, general feedback about the group's interactions, and responses to the following three criteria:

- The group member was present and attentive during group discussions.
- The group member provided input, listened to other people's ideas, and was agreeable to work with.
- The group member completed their fair share of work on time and at an acceptable quality.

These criteria can be structured using a rubric ("Groupmate did not meet expectations"; "Groupmate met expectations"; "Groupmate exceeded expectations") and include space for additional comments about each category.

We have found that most learners provide clear, straightforward responses without attempting to protect or attack their groupmates. Best of all, the vast majority of cases are incredibly consistent: Learners will, without hesitation, identify who did not participate in discussions, did not contribute to the work, or were difficult to work with; they also sing the praises of those who went above and beyond in coordinating group efforts, moderating differences of opinion, or diffusing arguments, particularly when those interactions happened outside the instructor's purview. Applied in conjunction with other ungrading methods, this helps the instructor to (1) develop a richer understanding of each learner's trajectory through the lesson, course, or program and (2) better direct learners toward specific goals they can continue pursuing in their respective domains of interest.

BIG, MESSY AFFAIRS

Worldbuilding projects are big, messy affairs with many moving parts, and it can be challenging to track individual learners' efforts amid emerging, unpredictable events (e.g., absences, late submissions, and unanticipated social conflicts). Likewise, the translation of qualitative information into quantitative grades and grade point averages can be headache-inducing, but conscientious educators understand that our evaluations must be able to speak across multiple audiences to satisfy the needs of learners as well as potential employers, scholarship grantors, and others.

The methods described in both chapter 5, "Assessment," and herein—self-assessment, one-on-one conferencing, large-group debriefing, self-accounting, and peer evaluation—can greatly inform such qualitative-to-quantitative translation by painting a holistic picture of learner performance. Doing so immediately upon completing the project encourages the normalization of healthy self-reflection, peer-to-peer discourse, and preparation for future self and peer reviews. Not only will this cement your learners' understanding of core content, but it should improve the likelihood of transfer and provide closure on what was hopefully a profound learning experience.

EPILOGUE: NOTES FROM THE END OF THE WORLD

Our combined thirty years of experience in the realm of playful learning has undoubtedly enriched our lives—many former students have contacted us long after graduation to extend thanks for an unforgettable experience, the lessons from which not only stuck with them but also proved invaluable to their careers and personal growth. Through workshops, mentoring, graduate courses, and professional development sessions, we have taught hundreds of people how to introduce the worldbuilding process into their curricula. To this day, we have never heard from someone whose attempt failed so miserably that they would never try again. Quite the contrary, everyone who has designed and implemented a worldbuilding assignment or unit in their classroom has reported that it went so well that they want another go with additional modifications and/or learning objectives. Thus, we have happily doomed many an educator to eternal tinkering.

Of course, as much as our students, trainees, friends, and colleagues inspire us, there are still moments when we are confronted with skepticism. We have both had disagreeable traditionalists turn up their noses and guffaw something to the effect of "Well *obviously* students respond well to games in the classroom! It's no different than children preferring candy to vegetables!" If they catch us in the mood for some back-and-forth, we dismantle their lazy argument by outlining the educational principles described in the first third of this book (e.g., situated cognition, constructionism, discovery learning, Communities of Practice). If we are tired, cranky, and less willing to tolerate a bad-faith argument, we roll our eyes, thank them for the critique, and walk away.

Perhaps we should have anticipated this trajectory sooner than the realization hit us. During the heady years of the early to mid-2010s—the peak of our early careers in academia—our goal was proselytizing to fellow teachers, professors, and instructional designers so we could win their conversion to the church of game-based learning. What we eventually discovered was that the interdisciplinary connections and collaborations emergent from events like the Games+Learning+Society Conference were more a product of who attended than any fundamental shift in the wider field of education. The most devout group of community members came with open minds and reasonably strong learning theory bona fides; people who "got it" without prompting and did not need our proselytization. Unfortunately, they were vastly outnumbered by a larger contingent consisting of instructors searching for turnkey gaming solutions that would make classroom problems disappear, industry developers happy to fabricate and sell snake oil for a quick buck, and administrators building professional credibility by buying up shiny technologies for their districts or universities. Those stories do not have particularly happy endings.

As it happens, there has never been—and never will be—a silver bullet or deus ex machina for educators. Teaching is very much a human endeavor, and playful approaches like worldbuilding can only work when educators are willing and able to leverage both good teaching and good design. That's the rub. Genuinely good teaching is extremely difficult to implement in the current educational ecosystem, and even the best designs inevitably surface old structural problems that we (as a society) have consistently failed to address.

- **Just like textbooks, film strips, computers, and tablets, games cannot replace quality educators**. The very best educational outcomes are the result of engaged instructors maintaining high levels of contact with each student, experimenting with creative pedagogical strategies, and interpreting data. In the absence of interpersonal connection, learners almost universally take the path of least resistance, idly playing phone games or flipping through a book to give the appearance of participation without internalizing instructional content. They need well-trained, highly qualified teachers whose compensation is commensurate with the gravity of their role in society.

- **Investment should be made to train educators, not buy equipment or prepackaged curricula**. For a board or video game to be successful, it must be able to teach its players the ruleset and why/how certain strategies yield specific outcomes. This is precisely the same thing educators do. Therefore, no one needs to be an expert on games to successfully integrate them into a curriculum; they need to be an expert on education. We should be using resources to help educators synthesize learning theories, instructional strategies, and assessment measures into learner-centered, discovery-based activities—a logical extension of which is game-based instruction.

- **Educators are overwhelmed and seldom have the administrative support necessary to implement new approaches.** The United States has experienced a multidecade, bipartisan effort to make teaching the worst job imaginable, and it feels like we have nearly achieved that goal. The majority of K–12 teachers have limited control over their curricula and are caught on the treadmill of preparing students for high-stakes standardized tests. Universities are similarly plagued with initiatives that sidestep innovation and creativity in favor of profitability and the adjunctification of faculty. Far too few institutions provide sufficient administrative backing for instructors to focus lessons on how to think, learn, or think about learning.
- **Many educators lack the interest or incentives to change how they teach.** Over time, instructors discover preferred methods and tend to stick with them even as the corresponding learning science evolves. If or when those methods become outdated, there are limited ways to induce change, especially if there is no will or available support to do so. Online courses, professional development workshops, and educator-focused conferences depend on individuals wanting change for themselves, doubly so when transitioning from didactic stand-and-deliver to anchored or play-based instruction. Hence, educators need more opportunities to practice intellectual risk-taking and additional benefits for their continued engagement with contemporary research (e.g., travel funds, paid professional development).
- **Good education is messy, and grades get in the way.** No two learners understand the same content in the same way or learn that content at the same speed. Yet, formal education treats learning outcomes as cemented in time (e.g., "By the end of this [lesson, assignment, unit, semester, year, etc.], students will demonstrate they have learned [insert some number of skills or facts]"). We issue one-and-done exams or essays to monitor comprehension, but as noted in chapter 5, "Assessment," these tools fail to measure change, and instructors often (incorrectly) conflate learner scores with their ability to transfer and apply knowledge. This discounts everything we know about the context-specific nature of learning and minimizes the degree to which life lessons—which are often equally or more valuable than course content—are made a primary, rather than secondary or tertiary, goal of education.
- **Good education requires ample time, space, and support.** The arms race spurred by neoliberal policy—namely, treating universities like businesses—has dramatically inflated tuition, but little of that money

has gone toward improved on-campus physical and mental healthcare, accessibility services for disabled learners, offices of diversity and inclusion, new tenure track faculty positions, additional paid assistantships for graduate students, or foundational humanities programs. Some of it has been spent on high-tech classrooms that do, in fact, facilitate better teaching and learning, but those gains have been undermined by immense administrative bloat, instructors remaining locked into rigid schedules and course formats, resources being unevenly distributed (almost universally in favor of STEM fields), and faculty service requirements exploding in the wake of COVID-19. No matter how successful, unorthodox instructional methods cannot be instantiated at scale unless something is done about the way twenty-first-century higher education is managed.

These are but a few reasons that education is collapsing under its own weight—capitalistic demand for unlimited growth meeting the hard reality of finite resources. K–12 superintendents cannot bank on teachers loving the job enough to stick with unreasonably low pay and substandard working conditions. Tuition cannot rise forever, meaning many institutions will simply cease to exist. University presidents are panicking about a looming enrollment cliff as shrinking pools of graduating high school seniors fail to feed this voracious machine.

Worse, politicians have made a cottage industry of cutting university funds while decrying rising costs and reduced quality. They call into question the value of anything that does not directly contribute to employer-demanded skills, as if Accounting II is essential for success, while subjects like history, philosophy, literature, and art have no utility whatsoever. Double up on STEM, get a master of business administration diploma, and gut the rest.

We are not suggesting that worldbuilding, simulations, and play will miraculously solve these problems. We are also not trying to turn non-believers into acolytes of games and learning. We simply posit that the incorporation of gameful and playful pedagogy produces meaningful experiences that can reshape the way you think about your role as an educator and how you interact with your organization or institution.

Your colleagues may not grasp or applaud your efforts.

You will not be guaranteed the provost's teaching award.

It is not some golden ticket to unlimited grant funding.

But it is still worth doing, for the benefit of yourself and your students.

And it needs to be something you want to do. Because it is interesting and fun and engaging, yes, but also because you care and want to implement a theoretically sound approach that can positively influence your students for years to come.

Meanwhile, we two authors will be drinking brandy old-fashioneds as we await the end of the world, figuratively or literally. One of us wound up jobless after their academic position and program were eliminated on the whims of a short-sighted, capricious dean; the other is still a professor watching with bemused resignation as faculty lines are reallocated away from the humanities and given to disciplines that cater to the business of making money. We have completed our transformation into Waldorf and Statler, a pair of cantankerous old Muppets yelling at nobody in particular about things over which they have no control.

Even so, we see the state of affairs at this moment—the worsening climate crisis, the rise in authoritarianism and fascism, the proliferation of misinformation, the untenable levels of wealth stratification, the apparent tolerance for racism and sexism, the threats to democracy, the dumpster fire that is higher education—and are strangely optimistic. Things may be bad, but the future is unwritten, and there are many ways that each of us can contribute to a better tomorrow.

Doing so will require acclimation to the death of this particular world, though, the post-World War II order in which the United States is the most powerful nation on earth and global capitalism concentrates wealth into the hands of as few people as possible. Will it be replaced by a sweltering, dystopian hellscape ruled by despots? A utopian solarpunk society with truly equitable economic, political, justice, and education systems? A high-tech, postnuclear federation led by corvids and octopi? Or will it become something entirely different—maybe one of the scenarios imagined by our worldbuilding students?

The only certainty is that things will not stay the same. There is no going back to some idyllic moment from the past. We are continually hurtling forward into the cold unknown on a tiny speck of rock locked in gravitational orbit around a middle-sized star along the edge of one galaxy among trillions.

Consequently, as human beings, intellectuals, and citizens, we feel compelled to step into the future each and every day, deconstructing the complexity of the present to make sense—as best we can—of which systems can be massaged into some new, more desirable shape, the tilting of the wheel described in our prologue. Somehow, in defiance of our cynicism, we persist in imparting that outlook onto others. It is the most significant thing we can do to aid our fellow raindrops in seeding the broader monsoon of change.

We appreciate you being part of that process.

Thank you so much for reading.

IV CASE STUDIES

CASE STUDY I HISTORY

Instructor: Eric J. Morgan
Institution: University of Wisconsin–Green Bay, Green Bay, WI
Class: The US and the World
Level: Undergraduate
Enrollment: 30
Project Duration: 1 semester

LEARNING OBJECTIVES

- Develop skills to express clear, concise, and critical analysis and arguments
- Refine the ability to think both historically and creatively
- Defend arguments and analyses on a variety of sources and questions related to the history of the United States and the world
- Discuss the history of the United States in the context of the broader world
- Compare and contrast US history with that of other nations
- Deconstruct the influence of historical events and their relevance to the present

WORLDBUILDING APPROACH

Worldbuilding in the discipline of history presented a fascinating challenge. How can one build a world that has already been constructed, where past events have already happened and their outcomes are immutable? My worldbuilding approach was to use immersive historical simulation role-playing games, which would allow my course to focus on primary sources—mainly government documents but also other sources such as speeches, photographs, memoirs and diary entries, letters, propaganda, and intelligence reports—and the actual past to create a dynamic world in which we could relive past events, experiencing them as the historical actors did.

I chose to integrate worldbuilding into this course because the history of US foreign relations, by its nature, has often involved opposing views and goals, tension, negotiation, compromise, and decision-making. A good simulation, for me, needs to have a strong sense of tension where the outcome is uncertain; there must be stakes that matter and the ability for individuals to influence others and the course of events. A situation, for example, where all the parties or individuals were already in agreement would not make for an engaging simulation experience. The course included four simulations, spread across the twentieth century that would engage students in the evolution of the United States' interaction with the larger world and a variety of critical issues that shaped both US foreign policy and international affairs: the Paris Peace Conference at the end of the First World War in 1919, the end of the Second World War and the decision to use the atomic bomb in 1945, the Cuban Missile Crisis of 1962 during the height of the Cold War confrontation between the United States and the Soviet Union, and the post-Cold War Rwandan genocide of 1994.

I began each simulation with a contextual lecture, laying out the broader historical background from which the simulation emerged, which was followed by the screening of a documentary film to immerse ourselves more deeply within the historical moment as we often heard commentary or analysis from the actual historical actors themselves. We then broke into various groups for the simulation, with each group composed of different characters and overarching goals. For example, the Cuban Missile Crisis simulation included three larger groups: President John F. Kennedy's Executive Committee of the National Security Council, Soviet officials, and Cuban officials. I provided a list of primary source documents that students were responsible for reviewing, and students were also tasked with researching the biographies and personalities of their individual characters. Each simulation also included a background reading to provide further historical context and analysis. Students were then given a workday to plan their strategies before we began the simulation in earnest.

The simulations did not have to unfold exactly as the real historical experiences did, and indeed we often trod down alternative paths. I had only two rules for the simulations: Students could not act out of character (e.g., President John F. Kennedy would not have ordered a preemptive nuclear strike of Cuba on the first day of the 1962 crisis, though some of his advisers advocated doing so and certainly other actors, had they been president, could have made that choice), and the decisions made could not be ahistorical (e.g., no matter how compelling the arguments of the colonized peoples who attended the Paris Peace Conference in 1919, the major powers were not going to grant independence to those countries at that time). My role was to help facilitate the simulation, moving it forward and offering consequences to the various decisions made by students.

COMPARISON APPROACHES

Since my graduate school days as a teaching assistant, my courses have almost always included discussion as a central pedagogy, which allows students to be at the center of their educational experience. I have also experimented with a variety of creative projects, including podcasts, virtual historical exhibits, nonlinear storytelling through Twine, historical fiction, board game creation, field trips, and experiential learning. Simulation role-playing games would allow a deeper immersive experience: students building a world through the act of becoming historical actors rather than hearing, reading, or watching a film about these characters. Doing so would force students to take ownership of their own learning while also better understanding both how historical decision-making happens and the importance of individual personalities in both the past and present. We would build this historical world together, immersing ourselves in primary source documents and the myriad personalities and nations that took part in these various events.

ASSESSMENT MEASURES

Students were assessed on three separate components, all intentionally connected with role-playing simulation games. First, students submitted character journals at the end of each simulation, written in the first person from the perspective of their historical actor. The purpose of the journals was to have students reflect and write on the simulation experience as their character. Doing so allowed students to express frustration, fear, anxiety, jubilation, hopefulness, and numerous other feelings that they may not have experienced firsthand in a lecture-oriented course. Second, students were assessed on their participation in the simulations. Since this upper-level course was fairly large with nearly thirty students, it was impossible for every student to be an active participant in each simulation. Thus, each simulation included several major characters, and every student was required to portray at least one major character throughout the semester. Finally, students were placed into small groups for a final project, tasked with creating the framework for their own simulation role-playing game on a topic of their choice relating to the history of the US and the world from the Spanish-American War in 1898 to the 9/11 terrorist attacks.

The final project was scaffolded with groups drafting a proposal and annotated bibliography, demonstrating their familiarity with some of the literature related to their topic. The project consisted of a simulation introduction and setting, learning outcomes, a list of at least fifteen playable historical characters, documents and other primary sources that students would use for the simulation, a bibliography, and a section titled "What We Learned." The concluding section asked students to discuss what they learned about US foreign relations through both their own simulation project as well as the course as a whole. How did simulation role-playing games—both engaging in them and creating one—help students to better understand the history of US foreign relations and various historical actors throughout the twentieth century? Students responded to this question in various ways. Several commented that they enjoyed the opportunity to play a variety of characters and characters from different viewpoints, for example, a character from the United States' perspective in one simulation and one from the Soviet Union's in the next, which stimulated creativity and comparative analysis. Others appreciated experiencing firsthand the challenges, complexities, and constraints that historical actors faced while better understanding the motivations and strategies that shaped US foreign policy. Students felt that the course's approach helped them to grapple with the complexities of international relations and US foreign policy in a more intimate way, especially the importance of individual personalities in the shaping of history. As one student noted, all of these historical characters were real human beings with their own strengths, flaws, biases, and interests (as well as families, love and loss, successes and failures, hobbies, etc.), and the course's approach allowed them to be humanized and thus empathy practiced. For many students, the simulations became personal and, as a result, more important to them than a research paper or exam as the stakes were perceived as real and thus worth fighting for. Finally, students observed that the making of US foreign policy and the United States' engagement with the larger world was often contentious. There were myriad conflicting opinions and approaches, and students had to develop and practice listening skills, negotiation, and compromise.

REFLECTION ON IMPLEMENTATION

Overall, the worldbuilding endeavor worked very well. Students were almost always prepared for the simulations after having engaged with the primary sources and other readings. The simulations themselves were dynamic and fun. The major weaknesses were of my own making: lack of preparation and a natural hands-off approach to teaching at times. Throughout all four simulations, I could have occasionally been a stronger facilitator, better guiding students through the simulations or engaging in more outside work to consider alternatives if different decisions were made than what happened during the actual historical event. Some students also expressed displeasure with the final group project since some group members failed to adequately contribute (though I have found that group projects in general are not a favorite of many students). Another issue I observed upon reflection was the lack of diversity in terms of characters. The first and final simulations included a broad range of historical actors—presidents, diplomats, politicians, citizens, women, colonized peoples—while the middle two focused far more on high-level decision-making, almost exclusively by the policymaking elite.

In conclusion, I will absolutely engage in this worldbuilding approach again, perhaps integrating role-playing simulation games into other courses as well. The opportunity for students to become historical actors and live through past events is too unique to limit to only one course. The overall experience was both thrilling and rewarding, with students learning about the past through rigorous research into both primary and secondary historical sources and cooperative worldbuilding.

CASE STUDY II   BRITISH LITERATURE

Instructor: Luke Strohm
Institution: Grand Valley High School, Orwell, OH
Class: British Literature
Level: High school (advanced)
Enrollment: 17
Project Duration: 23 weeks

LEARNING OBJECTIVES

- Ohio Common Core Standards for English Language Arts:
  - Reading Standards for Literature: RL.11–12.1/RL.11–12.2/RL.11–12.3/RL.11–12.7
  - Reading Standards for Informational Text: RI.11–12.1/RI.11–12.2/RI.11–12.7/RI.11–12.8/RI.11–12.9
  - Research and Writing Standards: W.11–12.2/W.11–12.4/W.11–12.7/W.11–12.8
  - Speaking and Listening Standards: SL.11–12.1/SL.11–12.4/SL.11–12.5
  - Language Standards: L.11–12.2/L.11–12.3/L.11–12.6

WORLDBUILDING APPROACH

The primary goal for my worldbuilding endeavor was to provide students with the chance to solve "real-world" problems in a safe, fictional setting that would encourage them to meaningfully consider the ways in which society operates. Ideally, it would connect fictional issues to real issues and transfer their learning outside the classroom setting.

We began the year by generating a series of fictional worlds using Trent Hergenrader's *Collaborative Worldbuilding* card deck. We did this as an entire class so that I could lead, guide, and model how discussions should proceed for each substructure, teaching students how to investigate real-world structures and apply their understanding to fictional settings. The final world we created during this introductory process was saved and repurposed for additional creative writing exercises during the spring semester.

Once students were comfortable with the system and understood how a given world's substructures should be numerically categorized, we integrated the process into different eras of British literature history. The class consisted of seventeen students who self-arranged into five groups of three or four students. Each group was randomly assigned a British city that would be theirs to manage throughout the semester. These cities were selected to maximize the diversity of size, location, and resources: London, Newcastle, Liverpool, Bath, and Cambridge. The eras we covered during the semester included Anglo-Saxon, medieval, Renaissance, Romantic, and Victorian. Each unit was structured in five-week increments.

We opened each unit with an introduction to the target era as well as student research in preparation for class discussion. We then assigned numerical values to each substructure from the card deck; rather than randomly drawing cards for worldbuilding, we intentionally assigned values based on what we knew and learned about the era. We did this as a whole class to generate a general, overarching value for the era as a whole; we also reviewed the text(s) attached to that era to discuss how structural values were portrayed through the literature of the time. In week two, students split into their groups, researched their assigned villages/cities, and applied the structural values we collaboratively formulated as a jumping-off point for assigning structural values to those villages/cities (including discussion of divergences from the overarching values; this was akin to assigning overall values to the entire United States but modifying those values based on the lived experience of someone in New York City versus Boise, Idaho).

During week three, I randomly assigned a "universal problem" that each group would have to troubleshoot and resolve for their specific village/city based on that village/city's unique circumstances. I used a twenty-sided die roll to randomly determine the "universal problem" with the stipulation that we could not have the same problem in back-to-back eras. The issues to be solved included Immigration, Poverty, Environment (subcategories randomly assigned on a six-sided die roll: Drought, Harsh Winter, or Flooding), Pandemic/Plague, and Economic Disaster/Depression. Groups then needed to research the problem; research potential solutions using only the resources, technology, and knowledge of the era; and draw ideas from textual evidence grounded in our text(s) related to the era.

Week four entailed a whole-class discussion of the era text(s) to scaffold group presentations. Students were encouraged to centralize their research by creating group wikis (i.e., websites with different pages and sections for each era); these would serve as visual aids while presenting relevant information and proposed solutions.

During week five—the final week of the era—each group shared their findings with the entire class. As all groups came together in the representation of different cities, we called this portion of the unit our "British Council"—an opportunity to discuss each group's proposal and compare/contrast how effectively they would address the shared universal problem. Each group was assigned a score between 1 and 10, corresponding to a modifier of anywhere from –3 to +3. Success was randomly determined by a twenty-sided die roll as even the most successful plans do not always work in the real world (and, conversely, poor plans sometimes work better than anticipated). After the die roll (plus/minus a modifier), all students individually submitted self-evaluations for the era and focused on their success rolls. If they had a really strong proposal but it happened to fail, they needed to consider what variables might have contributed to failure, what information or planning processes might have been overlooked, and how they could account for those issues in the future. Students whose proposals were successful reflected on the inverse: What events or variables might have contributed to their success, what variables were most influential, and what takeaways could be applied to future problems? Crucially, the self-evaluation focused on *process*, emphasizing context and environmental conditions emergent from complex systems rather than any one character, event, or idea.

Although each era was originally set on a five-week timeline, most were extended to six or seven weeks due to the sheer amount of information students were evaluating and synthesizing.

COMPARISON APPROACHES

I have found that worldbuilding allows me to challenge learners in ways that I might not be able to otherwise. Because it is (at some level) fictional, it provides a safe space for many students to examine issues, problems, and solutions that might be difficult to address when set in the real world. Specifically, it makes it safer for them to explore issues of race, gender, politics, religion, technology, and economics as well as how those structures impact a society and how social norms (and overarching complex systems) impact lived experience. They are able to evaluate how different beliefs influence societal events/institutions and follow those beliefs to their logical conclusions. With the inherent transferability built into the worldbuilding process, students can investigate the world in which they exist and deconstruct all of its components to make meaning. With respect to literature, students can also manipulate aspects of the worldbuilding process to create texts within a fictional world that help them better understand how (1) prose reflects specific societal standards and (2) codes are upheld or subverted through the use of symbolism, semiotics, word choice, and so forth.

Addressing sensitive topics through the traditional essay writing process can be exceptionally challenging. We can, of course, discuss their treatments in stories and novels, but many students have trouble seeing past their own biases—a by-product of merely existing within a society. Conversely, worldbuilding offers the opportunity to create a new or original society and figure out what problems would emerge based on interactions between the society's structures and substructures. The creation process forces students to abandon their biases by anchoring their fictional worlds in a wide array of real-world data, histories, and cultures.

ASSESSMENT MEASURES

- [Individual] Weekly participation
    - Google Sheets to track what each learner completed throughout the week
- [Group] British Council score
    - Score sheet (rubric) used to evaluate presentations and discussion/debate in class; the score determines the modifier on the success roll. The following are modifiers:
        - Score of 9–10 = +3
        - 8.8–8.9 = +2
        - 8.4–8.7 = +1
        - 8–8.3 = 0
        - 7.5–7.9 = −1
        - 7–7.4 = −2
        - 6–6.9 = −3

British Literature

- Under 6 = automatic failure due to no solution given or no presentation
- [Individual] Reading check
    - Formative evaluation to determine whether the learner read the assigned text for the era
- [Individual] Self-evaluation
    - Success is randomly generated by a D20 roll plus the addition/subtraction of the appropriate modifier from above:
        - 1–5 = Critical failure
        - 6–10 = Mild failure
        - 11–15 = Mild success
        - 16–20 = Resounding success
- [Group] Website
    - Collaboratively generated web content that reflects completeness, coherence, cohesiveness, and appropriate mechanics/grammar
- [Group] Presentation
    - Collaborative presentation of city facts during the current era, recap of previous era, extent problems and effects on city, and potential solutions (with evidence) capable of persuading the council that it will work

REFLECTION ON IMPLEMENTATION

Overall, the process worked really well. The students were engaged and began to critically analyze the world around them, even if they did not put 100 percent effort into the full process. After collecting feedback and reflections, they all claimed that this was much better than their standard process of learning and working through things in a typical style. They enjoyed themselves and enjoyed learning about daily life during different time periods. Likewise, they were able to better understand texts from each era because they had a broader frame of reference for specific author choices (e.g., vocabulary, content, characterization).

Although I will amend the process going forward, I plan to continue incorporating worldbuilding and gamification in my classroom. I would like to put greater emphasis on the texts and textual analysis, so I am investigating ways to draw on characters and/or thematic elements to better facilitate student problem-solving. Students recommended that I use "population" as a function of success or failure, accounting for how individual decisions might affect the population level of each city (or at least the population available to help or willing to take part in actualizing each proposed solution). Additionally, by threading the worldbuilding component through the full academic year, I can incorporate new opportunities for student writing practice (e.g., persuasive speeches, essays, original poems, and/or short stories aimed at persuading the target population to support students' ideas for helping the city).

CASE STUDY III PHILOSOPHY

Instructor: Rebecca Scott
Institution: Harper College, Palatine, IL
Class: Introduction to Philosophy
Level: Undergraduate
Enrollment: 20
Project Duration: Fall 2022–present

LEARNING OBJECTIVES

- Cultivate a habit of questioning the inevitability of the status quo
- Recognize the historical nature of norms and institutions
- Develop skills of critical imagination
- Develop an expansive understanding of what philosophy is/what philosophers do
- Improve academic reading and writing skills

WORLDBUILDING APPROACH

While it is not always recognized as such, philosophy is a discipline that has often engaged in worldbuilding. In fact, Plato's *Republic*, one of the foundational texts of European philosophy, can be read as an elaborate attempt at building a world. Plato imagines the ideal polis—its people, education, familial arrangements, governmental organization, and so on. In fact, across the discipline, philosophers have often been concerned with imagining otherwise—they conceive of possible worlds, construct thought experiments, and articulate new visions of what could be. This framing of philosophy as imaginative worldbuilding was the organizing principle for my Introduction to Philosophy course in the fall of 2022. Inspired by philosophical utopian imaginings from Plato to Afrofuturism, I invited students to work together to build their own version of a just world. Influenced by Brian Angus McKenzie's use of wikis for a worldbuilding first-year seminar, students built the world using a collaborative wiki in which they created and described their world's physical, social, and political features.

This particular course was offered at a community college and was part of my institution's Social Justice Studies (SJS) program. While the course was designated as an SJS course, it was open to all students with no prerequisites. SJS courses include the same learning outcomes as non-SJS sections of the course but focus particularly on social justice themes and include additional learning outcomes specific to the SJS program. Twenty students were enrolled, and a handful took the class because of its SJS distinction. Students had little to no background in philosophy before taking the course, and most students took the course as a way of earning credits for their associate of arts degree. For most of my students, this course will be the only philosophy course they will take.

COMPARISON APPROACHES

Many faculty members introduce philosophy either through a historical lens or by organizing the course around the central problems/questions of the discipline. My own approach focused less on content and more on introducing philosophy as a set of academic skills and critical dispositions. That is, my goals were not to cover specific philosophers or topics but rather for students to discover a new way of approaching reading, thinking, and writing. My hope was for them to develop a disposition of questioning the status quo and the skills to think critically and creatively about the world around them.

Because content was not a major concern, I invited students to choose which aspects of the world they wanted to develop. After an introductory unit providing the framework for the course, we brainstormed a list of possible aspects of the world they might work on, including the system of government, ethnic groups (if any), religion, education, technology, and the harm and accountability system. Once students chose a feature of the world to develop, I chose texts for us to read together. We then spent two weeks reading followed by one week dedicated to building our collective wiki. When I teach this course again, the world created by this first class will live on and continue to be edited and built upon by future classes.

In the initial unit, I introduced students to the notion of worldbuilding and the idea of using a wiki to build a world. We read the novella *Binti*, by Nnedi Okorafor, as an example of Afrofuturist worldbuilding with social justice themes, and I had students create a practice wiki for the novella describing various aspects of Okorafor's world. In this unit, students also chose the name Pendo for their own world, and we used random map-generating software to create a map of the continent. In this introductory unit, each student chose one aspect of the physical environment to describe in more detail for our wiki. While describing the physical aspects of the environment was not explicitly "philosophical" work, doing so allowed Pendo to take shape in our collective imaginations, and I found it to be crucial for grounding our project as a collective enterprise.

For our first main unit, students chose to develop the system of government. The first week, we read the Declaration of Independence alongside excerpts from Thomas Hobbes's *Leviathan* and John Locke's *Two Treatises on Government*. The following week, we considered an Indigenous critique of liberal democracy via excerpts from Taiaiake Alfred's *Peace, Power, and Righteousness: An Indigenous Manifesto*. Students were then divided into groups focusing on articulating the underlying values of the system of government, the composition of the legislative body, and the mechanisms for choosing those leaders. In the next unit, we focused on the harm and accountability system by reading works on prison abolition and restorative justice. And finally, students developed Pendo's system of education after reading work by Jean Anyon and Paulo Freire.

ASSESSMENT MEASURES

For assessments, I used a version of **specifications grading**. In this system, all assignments are graded on a complete/"not yet" basis with the overall course grade determined by the number of assignments successfully completed. Students were allowed to revise major assignments until they received a "complete" grade. The course assignments included structured annotations on the readings on the platform Perusall, individual journal reflections connecting course themes and questions to their own life experience, and worldbuilding wiki entries, which they worked on in small groups.

REFLECTION ON IMPLEMENTATION

Overall, I was pleased with the course, and I think we achieved several important goals.

First, the collaborative, authentic nature of the project increased student engagement in the course. In particular, the collaborative nature of the work gave students a greater purpose in completing the readings and assignments. Rather than reading the texts simply because I assigned them or to get a good grade or pass a test, students were reading with an eye toward the decisions that they would be making for our world. Our class discussions were similarly focused on the goal of developing the various institutional structures. Having a specific, collective task helped students to see the purpose of the class's work.

In addition, the worldbuilding project allowed students to have greater agency and a sense of ownership of the class. Students were able to decide which aspects of the world we developed and thereby shaped the course readings and discussions. In general, the worldbuilding project gave just enough structure for this kind of student decision-making to be effective. In the past, I have found that giving students too much agency in making decisions about a course can backfire. If we provide too little structure, students are unable to make good decisions that will benefit their learning. In this course, however, the worldbuilding process included enough scaffolding to allow for real, open-ended choices that were nevertheless informed and constrained by our collective efforts.

While the class was overall a success, there are some things that I plan to do differently in the next iteration of the course. One of the biggest challenges I faced was a lack of tension or friction in many of the decisions that the students made. I found that students agreed a bit too quickly and failed to question the status quo as deeply as I had hoped. Instead, they tended to recreate idealized versions of our current social and political institutions. For example, for the system of government, students mostly recreated a representative democracy that also tried to acknowledge Indigenous principles in their statement of values. This tendency for students to avoid conflict through an idealized compromise that fails to grapple with the genuine tension between ideas is a challenge that is not unique to this course, but it is something that I hope to work on moving forward. One possible way to counter this problem is to introduce "events" in the world where students have to make more concrete decisions that affect the inhabitants.

Another challenge was the interconnected nature of the social and political institutions we were creating. Because we were starting from scratch, we often had to make provisional decisions because we had not yet decided on other crucial aspects of the world (e.g., students began by creating the government of Pendo despite having not yet made decisions about technology, education, and other features of the world that would influence how the government was structured). As the world becomes more established with each iteration of the course, I hope that this will become less of a problem.

While there are several changes that I will make to the course and assignment design moving forward, I am excited to continue making improvements and learning along with my students as the world of Pendo continues to evolve. While worldbuilding may not immediately come to mind as an obvious pedagogical choice for philosophy courses, creatively reimagining the possible, in my view, lies at the heart of what philosophy is (or could be).

CASE STUDY IV   PHYSICS

Instructor: Tori Wagner
Institution: Staples High School, Westport, CT
Class: Physics
Level: High school
Enrollment: 16
Project Duration: 6 weeks

LEARNING OBJECTIVES

- NGSS HS-PS2–4: Use mathematical representations of Coulomb's law to describe and predict the electrostatic forces between objects.
- NGSS HS-PS2–1: Analyze data to support the claim that Newton's second law of motion describes the mathematical relationship between the net force on a macroscopic object, its mass, and its acceleration.

WORLDBUILDING APPROACH

My goal for this electrostatics unit was to nest the content in a fictional world designed for students to assume the roles of scientists or engineers tasked with solving community problems. I chose a world whose central theme revolves around electrostatics. My selection was the *Splatoon* universe, which is from a video game series owned by Nintendo. In these games, players take on the role of Inklings (squid humanoids) who defend their territory against Octolings (octopus humanoids) using splat guns to ink their territory. The game is set in Earth's postapocalyptic future, where dry land is becoming scarce. The *Splatoon* games feature a detailed backstory extensively documented by fans in various wikis, which made it easier to draw creative inspiration from the games.

The defining element of the *Splatoon* universe is the existence of Zapfish. These creatures, floating fish with an electric charge, power their entire world. In the game's narrative, Octolings frequently steal Zapfish from Inklings, jeopardizing the latter's access to essential electricity. The *Splatoon* universe includes time travel, allowing me to craft a unit premise where Inklings use this ability to bring my students to their current era. Inklings seek students' help to rediscover lost technological knowledge, which has been lost to time from the ravages of war. The primary aim for the students is to redesign Inklings' splat guns, enhancing defense capabilities. However, to grasp the mechanics of these guns, the students face a sequence of challenges set by some well-known characters in the *Splatoon* universe. These tasks aim to equip students with the necessary foundational knowledge before they begin redesigning the splat guns.

I created several simple, *Splatoon*-themed digital simulations to aid students' inquiry-based exploration of electrostatic equations.

FINDING ELEMENTARY CHARGE

$$|q| = n(1.6 \times 10^{-19})$$

In this lab, students initially interacted with a Zapfish, guided by an Inkling, to investigate how Zapfish store electrical charge. Students had preexisting knowledge that charge results from electron transfer and that electrons and protons possess equal but opposite charges. Students used a simple simulation to rub a Zapfish on a sweater, causing the Zapfish to gain a negative charge. This led to a classroom discussion on the triboelectric series and why certain materials gain or lose electrons upon friction. The simulation displayed the current charge on the Zapfish as they continued rubbing the sweater. In the code, the simulation increased the electron count on the Zapfish randomly between 2 and 5 electrons each time the Zapfish was rubbed against the sweater. Students recorded the evolving charge over multiple sessions and then reset and repeated the process. This iterative approach helped them deduce the quantized nature of charge, realizing that it increments in units no smaller than 1.6×10^{-19}C, and therefore the charge on a single electron must be -1.6×10^{-19}C. Students could then conclude that the amount of charge on an object ($|q|$) is equal to the number of missing or excess electrons multiplied by this elementary charge, 1.6×10^{-19}C. Understanding fundamental charge and electron transfer is crucial to comprehending electrostatic forces, which students explored when they met the next Inkling.

EXPLORING COULOMB'S LAW

$$F_e = \frac{k|q_1 q_2|}{r^2}$$

Students were then tasked by an Inkling farmer to help build a secure fence to contain his Zapfish. The problem with containing Zapfish is that when two or more are charged, they create an electrostatic force that can cause them to collide with the fencing and potentially knock it down. Students used a simulation to manipulate the charges of two Zapfish, their distance apart, and their masses. By completing this inquiry-based activity, students learned that the charges of the Zapfish, q_1 and q_2, are directly proportional to the electrostatic force (F_e). They also discovered that the distance between Zapfish (r) has an inverse square relationship with electrostatic force. Additionally, they observed that the mass of the Zapfish does not influence the electrostatic force. Students realized a constant (k) is required in the equation. Combining these relationships, students could derive Coulomb's law. Armed with an understanding of Coulomb's law, the students then applied this knowledge to assist the farmer in designing the most compact yet effective pen. This design is based on the maximum electrostatic force that can be sustained, considering the highest charge that Zapfish are capable of holding.

ELECTROSTATIC FORCE AND ELECTRIC POTENTIAL ENERGY IN A UNIFORM ELECTRIC FIELD

$$F_e = |q|E$$
$$PE_e = |q|Ed$$

The last task was for students to design a new splat gun to help Inklings defend against the encroaching Octolings. The mechanism of Inkling splat guns is akin to that of an inkjet printer, where ink droplets are charged and propelled through the gun's barrel by a uniform electric field. In a simulation, students were able to manipulate the mass of the ink droplet, the splat gun barrel length, the nozzle's position in the barrel, the charge of the ink droplet, and the strength of the uniform electric field. The resulting electrostatic force (F_e) and electric potential energy (PE_e) were displayed. Through inquiry-based experimentation, students learned that the electrostatic force is directly proportional to the charge of the ink droplet (q) and the electric field strength (E). They also discovered that the electric potential energy is directly proportional to the charge of the ink droplet, the electric field strength, and the distance the ink droplet could travel in the electric field (d, found by the barrel length and nozzle position). Once students determined these relationships, there was no single "correct" splat gun for them to design. The simulation allowed them to try any combination of variables, and students chose their favorite configuration based on the splat patterns produced on a test wall.

After designing their splat guns, the students faced an Octarian attack! In a series of word problems, Inklings placed students' splat guns on towers, and students used their newfound knowledge about electrostatic forces and electric potential energy paired with existing knowledge about Newton's second law to predict where their ink splats would land.

Comparison Approaches
Our standard electrostatics curriculum is anchored around the phenomenon of the inkjet printer. Similarly to the worldbuilding approach, students use inquiry-based lab experiences to derive equations for elementary charge, Coulomb's law, and electrostatic force and electric potential energy in a uniform electric field. However, these labs are unrelated to one another and supplemented by extensive lectures and traditional note-taking.

In the past, we have used a simulation for students to observe the effects of different variables on the behavior of charged ink droplets in a uniform electric field. A complexity in this simulation is that the electric field is perpendicular to the motion of the ink droplet, which maintains a constant horizontal velocity. This perpendicular arrangement between the electric field's direction and the droplet's motion presents a more intricate challenge for students, especially those at an introductory physics level, to comprehend. In the *Splatoon* splat gun, the droplet's motion and the electric field are parallel, simplifying the motion of the droplet and making it easier for students to interpret the relationships between variables.

ASSESSMENT MEASURES

For each activity, students were responsible for presenting their experimental outcomes to the Inkling character involved in the lab simulation. Write-ups included the question or problem they were trying to solve, relevant background information, their procedure, data, and results. The objective was to craft these reports comprehensively enough that an Inkling with only basic scientific knowledge could replicate the experiment and interpret the results. These write-ups were evaluated based on a standard lab report grading rubric.

In addition to the write-up for the splat gun lab, students were also required to present their findings to a panel of Inklings consisting of me and their classmates. Students had to present their proposed splat gun design and field a variety of questions from the Inklings panel. These questions focused on potential enhancements to their design, such as reducing the required charge, extending the range, increasing the speed or size of the splat, enhancing accuracy, or lowering production costs.

REFLECTION ON IMPLEMENTATION

My students and I had a blast with this unit. Students were more engaged than they had been in previous years. They seemed to be more interested in designing the splat guns compared to understanding how an inkjet printer works. Initially, I had some concerns about whether students unfamiliar with the *Splatoon* universe would find the unit engaging. I think kickstarting the unit with background on the *Splatoon* world and the ongoing war between Inklings and Octolings kept them interested. No prior knowledge of the *Splatoon* universe was required for students to engage meaningfully with the characters or the storyline.

The timing of this unit during the COVID-19 pandemic presented unique challenges and opportunities. Conducting the activities in a digital format was particularly beneficial, as a significant number of students were participating from home for portions of the unit. Even I had to quarantine for a couple of weeks during this unit, but it was successfully rolled out regardless. The adaptability of the unit's structure to remote learning was crucial to its successful implementation.

The unit could easily be scaled for more advanced courses. For example, students could be tasked with keeping more than two Zapfish in the farmer's pen, the splat gun design could be modified to include the impact of gravity on the ink droplet in the splat gun barrel, and students could be tasked with solving angled projectile problems with their splat guns.

If I were to repeat the experience, I would prefer to include additional discussions or debates about the ethics of scientists designing wartime weapons. This could involve exploring real-world parallels, such as the creation of the atomic bomb, to foster a deeper understanding and awareness of the ethical dimensions of scientific advancements. There were additional world details in the *Splatoon* wikis that would have led to difficult moral dilemmas. For example, while Octolings do frequently steal Inklings' Zapfish, they do so because Inklings hold a majority of the territory. Octolings were forced to live underground and steal Zapfish out of survival necessity. There were many other interesting facets of the *Splatoon* universe that I would draw from in future iterations of this unit.

CASE STUDY V HONORS

Instructor: Wendi Sierra
Institution: Texas Christian University, Fort Worth, TX
Class: Worldbuilding as Reflective Social Practice
Level: Undergraduate
Enrollment: 16
Project Duration: 16 weeks (full term)

LEARNING OBJECTIVES

- Students will learn a theoretical framework for describing fictional worlds.
- Students will critically apply and analyze this theoretical framework, applying it to both fictional and real-world environments.
- Students will compose according to this theoretical framework.

WORLDBUILDING APPROACH

Honors classes, as they are conceived of at Texas Christian University, offer students from majors across the university the opportunity to approach subjects from an interdisciplinary (or at least multidisciplinary) perspective. For a class on worldbuilding, this has two important implications. First, students will be coming to the subject material with no shared background but with a wide array of disciplinary knowledge and abilities. Out of sixteen students in this course, ten different majors were represented (with multiple double majors and minors as well), and every college on campus, from fine arts to nursing, was represented by at least one student. Second, students entered the course expecting to be challenged to think in multidisciplinary ways and to engage with a variety of approaches and perspectives. In response to this context, I found it essential that students should be pushed to make connections between how we discussed worldbuilding in tabletop role-playing games (TTRPGs) and how they conceived of real-world governments, histories, and social structures.

The course was structured so that students would (1) learn the worldbuilding framework and be able to define each aspect, (2) apply the framework in novel contexts, and (3) use the framework as a generative tool to create their own fictional world exploring a social issue. As students learned about the worldbuilding framework, they also learned about *Dungeons & Dragons*. They read sections from the *Player's Handbook* and chapters from various campaign settings and modules, and played in a one-shot session. Throughout this first unit, they both applied the key terms they were using as the terms came up and considered which terms seemed to be given minimal attention in the materials. In the second unit, students were split into three groups and assigned to either *Coyote and Crow, Call of Cthulhu*, or *Pathfinder*. The students again read selections from sourcebooks and campaign settings and then presented to the class how these various systems dealt with elements of the worldbuilding framework. Finally, after exploring *Dungeons & Dragons* and being introduced to three other systems, students grouped up and made their own fictional worlds in World Anvil. They were tasked to "explore a social issue" but given substantial leeway to determine what they identified as a social issue. Two groups chose to tackle climate change, while the third explored the tension between punishment and reform (though, interestingly, a climate disaster figured heavily into this group's fictional world history as well).

COMPARISON APPROACHES

This was a novel class created with the intention of using worldbuilding as a way to think through societal structures. Thus, there are no comparison approaches for the class itself. However, the worldbuilding approach is one that appealed greatly to me given my background in rhetoric and my current position as a professor of game studies. My pedagogical practice has always involved a substantial amount of experiential learning, group collaboration, and creative thinking. This matches nicely with a focus on TTRPGs, which themselves require the demonstration of these skills. Similarly, I frequently employ popular culture in my class as entryways into conversations about power, culture, and social relationships. I have found that popular culture frequently adds a level of critical distance that makes these issues more approachable for a number of students. Thus, the method of first exploring an issue or idea through a popular text and then applying it to real people and situations is one I use frequently in a variety of courses.

ASSESSMENT MEASURES

Students had three major assignments to match with the three parts of the course. First, they were required to play in a *Dungeons & Dragons* one-shot session and write a reflection paper. This assignment was meant to demonstrate their fluency with the worldbuilding framework and their ability to apply it to a common text, as we were all reading and working with *Dungeons & Dragons*. In the second unit, students were put into small groups, where they researched an assigned TTRPG system. They then presented the system to the rest of the class using the framework and guided the class through the character creation process. After the presentation, students individually wrote a reflection essay on how they felt their system handled/ignored various parts of the framework.

Finally, students created a fictional world in groups and were collaboratively responsible for creating a world overview, timeline, and framework outline. Individually, they wrote articles that were evaluated, in part, on how the articles adhered to the principles outlined in the collaborative sections. In other words, their individual articles—which could be on historical figures, events, places, artifacts, factions, or other elements of the world—had to fit within the collaboratively designed framework or be intentionally designed as an outlier (and explained as such). For this last unit, students again wrote a reflection essay, considering (1) what they hoped to accomplish with their world and how they explored their social issue, (2) which aspect of their individual compositions they were most proud of, and (3) what they would do if they had another month to work on the project.

REFLECTION ON IMPLEMENTATION

Overall, I was pleased with how the course progressed and with the final products students put together. This course has become part of my regular rotation and will be returning on a biannual basis.

I believe that using the worldbuilding framework was the greatest strength of this approach. Students, coming from a wide variety of disciplinary backgrounds, were able to ground themselves and their responses in the framework. Thus, it became an excellent organizing heuristic for the class. This is not to say that students accepted the framework whole; at various points in the course, we had discussions about what students felt might be missing from the framework or places where they felt like the framework was perhaps making unnecessary/unhelpful distinctions. However, in both cases, the framework was both generative and structural for our discussions. Ultimately, I presented this framework as one possible taxonomy for how to think about worlds and social relationships, a framework they had to become conversant in but were welcome to accept or reject.

Somewhat less successful was my decision to give them three systems to explore in the middle of the semester. My hope was that they would experience a variety of different TTRPGs and have more models to draw on when making the turn toward writing their own fictional world. However, I found that students sometimes lacked important context to understand any world but the one they were assigned. This was particularly true of *Coyote and Crow*, which is an example of Indigenous futurism, but even *Call of Cthulhu* presented some confusion to students who did not already have familiarity with the Cthulhu mythos. The groups assigned to these two systems had the time to engage with them deeply and gained some solid perspective, but those outside these groups did not seem to take much from the character creation activities or presentations (which were likely too short to be brief). Similarly, I felt rushed in both the *Dungeons & Dragons* and three systems units to ensure we would have enough time for their creative process in the fictional worlds unit. In the future, I intend to pick one system for us to work on for half the class instead of doing one system for a third and the three systems for another third. This will also lead to more time for their final creative unit, which will allow them to do more sharing and peer reviewing with the other groups.

CASE STUDY VI LABOR STORIES

Instructor: Ching-In Chen
Institution: University of Washington Bothell, Bothell, WA
Class: Labor Stories During Pandemic Times
Level: Advanced undergraduate for a regional state campus
Enrollment: 24
Project Duration: 5 weeks

LEARNING OBJECTIVES

- Read and investigate creative and critical texts to understand historical and current conditions of work, labor, and educational pathways to work and labor as well as alternative and solidarity economies
- Investigate students' own work, labor, and educational pathway narrative through individual writing and research, and learn about other work, labor, and educational pathways

WORLDBUILDING APPROACH

The class was a writing class focused on investigating and exploring the exacerbated, economic fault lines for working-class lives in times of crisis. The course also served as the culmination of a year of talks featuring visiting scholars and artists, coordinated by the University of Washington Bothell Labor Studies Colloquium.

My approach was to have students engage in speculative storytelling to reimagine work, labor, and educational pathways as well as alternative and solidarity economies.

In the first weeks of class, I focused on having the students read nonfiction and realistic fictional accounts of working-class stories while having them consider and write about the intersections of labor and equity within their own lives. Students read labor stories with intersectional analyses of gender, race, and/or language access as well as some related theories around reimagining alternative and solidarity economies.

In the middle of the quarter, I introduced students to the idea of visionary fiction via Walidah Imarisha and adrienne maree brown's *Octavia's Brood: Science Fiction Stories from Social Justice Movements* and discussed using speculative storytelling methods to speculate and reimagine a more just and equitable world, with a special emphasis on work and labor. We discussed specific stories with an eye to how they engaged in worldbuilding.

I created a universe census poll, which asked the students to vote on the conditions of the fictional universe that everyone would be operating under. I asked them to consider what kind of circumstances would be the most interesting to think about regarding current world challenges such as police brutality, lack of access to fresh water, or a worldwide pandemic. Once they voted, I created a fictional story using these details and led the students through an envisioning process to develop a new character in this world. Students would freewrite about what kind of social change their characters might care about. Then, I played a short clip from the *Fourth World War* documentary, divided the students up into smaller neighborhoods, and asked them to devise a method of how the neighbors stopped being afraid and came together as a community based on the clip.

Each neighborhood was tasked with devising an origin story of how the neighborhood had come to be and what challenges and resources were needed, with the goal for each neighborhood to introduce their neighborhood to the universe in a resource-sharing meeting where the universe would vote on how to redistribute a collective pot of resources. Each neighborhood was tasked with creating a map of their neighborhood with specific locations and timelines (which were both devised for the specific neighborhoods by myself and my teaching assistant as well as chosen by chance) along with developing a story of how their characters interacted with each other and the neighborhood locations and timelines. Individually, students developed characters by writing personal ads for them as well as choosing and describing objects that were important to them.

After the neighborhoods had some time to develop their neighborhoods, we did a neighborhood exchange where each neighborhood elected one traveler and the rest stayed behind to receive diplomatic guests. Each neighborhood was tasked with preparing something of the neighborhood to offer.

In addition, my teaching assistant and I created "wrenches" that we provided to each neighborhood to encourage them to develop specific areas that we thought were either underdeveloped or challenges too easily solved. During the last meeting, each neighborhood presented their story and their requests alongside a zine as a guide to the community to be shared during the gathering. After the storytelling presentations, each neighborhood deliberated on how they would allocate their resources (with the rule that they could not award the resources to their own neighborhood), with bartering acceptable. At the end, students wrote evaluations of their own participation as well as the participation of their teammates, and they were given a final prompt to respond as their character to the determination of the resource-sharing universe meeting.

COMPARISON APPROACHES

I find that using this worldbuilding approach encourages students to approach often heated subjects in ways that might not surface otherwise. I have noticed a desire among students to envision other kinds of social structures than our current one, which is one of the goals of this approach.

For instance, though the project was devised as giving each neighborhood $1,000 in a pot to redistribute, one team notably pushed back against the idea that a monetary system would necessarily be used and proactively engaged in bartering for their needs instead.

In addition, I found that students learned from seeing how varied the neighborhoods and individual characters were in what they came up with. It also helped them consider other aspects of social equity and power.

ASSESSMENT MEASURES

- [Individual] Conversation entries
  - Analysis and creative prompts related to the *Octavia's Brood* reading
- [Group] Communal class notes
  - Each neighborhood chose assigned roles, including a notetaker. Notetakers kept communal notes on Google Docs, which responded to specific questions for prompts for the neighborhood.
- [Individual] Creative experiments
  - Individual writing prompts to help develop individual characters and their backstory

- [Group] Storytelling presentation and zine
  - Collaborative storytelling about the origin of their neighborhood, challenges, and needs as well as the origin story of each character
  - Collaborative zine
- [Individual] Self and team evaluation
  - Each participant wrote about their own contributions, their team members' contributions as well as reflections on how their team worked together.

REFLECTION ON IMPLEMENTATION

Overall, I felt that the worldbuilding approach engaged many of my students in some of the fundamental questions of the class, especially in the work it takes to rebuild a new kind of world. For the most part, the students had more fun with this way of writing and storytelling.

I found it interesting that many of the students desired to reimagine a new kind of society but had difficulty implementing this in the way that they developed their characters. For instance, the whole group chose the condition that gender identity and sexuality looked completely different in this new world than it had before, but had a hard time creating characters reflecting this reality despite having some examples in the reading. In the future, I think I will put more scaffolding in earlier on to help students better envision what might be possible without resorting to "magic pollution" or other kinds of fantastical fix-it solutions.

In addition, one of the challenges I faced had more to do with the nature of teamwork, especially when teaching on a regional state campus during a pandemic with a student body that was juggling many responsibilities. It impacted teamwork when students would miss the class periods I had set aside for developing the project, and some neighborhoods had a challenging time meeting outside of the class.

Despite these challenges, I think that this kind of engagement is exciting for both the students and me as an instructor, and I am committed to continuing to use this kind of approach in my future teaching.

NOTES

FOREWORD

1. J. R. R. Tolkien, *The Tolkien Reader* (Ballantine, 1966).

PROLOGUE

1. Amy Bruckman, "Can Educational Be Fun?," paper presented at the Game Developers Conference, San Jose, CA, March 17, 1999, http://www.cc.gatech.edu/~asb/papers/bruckman-gdc99.pdf.

2. *Jurassic Park*, directed by Steven Spielberg (Universal Pictures, 1993).

3. James Paul Gee, *What Video Games Have to Teach Us About Learning and Literacy* (Palgrave Macmillan, 2003).

4. *Majesty: The Fantasy Kingdom Sim*, Cyberlore Studios, Hasbro Interactive, released March 2000.

5. William Sleator, *Interstellar Pig* (E. P. Dutton, 1984).

6. *World of Warcraft*, Blizzard Entertainment, released November 23, 2004.

7. *The Nightmare Before Christmas*, directed by Henry Selick (Touchstone Pictures, 1993).

8. *Spore*, Maxis, Electronic Arts, released September 7, 2008.

9. Noah Wardrip-Fruin and Pat Harrigan, eds., *First Person: New Media as Story, Performance, and Game* (MIT Press, 2006).

10. Noah Wardrip-Fruin and Pat Harrigan, eds., *Second Person: Role-Playing and Story in Games and Playable Media* (MIT Press, 2010).

11. Gee, *What Video Games Have to Teach Us About Learning and Literacy*.

12. John Gardner, *The Art of Fiction* (Alfred A. Knopf, 1984).

13. Flannery O'Connor, *Mystery and Manners: Occasional Prose* (Farrar, Straus and Giroux, 1969).

14. *Fallout 3*, Bethesda Game Studios, Bethesda Softworks, released October 28, 2008.

15. John Joseph Adams, *Wastelands: Stories of the Apocalypse* (Night Shade Books, 2008).

16. *Mad Max Beyond Thunderdome*, directed by George Miller and George Ogilvie (Kennedy Miller Productions, 1985).

17. *The Road*, directed by John Hillcoat (2929 Productions, 2009).

18. Gerald Voorhees, Joshua Call, and Katie Whitlock, eds., *Dungeons, Dragons, and Digital Denizens: The Digital Role-Playing Game* (Bloomsbury Publication, 2012).

19. Trent Hergenrader, "Gaming, World Building, and Narrative: Using Role-Playing Games to Teach Fiction Writing," in *GLS'11: Proceedings of the 7th International Conference on Games + Learning + Society Conference*, ed. Constance Steinkuehler, Crystal Martin, and Amanda Oschsner (ETC Press, 2011), https://dl.acm.org/doi/10.5555/2206376.2206389.

20. Michael F. Young et al., "Our Princess Is in Another Castle: A Review of Trends in Serious Gaming for Education," *Review of Educational Research* 82, no. 1 (2012): 61–89, https://doi.org/10.3102/0034654312436980.

21. Michael F. Young and Stephen T. Slota, eds., *Exploding the Castle: Rethinking How Video Games & Game Mechanics Can Shape the Future of Education* (Information Age Publishing, 2017).

22. Trent Hergenrader, *Collaborative Worldbuilding for Writers and Gamers* (Bloomsbury Academic, 2018).

CHAPTER 1

1. Isaac Asimov, *I, Robot* (Doubleday, 1950), 133.

2.

3. Karl Popper, *The Open Society and Its Enemies* (Routledge, 1945).

4. Michel Rosenfeld, "Extremist Speech and the Paradox of Tolerance," review of *The Tolerant Society: Freedom of Speech and Extremist Speech in America*, by L. C. Bollinger, *Harvard Law Review* 100, no. 6 (1987): 1457–1481, https://doi.org/10.2307/1341168.

5. Jonathan Haber, *Critical Thinking* (MIT Press, 2020).

6. Michael Scriven and Richard Paul, "Defining Critical Thinking," presentation at the Eighth Annual International Conference on Critical Thinking and Education Reform, Summer 1987, http://www.criticalthinking.org/pages/defining-critical-thinking/766.

CHAPTER 2

1. Xun Kuang, *The Teachings of the Ru*, book 8, chapter 11, compiled by Liu Xiang (818 CE), trans. H. H. Dubs (1928).

2. Brown v. Board of Education, 347 U.S. 483 (1954).

3. Sheff v. O'Neill, 678 A.2d 1267, 1274 (1996).

4. Education Amendments Act of 1972, 20 U.S.C. §§1681–1688 (2018).

5. Individuals with Disabilities Education Act, 20 U.S.C. §1400 (as reauthorized in 2004).

6. Section 504 of the Rehabilitation Act of 1973, 29 U.S.C. § 794; 28 C.F.R. § (2002).

7. Americans with Disabilities Act of 1990, 42 U.S.C. §12101 et. seq. (1990).

8. Rene Descartes, "Discourse on Method: Part One," in *The Philosophical Writings of Descartes*, trans. John Cottingham, Robert Stoothoff, and Dugald Murdoch (Cambridge University Press, 1985), 11–16.

9. Stanley Finger and Paul Eling, *Franz Joseph Gall: Naturalist of the Mind, Visionary of the Brain* (Oxford University Press, 2019).

10. Charles Darwin, *On the Origin of Species by Means of Natural Selection, or the Preservation of Favoured Races in the Struggle for Life* (J. Murray, 1859).

11. Wilhelm Wundt, "Principles of Physiological Psychology, 1873," in *Readings in the History of Psychology*, ed. Wayne Dennis (Appleton-Century-Crofts, 1948), 248–250, https://doi.org/10.1037/11304-029.

12. William James, *The Principles of Psychology* (Henry Holt and Company, 1890).

13. Edward Thorndike, *The Elements of Psychology* (A. G. Seiler, 1905), 205.

14. W. E. B. Du Bois, *Souls of Black Folk* (A. C. McClurg, 1903).

15. John Dewey, *Democracy and Education: An Introduction to the Philosophy of Education* (MacMillan, 1916).

16. John Dewey, *Experience and Education* (Macmillan, 1938).

17. Edward Thorndike, "Eugenics: With Special Reference to Intellect and Character," *Popular Science Monthly* 83 (1913): 130.

18. The term "metaphysical" derives from the Greek words μετά (metà, "after") and φυσικά (physiká, "physics"), referring to concepts and conditions that are not grounded in the physical world. By definition, they cannot be perceived using sensory organs nor falsified through the scientific method; they exist outside the bounds of material reality.

19. The homunculus problem refers to a logical dilemma following from the presumption that the "mind" (i.e., an encapsulation of one's personality, emotions, thoughts, hopes, etc.) is managed by a metaphysical entity (the homunculus). Because the homunculus cannot be directly observed or measured, its existence cannot be falsified, and there is no way to detect whether it may be controlled by another homunculus (an infinite recursion—turtles all the way down).

20. Noam Chomsky, "Review of B. F. Skinner's Verbal Behavior," In *Readings in the Psychology of Language*, eds. Leon A. Jakobovits and M. S. Miron (Prentice-Hall, 1967), 142–143.

21. B. F. Skinner, *Verbal Behavior* (Appleton-Century-Crofts, 1957).

22. Albert J. Bandura, *Social Learning Theory* (Prentice Hall, 1977).

23. Lev S. Vygotsky, *Mind in Society: The Development of Higher Psychological Processes*, eds. Michael Cole, Vera John-Steiner, Sylvia Scribner, and Ellen Souberman, trans. Alexander R. Luria, Martin Lopez-Morillas, Michael Cole, and James V. Wertsch (Harvard University Press, 1978).

24. Julien Offray de La Mettrie, *Man a Machine. Translated from the French of the Marquiss D'Argens* (W. Owen, 1749; repr. Gale Ecco, 2018).

25. Hermann von Helmholtz, *On the Sensations of Tone as a Physiological Basis for the Theory of Music* (Longmans, Green, and Co., 1875), doi: 10.1037/10838-000.

26. Henri Bergson, *Matter and Memory* (Allen and Unwin, 1911).

27. Alan M. Turing, "Computing Machinery and Intelligence," *Mind* 49 (1950): 433–460.

28. Seymour Papert, *Mindstorms* (Basic Books, 1980), 7.

29. James J. Gibson, *The Perception of the Visual World* (Houghton Mifflin, 1950).

30. James J. Gibson, *The Senses Considered as Perceptual Systems* (Houghton Mifflin, 1966).

31. Eleanor J. Gibson, *Principles of Perceptual Learning and Development* (Appleton-Century-Crofts, 1969).

32. James J. Gibson, *The Ecological Approach to Visual Perception* (Psychology Press, 1979).

33. John Seely Brown, Allan Collins, and Paul Duguid, "Situated Cognition and the Culture of Learning," *Educational Researcher* 18, no. 1 (1989): 32–42.

34. Jean Lave and Étienne Wenger, *Situated Learning: Legitimate Peripheral Participation* (University of Cambridge Press, 1991).

35. Malcolm Knowles, *Self-Directed Learning* (Follet, 1975).

36. Malcolm Knowles, *Andragogy in Action* (Jossey-Bass, 1984).

37. Jack Mezirow, "Understanding Transformational Learning," *Adult Education Quarterly* 44, no. 4 (1994): 222–232.

38. Paulo Freire, *Pedagogy of the Oppressed* (Seabury Press, 1970).

39. Jack Mezirow, *Transformative Dimensions of Adult Learning* (Jossey-Bass, 1991).

40. Jerome Bruner, *Actual Minds, Possible Worlds* (Harvard University Press, 1986).

41. James Paul Gee, *What Video Games Have to Teach Us About Learning and Literacy* (Palgrave Macmillan, 2003).

42. Jane McGonigal, *Reality Is Broken: Why Games Make Us Better and How They Can Change the World* (Penguin Press, 2011).

43. Sigmund Tobias and J. D. Fletcher, eds., *Computer Games and Instruction* (Information Age Publishing, 2011).

44. Michael F. Young et al., "Our Princess Is in Another Castle: A Review of Trends in Serious Gaming for Education," *Review of Educational Research* 82, no. 1 (2012): 61–89, https://doi.org/10.3102/0034654312436980.

45. Pieter Wouters, Christof van Nimwegen, Herre van Oostendorp, and Erik D. van der Spek, "A Meta-Analysis of the Cognitive and Motivational Effects of Serious Games," *Journal of Educational Psychology* 105, no. 2 (2013): 249–265, https://doi.org/10.1037/a0031311.

46. Douglas B. Clark, Emily E. Tanner-Smith, and Stephen S. Killingsworth, "Digital Games, Design, and Learning: A Systematic Review and Meta-Analysis," *Review of Educational Research* 86, no. 1 (2016): 79–122, https://doi.org/10.3102/0034654315582065.

47. Michael F. Young and Stephen T. Slota, eds., *Exploding the Castle: Rethinking How Video Games & Game Mechanics Can Shape the Future of Education* (Information Age Publishing, 2017).

CHAPTER 3

1. Brandon Sanderson, *The Way of Kings* (Tor Books, 2010), 1005–1006.

2. John D. Bransford, Ann L. Brown, and Rodney R. Cocking, eds. *How People Learn: Brain, Mind, Experience, and School* (National Academy Press, 1999), 19.

3. Edward L. Thorndike and Robert S. Woodworth, "The Influence of Improvement in One Mental Function upon the Efficiency of Other Functions," *Psychological Review* 8, no. 3 (1901): 247–261.

4. Douglas K. Detterman and Robert J. Sternberg, eds., *Transfer on Trial: Intelligence, Cognition, and Instruction* (Ablex Publishing, 1993).

5. Upton Sinclair, *The Jungle* (Doubleday, Jabber, and Co., 1906).

6. Mary L. Gick and Keith J. Holyoak, "Analogical Problem Solving," *Cognitive Psychology* 12, no. 3 (1980): 306–355, https://doi.org/10.1016/0010-0285(80)90013-4.

7. Karl Duncker, "On Problem-Solving," trans. L. S. Lees, *Psychological Monographs* 58, no. 5 (1945): i–113, https://doi.org/10.1037/h0093599.

8. Duncker presented a hypothetical scenario in which a doctor is treating a patient with a malignant brain tumor. The tumor cannot be surgically removed, but the doctor can use radiation to destroy the cancer cells. Unfortunately, the radiation will destroy healthy tissue at high intensity; at low intensity, treatment will fail. This leaves us with the question: How do we fully eliminate the tumor without harming the patient?

9. Michael Crichton, *Jurassic Park* (Knopf Publishing, 1990).

10. *Monty Python and the Holy Grail*, directed by Terry Gilliam and Terry Jones (Python (Monty) Pictures, 1975).

11. Burton Bennett, Michael Repacholi, and Zhanat Carr, *Health Effects of the Chernobyl Accident and Special Health Care Programmes* (World Health Organization, 2006).

12. Svetlana Aleksievich, *Voices from Chernobyl: The Oral History of a Nuclear Disaster*, trans. Keith Gessen (Picador, 2006).

13. *Chernobyl*, directed by Johan Renck (2019, HBO; Sky UK), streaming video.

14. Stephen Slota (author) and Michael Young's "Narrative & Situated Cognition" recommended that educators treat learning theory as a fourth, separate TPACK Venn diagram bubble to emphasize that theory and pedagogy are related but distinct entities; theory can and should inform pedagogy, but different pedagogies are not inherently bound to any individual theory and can be applied in multiple ways alongside various assessment methods.

15. Stephen T. Slota and Michael F. Young, "Narrative & Situated Cognition," in *Handbook of Research on Serious Games for Educational Applications*, eds. Robert Z. Zheng and Michael K. Gardner (IGI Global, 2016).

16. Sasha A. Barab and Wolff-Michael Roth, "Curriculum-Based Ecosystems: Supporting Knowing from an Ecological Perspective," *Educational Researcher* 35, no. 5 (2006): 3–13, https://doi.org/10.3102/0013189X035005003.

17. Stephen T. Slota and Kevin Ballestrini, "Una Vita: Exploring the Relationship Between Play, Learning Science, and Cultural Competency," in *Teaching Classics with Technology*, eds. Bartolo Natoli and Steven Hunt (Bloomsbury Publishing, 2019), 81.

18. Cognition and Technology Group at Vanderbilt, "Anchored Instruction and Its Relationship to Situated Cognition," *Educational Research* 19, no. 6 (1990): 2–10.

19. Similar anchored instruction resources were deployed around the same time as CTGV's *The Adventures of Jasper Woodbury*, including Bank Street College of

Education's (1984) *The Voyage of the Mimi*, which followed an expeditionary seafaring crew as they ventured across the ocean and took a census of humpback whales. The series introduced middle schoolers to numerous scientific and mathematical concepts, including principles of heat transfer, condensation, marine mammal biology, navigation techniques, map reading, and states of matter.

20. Cognition and Technology Group at Vanderbilt, "Anchored Instruction and Situated Cognition Revisited," *Educational Technology* 33, no. 3 (1993): 52–70.

21. Cognition and Technology Group at Vanderbilt, "From Visual Word Problems to Learning Communities: Changing Conceptions of Cognitive Research," in *Classroom Lessons: Integrating Cognitive Theory and Classroom Practice*, ed. Kate McGilly (MIT Press, 1994).

CHAPTER 4

1. *The Simpsons*, season 7, episode 12, "Team Homer," directed by Mark Kirkland, written by Michael Scully, aired January 7, 1996, in broadcast syndication, Disney+, 2024, streaming video.

2. Ben Rhodes, *After the Fall: Being American in the World We've Made* (Random House, 2021).

3. Peter N. Kugler, Robert E. Shaw, Kim J. Vicente, and Jeffrey Kinsella-Shaw, "The Role of Attractors in the Self-Organization of Intentional Systems" in *Cognition and the Symbolic Processes: Applied and Ecological Perspectives*, eds. Robert R. Hoffman and David S. Palermo (Lawrence Erlbaum Associates, Inc., 1991), 387–431.

4. Ulrich Lüttge, Francisco Cánovas, and Rainer Matyssek, *Progress in Botany Vol. 77* (Springer International Publishing, 2016), https://doi.org/10.1007/978-3-319-25688-7.

5. Jean Lave and Étienne Wenger, *Situated Learning: Legitimate Peripheral Participation* (Cambridge University Press, 1991).

6. Lave and Wenger, *Situated Learning*, 35.

7. Kugler and Turvey, *Information, Natural Law, and the Self-Assembly of Rhythmic Movements*.

8. Andy Clark, *Being There: Putting Brain, Body, and World Together Again* (MIT Press, 1998).

9. Edwin Hutchins, *Cognition in the Wild* (MIT Press, 1995).

CHAPTER 5

1. Bill Watterson, *Calvin and Hobbes* (Andrews McNeel Publication, 1993).

2. Brian Palmer, "E Is for Fail," *Slate*, August 9, 2010, https://slate.com/news-and-politics/2010/08/how-come-schools-assign-grades-of-a-b-c-d-and-f-but-not-e.html.

3. *Whose Line Is It Anyway?*, created by Dan Patterson and Mark Leveson, originally aired August 5, 1998, in broadcast syndication, ABC Family and the CW, 2024, streaming video.

4. Jesse Stommel, "Ungrading: An Introduction," Jesse Stommel, June 11, 2021, https://www.jessestommel.com/ungrading-an-introduction/.

5. Paulo Freire, *Pedagogy of the Oppressed* (Seabury Press, 1970).

CHAPTER 6

1. Cormac McCarthy, *Blood Meridian, or, The Evening Redness in the West* (Random House, 1985).

2. Eames Office, "Powers of Ten," October 2, 2008, YouTube, 9:00, https://www.youtube.com/watch?v=0fKBhvDjuy0.

3. Robert Crumb, *A Short History of America* (Co-Evolution Quarterly, 1993).

CHAPTER 7

1. Chicago Humanities Festival, "An Evening with George R. R. Martin," October 11, 2019, YouTube, 1:20:32, https://youtu.be/IfIpY0eEA84.

2. Gallup Inc., *2009 Gallup Inc. Religion Survey* (Gallup Inc., 2009), https://news.gallup.com/poll/142727/religiosity-highest-world-poorest-nations.aspx

3. Margaret Atwood, *The Handmaid's Tale* (McClelland and Stewart, 1985).

4. George Orwell, *Nineteen Eighty-Four* (Secker & Warburg, 1949).

CHAPTER 8

1. *Charlie Rose*, "Octavia Butler on 'The Parable of Talents,'" aired June 1, 2000, https://charlierose.com/videos/28978.

2. Office of the Assistant Secretary for Planning and Evaluation, *Engaging People with Lived Experience to Improve Federal Research, Policy, and Practice*, https://aspe.hhs.gov/lived-experience.

CHAPTER 9

1. Ursula K. Le Guin, *The Left Hand of Darkness* (Walker, 1969), 220.

2. Steven L. Piott, *Daily Life in the Progressive Era* (Greenwood Press, 2011).

3. Dane Gordon, *Rochester Institute of Technology: Industrial Development and Educational Innovation in an American City, 1829–2006* (RIT Press, 2007).

4. Extra Credits, "Tangential Learning: How Games Can Teach Us While We Play," March 23, 2011, YouTube, 7:21, https://youtu.be/rlQrTHrwyxQ.

5. Aurélien Catros and Maxime Leblanc, "When Boston Isn't Boston: Useful Lies of Reconstructive Game Models," *Traditional Dwellings and Settlements Review* 32, no. 2 (2021): 35.

6. Catros and Leblanc, "When Boston Isn't Boston," 36.

CHAPTER 10

1. *The Office*, season 3, episode 18, "The Negotiation," directed by Jeffrey Blitz, written by Greg Daniels, Michael Schur, and Ricky Gervais, aired April 5, 2007, in broadcast syndication, Peacock, 2024, streaming video.

CHAPTER 11

1. Douglas Adams, *The Restaurant at the End of the Universe* (Pan Books, 1980).

2. *The Colbert Report*, "Neil deGrasse Tyson," aired March 10, 2014, Comedy Central, https://www.cc.com/video/gh6urb/the-colbert-report-neil-degrasse-tyson-pt-1.

3. Trent Hergenrader, *Collaborative Worldbuilding for Writers and Gamers* (Bloomsbury Academic, 2018).

4. Octavia Butler, *Parable of the Sower* (Four Walls Eight Windows, 1993).

CHAPTER 12

1. Alain de Botton, *The News: A User's Manual* (Pantheon Books, 2014).

CHAPTER 13

1. Chip Heath and Dan Heath, *Made to Stick: Why Some Ideas Survive and Others Die* (Random House, 2007), 213.

2. Nassim Nicholas Taleb, *The Black Swan: The Impact of the Highly Improbable* (Random House, 2007), xvii–xviii.

3. C. West Churchman, "Guest Editorial: Wicked Problems," *Management Science* 14, no. 4 (1967): B141–B142.

CHAPTER 14

1. William Shakespeare, *As You Like It*, ed. Frances E. Dolan (Penguin Books, 2000).

2. José Zagal and Sebastian Deterding, eds., *Role-Playing Game Studies: A Transmedia Approach* (Routledge, 2018).

3. Zagal and Deterding, *Role-Playing Game Studies*, 47.

4. William Offutt, *Patriots, Loyalists, and Revolution in New York, 1775–1776*, Reacting to the Past (Pearson Education, 2010).

5. *Mission US: For Crown or Colony?*, The WNET Group, released 2010, https://www.mission-us.org/.

6. Richard Iorio and Daniel D. Fox, *Flames of Freedom: Grim & Perilous RPG* (Andrews McMeel Publishing, 2021).

7. *The New World*, developed by Brenda Romero (Brenda Romero, 2008), https://brenda.games/the-new-world.

8. *Train*, developed by Brenda Romero (Brenda Romero, 2009), https://brenda.games/train.

9. Jennifer Gonzalez, "Think Twice Before Doing Another Historical Simulation," Cult of Pedagogy, July 7, 2019, https://www.cultofpedagogy.com/classroom-simulations/.

10. Gonzalez, "Think Twice."

11. Gonzalez, "Think Twice."

12. Benjamin Franklin, "On Protection of Towns from Fire," *Pennsylvania Gazette*, February 4, 1735, https://founders.archives.gov/documents/Franklin/01-02-02-0002.

13. Ingrid Drake, "Classroom Simulations: Proceed with Caution," *Teaching Tolerance Magazine*, no. 33 (2008), https://www.learningforjustice.org/magazine/spring-2008/classroom-simulations-proceed-with-caution.

14. United Press International, "King Predicted He Too Would Be Assassinated—Like JFK," *Washington Afro-American*, September 9, 1969, https://news.google.com/newspapers?id=ZrYlAAAAIBAJ&pg=3439%2C4781621.

15. Daniel W. Graham, "Heraclitus," in *Stanford Encyclopedia of Philosophy* (Stanford University, 1997–), published February 8, 2007; substantive revision December 8, 2023, https://plato.stanford.edu/entries/heraclitus/.

CHAPTER 15

1. Francis Bacon, "Of Studies," in *The Essays* (Penguin Random House, 1986).

INDEX

Actual Minds, Possible Worlds, 39
Adams, Douglas, 161
Adult learning theory, 37
Adventures of Jasper Woodbury, The, 62
Affordances, 40
Age of Empires, 187
Agriculture, 111, 115
Alexievich, Svetlana, 47, 65
Alphanumeric grading, 79–80
American Revolution, 100–101, 105–106
Americans with Disabilities Act of 1990, 24
Analogical Problem Solving, 45–46
Analysis Design Development Implementation Evaluation (ADDIE) instructional design model, 56–57, 65–67
Anchored instruction, 62–63
Andragogy, 37, 53
 actualizing, 63–65
Andragogy in Action, 37
Arici, Anna, 18
Arts and culture influence, 116
Asimov, Isaac, 3
Assassin's Creed, 143
Assassin's Creed III, 143–144
Assessment
 alphanumeric grading in, 79–80
 feedback and, 92–94
 scaling, 94

self-, 87–91
standards-based, 80–86
ungrading, 86–92
As You Like It, 199
Atwood, Margaret, 116
Authentic learning environments, 36–37

Bacon, Francis, 219
Bandura, Albert, 30–31
Barab, Sasha, 18
Behaviorism, 51, *52*
Black Swan events, 193–194
Black Swan: The Impact of the Highly Improbable, The, 193
Bloom, Benjamin, 50
Branching and nesting on Wikipedia, 155–156
Bransford, John, 36, 39, 62
British literature case study, 239–244
Brown, John Seely, 36
Brown v. Board of Education, 24
Bruner, Jerome, 39, 62
Butler, Octavia, 121, 163

Calvin and Hobbes, 79
Canadian history, 7
Case studies
 British literature, 239–244
 history, 233–237
 honors class, 257–260

Case studies (cont.)
  labor stories, 261–264
  philosophy, 245–249
  physics, 251–256
Cataloging, 173–174
  of groups, events, and other types of entries, 183–184
  how many entries per category in, 174–175
  of people, 175–179
  of places, 179–181
  of things, 181–183
  world built from, 184–185
Catros, Aurélien, 143–144
Center for the Ecological Study of Perception & Action, 36
Chen, Ching-In, 261–264
Chernobyl, 47, 65
Chernobyl nuclear disaster, 47–48, 54–55
Chicago, downtown, 102–105
Chomsky, Noam, 29–30
Civilization, 187
Clark, Douglas, 18, 40
Classical conditioning, 27
Class preparations, 137
  completion of, 146–147
  developing your project overview in, 138
  introducing the project in, 145–146
  primary and secondary sources for, 140–143
  project purpose and length, 138–139
  scheduling, 139–140
  unlearning what you have learned in, 143–144
  Wikipedia as source of information for, 144–145
Coffee consumption, 8–11, 14–15
Cognition, 33–38
Cognition and Technology Group at Vanderbilt (CTGV), 62–63
Cognitive development, phases of, 29

Cognitive information processing (CIP) theory, 32, 39
Cognitivism, 51, *52*
Colbert Report, The, 163
Collaboration and community, 69
  in communities of practice, 73–76
  communities of practice for the classroom, 76–78
  cultivating, 78
  identity, positioning, and social constructivism in, 70–71
  by termites compared to humans, 71–73
Collaborative Worldbuilding for Writers and Gamers, 163
Collins, Allan, 36
Communities of Practice (CoPs), 36–37, 73–76, 225
  for the classroom, 76–78
Complexity, charting, 161–162
Compulsory education, 24
Computer Games and Instruction, 39
Computers, development of, 31–33
Concept-oriented simulations, 188–189
Conferencing, one-on-one, 91–92
Conservatism, *49*
Constructionism, 33, *52*
Constructivism, *52*
Contributor pages on Wikipedia, 157
COVID-19 pandemic, 193, 194
Crichton, Michael, 47
Critical pedagogy, 37–38, 87
Critical thinking, 15–16
Crumb, Robert, 106
Cultural influences, 113, 115
Cultural relativity, 13–14, 127
Curriculum development, 47–48
  example of putting learning theory and instructional design together for, 65–67
  instructional design in, 57–59
  philosophy and psychology in, 48–55
  steps in, 55–57

Daily Life in the Progressive Era, 141–142
Darwin, Charles, 26–27
De Botton, Alain, 173
Debriefing, large-group, 220
Democracy and Education: An Introduction to the Philosophy of Education, 28
Democratization, 50
Demographic data, 121–122
  nominal and quantitative descriptions in, 122–123
  used to explore lived experiences, 128–133
Descartes, René, 25
Desegregation, 24
Deterding, Sebastian, 199
Detterman, Douglas, 45
Dewey, John, 28, 33, 38, 50, 62
Digital Games, Design, and Learning: A Systematic Review and Meta-Analysis, 40
Disassociated learning, 32
Drake, Ingrid, 203
Du Bois, W. E. B., 28, 50
Duguid, Paul, 36
Duncker, Karl, 45–46
Dungeons & Dragons, 216

Eastman, George, 142
Ecological Approach to Visual Perception, The, 34
Economic equalization, 48, 50
Economic strength, 111, 115
Education
  advancements in instructional technology in, 4, 6
  compulsory, 24
  curriculum building in, 47–48
  deluge of information sources and, 7
  desegregation in, 24
  development of computers and, 31–33
  different philosophies applied to, 48–51
  and framework for good teaching, 226–228
  game-based (*see* Game-based education)
  learning theory in, 19
  philosophy and psychology of, 25–26, 48–55, 245–249
  play-based (*see* Play-based education)
  preparing students for "the real world," 7
  reconfigured for the challenges of modernity, 7–8
  research of early learning theorists in, 28–31
  roots of educational psychology and, 26–28
  seventeenth and eighteenth century American, 23–24
  student-centered, 38–39
  transfer in, 44–46
  understanding of situated cognition in, 33–38
Educational psychology, 26–28
El Cid, 206–214
Empathy, 16–17
  in understanding other life-worlds, 133–135
Essentialism, *49*, 124–127
Events, cataloging of, 183–184
Exact locations, identification of, 180
Experience and Education, 28
Exploding the Castle: Rethinking How Video Games & Game Mechanics Can Shape the Future of Education, 40
Exxon Valdez oil spill, 191–192

Fallout 3, 54, 64, 65–66, 143
Farber, Matthew, 18
Feedback, 92–94
Fields, Deborah, 18
First-person scenarios, 204–205
Fletcher, J. D., 39

Foreign relations, 110
Franklin, Benjamin, 202
Freire, Paolo, 37, 87

Gage, Phineas, 25–26
Gall, Franz Joseph, 25
Game-based education, 18–19, 39–40, 140–141, 225–226
  role-play in (*see* Role-play)
  storytelling in, 143–144
  in Technology, Pedagogy, and Content Knowledge (TPACK) framework, 54–55
Gee, James Paul, 18, 39
Gibson, Eleanor, 33–36
Gibson, James, 33–36
Gick, Mary, 45
Gonzalez, Jennifer, 201
Gordon, Dane, 141–142
Governance, 109–110
Government presence, 114–115
Grading, alphnumeric, 79–80
Grand Theft Auto, 143
Groups, cataloging of, 183–184

Haber, Jonathan, 15
Handmaid's Tale, The, 116
Heath, Chip, 187
Heath, Dan, 187
History case study, 233–237
Holyoak, Keith, 45
Honor class case study, 257–260
How People Learn, 44
Hyperlinks, 154–155

Identity, 70–71, 129
Images and media on Wikipedia, 156
Imposter syndrome, 137
Individuals with Disabilities Education Act of 1975, 24
Information Age, 32
Instructional design, 57–59

Instructional technology, 4
Interdisciplinary programs of study, 66–67

James, William, 27
Jeffries, Hasan Kwame, 201
Jungle, The, 45
Jurassic Park, 47

Kafai, Yasmin, 18
Ke, Fengfeng, 18
Killingsworth, Stephen, 40
Knowing as doing, 61
Knowles, Malcolm, 37
Koehler, Matthew, 53
Kugler, Peter, 71–72

Labor stories case study, 261–264
Language acquisition, 29–30
Large-group debriefing, 220
Lave, Jean, 36, 73–74, 77
Law of effect, 28
Learning as education of intention and attention, 61
Learning theory, 19
  adult, 37
  Analysis Design Development Implementation Evaluation (ADDIE) instructional design model and, 56–57
  connected to different philosophies, 50–51
  curriculum development and, 55–57
  details of major, 51–53
  early American education and, 23–25
  instructional design and, 57–59
  put into practice, 43–44
  situated cognition and, 33–38
Leblanc, Maxime, 143–144
Legitimate peripheral participation (LPP), 74
Le Guin, Ursula K., 137

Life-transformative education, 37
Life-worlds, 60–61, 121–122
  demographic data on, 121–122
  empathy in understanding other, 133–135
  essentialisms, stereotypes, and drawing wrong conclusions on, 124–127
  narrative and qualitative descriptions of, 124
  nominal and quantitative descriptions of, 122–123
  using demographics to explore lived experiences in, 128–133
Lived experiences, 128–133
Local culture, 180
Logo Turtle, 33

Macro and micro worlds, 106–107
Mann, Horace, 50
Martin, George R. R., 109
Marxism, *49*, 50
McCarthy, Cormac, 99
McGonigal, Jane, 39
Meaningful generalization, 12–13, 125–126
Meta-Analysis of the Cognitive and Motivational Effects of Serious Games, A, 40
Metanarrative construction
  charting complexity in, 161–162
  drafting of world, 166–171
  qualitative approaches in, 164–165
  quantitative approaches in, 163–164
Mexican history, 7
Mezirow, Jack, 37
Military influence, 116
Mindstorms, 32
Mishra, Punya, 53
Montessori, Maria, 38, 50
Monty Python and the Holy Grail, 47
Morgan, Eric J., 233–237

Narrative and qualitative descriptions of life-worlds, 124
National Research Council, 44
Needs Analysis, 57–58
Neutral Point of View (NPOV), 151
New World, The, 201
Nineteen Eighty-Four, 117
Nominal and quantitative descriptions of life-worlds, 122–123

Office, The, 149
One-on-one conferencing, 91–92
On the Origin of Species, 27
Operant conditioning, 29
Operating rooms, 3–6
Orwell, George, 117
Our Princess Is in Another Castle: A Review of Trends in Serious Gaming for Education, 39

Papert, Seymour, 32–33, 39, 62
Parable of the Sower, The, 163
Paradox of tolerance, 14
Paul, Richard, 16
Pavlov, Ivan, 27
Peer evaluation, 221–222
Pemberton Memorial Operating Room, 3–5
People, cataloging of, 175–179
Perception of the Visual World, The, 34
Perennialism, *49*
Philosophy
  case study in, 245–249
  in curricular design, 48–55
  emergence of, 25–26
Physics case study, 251–256
Piaget, Jean, 28–29, 30, 31, 32, 50
Piott, Steven L., 141
Place, cataloging of, 179–181
Play-based education, 33, 38–39, 225
Popper, Karl, 14
Positioning, 70–71
Positive reinforcement, 29

Powered by the Apocalypse, 216
Powers of Ten, 102
Primary sources, 140–143
Principles of Perceptual Learning and Development, 34
Principles of Physiological Psychology, 27
Principles of Psychology, The, 27
Privilege, 112
Problem-solving, 16
Progressivism, *49*, 50
Project overview, 138
  introducing the project, 145–146
  project purpose and length in, 138–139
  scheduling in, 139–140
Prosocial behaviors, 30
Psychology, 25–26
  in curricular design, 48–55
  roots of educational, 26–28
Pu, Bao, 70
Puritan New England, education in, 23–24

Qualitative approaches in metanarrative construction, 164–165
Quantitative approaches in metanarrative construction, 163–164

Radical behaviorism, 29
Rationalism, 35
Reacting to the Past (RTTP), 140–141, 199
Reality Is Broken: Why Games Make Us Better and How They Can Change the World, 39
Rehabilitation Act of 1973, 24
Religious influence, 115–116, 125
Review of Educational Research, 39, 40
Rochester Institute of Technology: Industrial Development and Educational Innovation in an American City, 142
Role-play, 199–201
  cautionary tale on, 201–204
  consequences for actions in, 214

  first-person scenarios in, 204–205, 210–214
  perspectives on, 204–206
  successes and failures in, 215–216
  third-person distant in, 205, 206–208
  third-person limited in, 205, 208–210
  used to virtually experience worlds, 217
  using cards, 215
  using dice, 215
  in worlds of *El Cid*, 206–214
Role-Playing Game Studies: A Transmedia Approach, 199
Romanticism, *49*
Romero, Brenda, 201
Rosenfeld, Michel, 14
Rule of law, 110, 115

Scaling assessment, 94
Scheduling, 139–140
Schema, 28–29
Schrier, Kat, 18
Schute, Valerie, 18
Scope, world, 101–105
Scott, Rebecca, 245–249
Scriven, Michael, 16
Secondary sources, 140–143
Section 504, 24
Self-accounting, 220–221
Self-actualization, 50
Self-assessment, 87–91
Self-Directed Learning, 37
Senses Considered as Perceptual Systems, The, 34
Sequence, 105–106
Shaw, Robert, 36
Sheff v. O'Neill, 24
Short History of America, A, 106
Sierra, Wendi, 257–260
SimCity, 187
Simpsons, The, 69
Simulations, 187–188
  Black Swan events, 193–194

in the classroom, 197–198
concept-oriented, 188–189
social and environmental changes on a timeline in, 189–192
wicked problems, 194–197
for worldbuilding, 189
Sinclair, Upton, 45
Situated cognition, 36, 53
Situated Cognition and the Culture of Learning, 36
Situated Learning: Legitimate Peripheral Participation, 36–37, 73–74
Situativity, 60–61
Skinner, B. F., 28–29, 30, 31
Slota, Stephen, 40
Social and environmental changes on a timeline, 189–192
Social cognitive model, 30
Social constructivist framework, 31, 70–71
Social forces, 117–119
Social interactivity, 36
Social learning theory, 30, 52
Social Learning Theory, 30
Social relations, 111–113
Social services, 110, 115
Souls of Black Folk, The, 28
Space, worlds in, 101–105
Spatial relationships, 180
Squire, Kurt, 18
Standards-based assessment, 80–86
Steinkuehler, Constance, 18
Stereotypes, 13, 124–127
Sternberg, Robert, 45
Stommel, Jesse, 87
Strohm, Luke, 239–244
Structures and substructures
  cultural influences, 113
  economics, 111
  governance, 109–110
  social forces, 117–119
  social relations, 111–113
  synthesis, 113–117

Sympathy, 17
Synthesis, 113–117
Syntonic learning, 33

Taleb, Nassim Nicholas, 193
"Tangential Learning: How Games Can Teach Us While We Play," 143
Tanner-Smith, Emily, 40
Teaching, framework for good, 226–228
Technology, Pedagogy, and Content Knowledge (TPACK) framework, 53–55, 56, 65–67
Technology influence, 116
Termite behavior, 71–73
Things, cataloging of, 181–183
Thirteen Colonies, 100–101
Thorndike, Edward, 28, 44–45
Time, worlds in, 105–106
Title IX, 24
Tobias, Sigmund, 39
Trade, 111, 115
Train, 201
Transfer, 44–46
Transfer on Trial: Intelligence, Cognition, and Instruction, 45
Truth-seeking, 70
Turvey, Michael, 36
Tyson, Neil DeGrasse, 163

Ungrading, 86–92
  one-on-one conferencing in, 91–92
  self-assessment in, 87–91
United States history
  basic outline of, 6–7
  education in early, 23–25
Unlearning what you have learned, 143–144

Values and cultural influences, 113
Verbal Behavior, 29–30
Voices from Chernobyl, 47, 65
Vygotsky, Lev, 30–31, 32, 38, 50, 62

Wagner, Tori, 251–256
Watson, John, 27
Wealth distribution, 111, 115
Wenger, Étienne, 36, 73–74, 77
What Video Games Have to Teach Us About Learning and Literacy, 18, 39
Wicked problems, 194–197
Wikipedia
  branching and nesting on, 155–156
  commonly recurring sections of location pages in, 150
  contributor pages on, 157
  getting started with, 149–152
  hyperlinks on, 154–155
  images and media on, 156
  as model for drafting world metanarrative, 166–171
  Neutral Point of View (NPOV) on, 151
  organizing entries on, 152–153
  as source of information, 144–145
  wiki management and, 154–157
  writing style on, 150–151
Women's suffrage movement, 190–191
Woodworth, Robert, 44–45
Worldbuilding
  actualizing andragogy in, 63–65
  analyzing life-worlds in, 60–61
  anchored instruction in, 62–63
  attitudes, beliefs, and values in, 10–11
  benefits of, 228–229
  as big, messy affairs, 222–223
  in British history case study, 239–244
  cataloging in (*see* Cataloging)
  characteristics of, 17–18
  class preparations in (*see* Class preparations)
  coffee consumption as illustrative of, 8–11, 14–15
  complexity of the world and, 8–12
  critical reflection on, 219–223
  critical thinking and empathy in, 15–17
  cultural relativity and, 13–14
  curriculum building in, 47–48
  definition of, 8, 17–19
  in history case study, 233–237
  in honors class case study, 257–260
  inequality in, 11–12
  in interdisciplinary programs of study, 66–67
  in labor stories case study, 261–264
  large-group debriefing in, 220
  life-worlds in (*see* Life-worlds)
  meaningful generalization in, 12–13
  metanarrative construction in (*see* Metanarrative construction)
  peer evaluation in, 221–222
  in philosophy case study, 245–249
  in physics case study, 251–256
  role-play in (*see* Role-play)
  self-accounting in, 220–221
  simulations in (*see* Simulations)
  structures and substructures in, 109–119
  theory of, 59–65
  transfer in, 44–46
  Wikipedia and (*see* Wikipedia)
  worlds in space and time and, 99–107
Worlds, 99–101
  macro and micro, 106–107
  in space, 101–105
  in time, 105–106
Wouters, Pieter, 40
Wrong conclusions, 124–127
Wundt, William, 27

Xun Kuang, 23

Year Zero Engine, 216
Young, Michael, 39–40

Zagal, José, 199
Zones of proximal development, 31

Publisher contact:
The MIT Press
Massachusetts Institute of Technology
77 Massachusetts Avenue, Cambridge, MA 02139
mitpress.mit.edu

EU Authorised Representative:
Easy Access System Europe, Mustamäe tee 50,
10621 Tallinn, Estonia
gpsr.requests@easproject.com

Printed by Integrated Books International,
United States of America